THE SOCIAL SIGNIFICANCE OF TELEMATICS

Pragmatics & Beyond

An Interdisciplinary Series of Language Studies

V:7

Lars Qvortrup

The Social Significance of Telematics:
An Essay on the Information Society

THE SOCIAL SIGNIFICANCE OF TELEMATICS

An Essay on the Information Society

Lars Qvortrup
Odense University

Translated by Philip Edmonds

JOHN BENJAMINS PUBLISHING COMPANY
AMSTERDAM/PHILADELPHIA

1984

Library of Congress Cataloging in Publication Data

Qvortrup, Lars.
The social significance of telematics.

(Pragmatics & beyond, ISSN 0166-6258; V:7)
Bibliography: p. 237
1. Communication -- Technological innovations. 2. Communication -- Social aspects. I. Title. II. Title: Telematics. III. Series.
P96.T42Q9 1984 001.51 85-7493
ISBN 90-272-2540-0 (European)/0-915027-04-6 (U.S.)

TABLE OF CONTENTS

AUTHOR'S PREFACE

The assumption underlying *The Social Significance of Telematics: an Essay on the Information Society* is that we are facing a social upheaval, a revolution in fact, with consequences at least as far-reaching as those of the Industrial Revolution. With this book I want to intervene in the current discussion about this revolution, a discussion which is normally coloured by a resigned determinism maintaining that the revolution will come about all by itself as an automatic consequence of the development of technology. Normally, too, the discussion is characterized by *quantitative* argumentation — the social upheaval will mean *less* work, *more* democracy ...

As opposed to this, I want to politicize the discussion here — to politicize it by insisting on the fact that this social revolution is not inextricably tied to the automatically whirring wheels of technological development, but is dependent on a number of political choices. The discussion is politicized further by the book's emphasis on the fact that the arguments *cannot* be quantitative — they *have to* be qualitative. For what we are talking about is not more — or less — work, but a qualitative change in the concept of work itself. And similarly we are not dealing with increased or diminished democracy but with changes in democracy's very essence.

All this naturally requires a change of focus. We must concentrate less on the *technical* appreciation of information and communications technology, and instead cultivate our understanding of such technology as a complex of socially significant systems. To this end, I have tried to outline the rudiments of a 'semantics' of computerized telecommunication: the foundation of a science of such systems' sociological *meaning*, of the normative cultural, political and social *content* which they subliminally contain. A number of examples are given in the book of the socially significant content of computerized telecommunications systems, as they are administered in different ways and under different social and political conditions.

A further consequence of my argument is that we *must* try to work out *how* this social revolution is to take place in accordance with the real needs and desires of the population at large. It is my belief that the revolution *can* be a democratically controlled social experiment. To this end, in my opinion, so-called "social experiments" with computerized telecommunication systems would be of considerable assistance. My final chapter provides a terminology and some guidelines for such experiments.

The book addresses itself to a variety of readerships. Human, organizational, and societal aspects of telematics have been the objects of awareness, consideration and analysis for some time now, but we have lacked a theoretical foundation for such analysis, and a theoretical tool which could lend an element of sobriety to the facile judgements of the humanities. So, such readers as have already been dealing with the new technology's human, organizational, and societal aspects will find chapters 2, 4 and 10 particularly interesting.

But the book is also intended for readers with technical insight in telematics, i.e. for engineers, and technicians, who are familiar with information and telecommunications technology, and who are interested in getting an orientation in the theoretical research regarding the societal aspects of this technology. It might be an advantage for such readers to start by reading chapters 5-10, which contain a relative number of concrete examples, before tackling the more theoretical considerations in the earlier chapters. The rudimentary facts in chapter 1 will of course be known to such readers already.

Finally, however, the book is also intended for a more general intellectually enquiring readership. If such readers are starting from scratch they may perhaps find chapters 2 and 4 rather heavygoing. Temporary postponement or subsequent re-reading should make life easier as far as those chapters are concerned.

The book would never have materialized without the help of a large number of people. First and foremost I am indebted to Philip Edmonds who has demonstrated that true translation includes critical examination — sometimes even re-creation — of the book translated. I am grateful, as well, to the Danish Research Council For the Humanities, which has granted the translation.

I am very much obliged to Aage Edvardsen and Jacob Mey. If the Danish state R. and D. appointments policy were not such that innovative research and development in the Humanities are virtually under boycott at the time of writing, Aage Edvardsen would have been the joint author of this book. Much of the thought expressed in the book has evolved out of conversations with him, and some of the chapters are revised versions of the fruits of earlier collaborations with Aage Edvardsen. Jacob Mey, both as colleague and as editor, has given me a great deal of inspiration and constructive criticism. And I would also like to express my gratitude to colleagues on the research project *Telematics and the Individual's Situation* Keld Vorup Sørensen and Niels Jørgen Jensen, and to our secretaries Kirsten Albjerg and Hanne Christensen, who have had the ungrateful task of deciphering my own, and my translator's, handwriting.

TRANSLATOR'S PREFACE

It is now almost forty years ago that George Orwell changed the last two digits around in his calendar and produced his famous *1984*. In retrospect there can be no doubt that what he presented as a terrible future was, in reality, a dramatised continuation of a terrible past. Yet another legacy of World War II which is still very much with us was the creation of NATO and the Warsaw Pact, and the start of the competition for the development of advanced information processing and communications systems, to guide and control the increasingly sophisticated weaponry which has been developed as the inevitable result of the logic of the life and death competition between East and West.

In the last quarter of the 20th C. it has, however, become increasingly clear that such advances in information processing and communications may also be put to peace-time use, in the same way as atomic physics was discovered to have valuable peacetime applications in the years following the Second World War. In a civilian context, however, just as atomic power has been bedevilled by ignorance and fear on the one hand, and extravagant claims for its usefulness on the other, so too modern I.T. (information technology) and telematics technology have provoked over-enthusiastic reactions, for suspect reasons, from P.R. people on the one hand, and ignorant and suspicious demands for their rejection on the other.

Future readers of this book will doubtless acknowledge that, by the fateful year of 1984, it had become abundantly clear that — if 'war' were to be 'peace' (as Orwell had predicted) for the advanced industrial nations of the world for an indefinite future period of time — the adaptation of military technology to peacetime ends was crying out for a book like Qvortrup's which could dispel the mists of ignorance and fear, as well as all the smoke with which the sophisticated P.R. people had for too long endeavoured to blind too many — especially within the well-heeled business community. In fact the fundamental reason for the success awaiting a book like this is precisely the degree of urgency with which it is needed. For not only does the book sweep away the cobwebs of half truths and misconceptions, of ungrounded hopes and fears surrounding I.T. and telematics technology, replacing them with a clear and consistent conceptual framework for our understanding of precisely what the new technology is, and what it actually can be used for. But it also provides us with a concrete strategy for the realisation of the very best that the late 20th and 21st centuries can hope for from the technology in terms of the improvement of our existing highly industrialised societies.

In acting as the medium through which this — unquestionably immensely valuable — work could become known to an English-speaking audience throughout the world, I have seen my own task as a twofold one. In the first place, I have endeavoured to translate as clearly, concisely and fluently as I could, the philosophical and technical language which is Qvortrup's natural element in his own language. And, secondly, I have seen it as my task to familiarise Qvortrup's larger global public with such detailed aspects of Danish culture and society as are not matters of common knowledge outside the little nation's own borders. This latter task, however, struck me as incomplete without a short account of the author himself, and I have therefore availed myself of the opportunity afforded by this preface to satisfy the curiosity of the world at large with a few brief details concerning Qvortrup and his position in the intellectual life of Denmark and of late 20th C. continental Europe generally.

In the aftermath of the 1968 student uprisings, it was, in a sense, no accident that the German student power leader, Rudi Dutschke, should seek refuge in Aarhus, the Danish capital of Jutland and Denmark's largest metropolis outside Copenhagen. Dutschke, who had been wounded in the head by a police bullet, was nevertheless able to hold a number of seminars at Aarhus University before his tragically premature death. And it was here, at this beautifully situated seat of learning, that Lars Qvortrup received his education. But the reason why Aarhus University should welcome Dutschke with open arms at this time was due to the fact that the Danish universities had just, more or less peacefully, broken the traditional power of their professorial élites, and had introduced one of the most liberal university administrations in Europe.

Combined with an enormous influx of students — thanks to the Danish Social Democratic tradition of free access to a university education, free university tuition, and a very liberal student grant system covering the typical eight-year study period — this administrative system ensured that many very young and relatively unknown academics, often of radical persuasion, were hired to teach courses on an hour by hour basis. The more popular the course, the more the young teachers' economic position was consolidated and improved. Of course they were pitifully underpaid, but all contributions were welcome to eke out the grants and interest-free loans, which the increasingly right-wing governments tended almost annually to reduce throughout the 'seventies, in reaction to the energy crisis, which rapidly, and painfully, made itself felt in a little country with relatively few mineral resources of its own and no atomic power.

So, throughout Lars Qvortrup's university education, the most popular courses were the courses which threw open doors and windows onto the radical intellectual traditions of Europe, and especially those of France and Germany. The younger Danish academics absorbed these new schools of thought ravenously, and developed them indigenously through an ongoing process of intellectual cross-fertilization, applying the latest ideas to virtually every traditional field of academic study, and even developing new fields of study, where the older boundaries seemed inadequate to cope with late 20th C. realities, or abolishing intellectual boundaries altogether, in order to tackle specific problem complexes on an interdisciplinary basis. New 'university centres' opened in three other major Danish cities — at Aalborg in Northern Jutland; at the royal cathedral town of Roskilde near Copenhagen, where salvaged Viking ships have been imaginatively housed in a new glass museum overlooking the bay only a few kilometers from Denmark's world-famous nuclear research institute, founded by Niels Bohr; and at Hans Christian Andersen's birthplace, Odense, on the beautiful island of Funen. Lars Qvortrup is now a fellow of the latter university, where he is at present working with his team on a characteristic project investigating 'Telematics and the Individual's Situation'. His time is divided between his theoretical work and his more practical role as adviser in connection with various current Danish social experiments with telematics. The constant endeavour to integrate pure and applied research, to bring academics out of their ivory tower seclusion, is typical of Denmark's new university centres, which have from the first been characteristically open towards the new radical ideas sweeping northwards from Foucault's and Althusser's Paris, and from East, as well as West Germany.

Yet at Odense, as well as at all the other Danish universities, the newest ideas have constantly had to fight against the old, and, of course, to vie with each other for the younger academics' favour. The students have been constantly forced to weigh the alternative approaches, the alternative lines of thought against each other, and the battles have been lively and enormously fruitful, though inevitably at times bitter and puerile, between Frankfurt School 'Idealists' on the one hand, and determinist adherents of French Structuralism on the other, while Popperesque Positivists and self-congratulatory New Critics have been hovering anxiously on the sidelines, wondering whether traditional scientific method or the traditional moral concerns of the humanities would survive the impact of the new 'subjectless' concept of history, or the new 'objectless' concept of science ...

Qvortrup, then, has made his detailed exploration of the 'internal logic' of *Das Kapital*, but he has also read much more of the early Marx than is generally known in the English-speaking world. He has read and despaired with Althusser and Foucault, but he has also received enormous optimistic inspiration from Ernst Bloch, the German utopian thinker who figures most prominently in the present book. Perhaps most important of all, Qvortrup, originally a student of literature, has an extensive knowledge and deep love of the great 19th C. Danish authors, including Hans Christian Andersen and N.F.S. Grundtvig; the former as culturally pessimistic as the latter was optimistic. And, rather unusually in Denmark, Qvortrup possesses, of course, a very extensive knowledge of the serious North American intellectual scene, from Marcuse to McLuhan, Bell, Toffler, Porat and Lasch.

Ernst Bloch, Lars Qvortrup's main inspiration, was both an admirer and a critic of the early pioneers of Critical Theory: Adorno, Marcuse, Pollock, Fromm, Leo Löwenthal and Walter Benjamin. Their aim was then — as Qvortrup's is now — to unite philosophical speculation and empiricism, and in accordance with the concept of totality in the Hegelian Marxism of the young Georg Lukács, for example, to reject any partial aspect of social life or any isolated phenomenon as incomprehensible unless related to the historical whole, to the social structure conceived as global entity.

Together with Horkheimer, Adorno and Marcuse, as well as Habermas, Lars Qvortrup patently disbelieves, however, in some Hegelian logic of history 'guaranteed' by the historical action of a Marxist proletariat. Yet, just as Horkheimer was unable to resist the temptation to reinterpret Kant's *Critique of Pure Reason* in 'concrete utopian' terms, substituting humanity itself for Kant's transcendental subject, so Qvortrup would seem to be reluctant to abandon a fundamental belief in history as an all-embracing process in which an historical subject attains its essence. Like Habermas, he seems to believe in the possibility of controlling the development of societies by institutionalized and politically effective public discussion: a possibility which his concept of the social experiment with telematics is obviously intended to go some way towards realising.

Lars Qvortrup, then, is an exponent of a very valuable European intellectual tradition rooted in the Enlightenment and hardened in opposition to the most perverted form of social development ever to be witnessed in any 20th C. industrial society — the totalitarian Fascism which Orwell so disconcertingly immortalized in *1984*. With his peculiarly Danish emphasis on pragmatism, his searching irony and his far-ranging impartiality — with his refusal, ultimately, to give in to the enormous forces of ignorance, fear, stupidity and short-sighted self-interest which surround us on all sides — Lars Qvortrup reminds us again and again of the relevance of that tradition.

Enjoying Lars's wisdom and humour as I have been privileged to be able to do at regular intervals for almost a year now — having been given the freedom to 'write whatever I liked', to expand his manuscript or to curtail it where I thought fit, to restructure the entire work, and to go back to his sources and quote more or less from them as I felt would be most appropriate — I have learnt at first hand something of what he meant by his idealistic, and yet pragmatic and essentially humane concept of the 'social experiment'. For every single change which I have offered to make in the original manuscript, and every single suggestion I have made for the translation of every 'difficult' word, has been the subject of shorter or longer — and always deeply cordial — discussion between us. They are discussions for which I have been immeasurably the richer. And yet, not content with all that he has already given me throughout the actual work process, with typical generosity Lars himself has insisted on taking full responsibility for every word in this English version, while at the same time acknowledging my collaboration with gratitude! No translator could wish for fairer treatment: few other authors would ever let their translator so easily off the hook!

At the time of writing this preface I have no knowledge of Lars's intentions concerning the dedication of this work, which is destined to pass through the hands of countless students of philosophy, sociology, political science and business economics, as well as finding its way onto the desks of numerous policymakers, whether in government or in private industry. But I would like to dedicate my own humble contribution to its success to my parents, whose help and support in earlier life did so much to render me as fit for this task as the most generous and loyally biased reader may deem me to have been. Like Lars Qvortrup, I have had the invaluable advantage of an old-fashioned and sincerely Christian upbringing — a fact which, despite ali our subsequent fascination with philosophical materialism, is no doubt ultimately largely responsible for our shared critical idealism, for our shared belief (which is fundamental to the moral project of the humanities) that to do as you would be done by is, as Kant considered, not necessarily a bad place to start ...

List of technical abbreviations

CAL: Computer Aided Learning.
CATV: Cable Television (earlier: Community Antenna Television).
DBS: Direct Broadcasting Satellite.
DP: Data Processing
EDP: Electronic Data Processing.
ISDN: Integrated Services Digital Network.
LAN: Local Area Network.
Modem: Modulator-Demodulator. A device that connects peripherals and that converts and reconverts digital signals into tone variations (in serial form).
RAM: Random Access Memory.
VDU: Video Display Unit.
VLSI: Very Large Scale Integration. Integrated circuits on a silicon chip that contains a large number of semiconductor devices.
WP: Word Processing.

INTRODUCTION

The word 'telematics' means much less in technological terms than it does in sociological terms. Technically we're talking about 'an integrated system of telecommunications and information processing'. But telematics can also mean a higher standard of living, democracy, happiness — or equally, it can mean unemployment, repression and cultural impoverishment. Telematics is one of those rare terms arousing simultaneous enthusiasm and fear around the world, on the one hand inspiring grandiose national development projects, while, on the other hand, sceptics claim that perhaps George Orwell got his dates right after all ... For some, telematics augurs well for the realisation of Popper's 'Open Society', a reign of freedom, while for others it portends a return to a Benthamite 'panopticon', where everyone would have to spy on everyone else in order to maintain a 'democratic' balance of power. More markedly than any other form of technology, perhaps, information and communications technology seems to inspire visions of the future — rose-coloured visions as well as nightmares. In 1980, Alvin Toffler wrote in his widely-read volume *The Third Wave* that "[...] communications, selectively applied, can serve the goal of telecommunity." (1980: 389) — A community created by the replacement of transport by electronic communication, bringing back a world of cottage industries, where people work at or near their homes with their families and friends, where individual knowledge is increased and individual loneliness is relieved.

But only a year earlier, Christopher Lasch published his book *The Culture of Narcissism* with a very different message: "The media give substance to and thus intensify narcissistic dreams of fame and glory, encourage the common man to identify himself with the stars and to hate the 'herd', and make it more and more difficult for him to accept the banality of everyday existence." (1978) In Lasch's vision the prospect is not one of fellowship and interpersonal collaboration but of unemployment and loneliness: and, even worse, the existential loneliness of people who have no personal identity of their own but who only 'imitate' — who, in other words, are mere copies of remote idols.

So the new information and telecommunications techniques and their related sciences call up visions of the future — they fascinate and provoke debate. But why? In my opinion it is because computerized telecommunications systems bring into play a number of 'grand themes'.

What are these 'grand themes'? They are those which have occupied a central place in public debate since the middle of the 18th century, and have been the preoccupation of 'grand theme specialists' — philosophers, in other words. There are a considerable number of such themes, of course, but the two I want to mention here are 'education' and 'democracy'.

Ever since Rousseau produced his educational theories in the 18th century, some hard and fast ideas have prevailed about the education of the individual, i.e. each individual's development from child into adult. According to these ideas, this is a process with well-defined aims, which is continuous over a number of years, is realised through interaction between adults (parents or teachers) and children, and involves a certain degree of compulsion.

But today the theme of education has again become a matter of moment because some of these basic tenets have been questioned. Many people feel that educational ideals are under threat: adult authority seems to be threatened; the media play an increasingly larger part in the educational process; and young people seem more and more to be educating themselves, in the absence of the traditional degree of external pressure and unity of purpose. Some regard these trends with anxiety, others welcome them as progress, but few deny their existence. In any event, the classic education debate has been reopened, and to a considerable extent this is due to developments in information and communications technology.

Similarly, the democracy debate has been revived. What is going to happen to the public life of the individual — his participation in political decision-making processes and his free-time participation in clubs and associations, for instance? On the one hand it is claimed that computerized telecommunications will ease access to information and facilitate point-to-point communication — with mini- and microcomputers, new local community T.V. media, electronic 'postal services' with word-processors sending out circulars to a closed circle of recipients (members of a club or society, for instance), etc. etc. On the other hand, attention is drawn to the growing possibility of keeping tabs on individuals via centralized state-controlled or privately owned databanks. The gap between the very knowledgeable and the less knowledgeable will become wider, it is claimed, and so-called 'electronic democracy' is considered to be a mere parody of what we now understand by democracy, reducing broadly-based public decision-making processes to tendentiously prefabricated opinion polls.

Developments in information and communications technology actually involve a considerable number of such 'grand themes', and those who are unaware of this fact may well become the blind and hapless victims of the play of such themes in their most debased and truistic versions.

But aren't people generally aware of this state of affairs already? In my opinion the answer is 'no' — or, at least, that they are not sufficiently aware of it. Only too typically, awareness of the ways in which technology and the grand themes impinge on each other fails to get beyond a few facile words of warning. In Denmark, for example, a recent government report on telecommunications rather anxiously wondered whether we could 'manage to make such comprehensive machinery available to the public without doing damage to central values in human intercourse'. But this worry was rapidly brushed aside to make way for an unreserved paean to Progress: "Such questions may arise, but they are not such obstacles as ought to prevent us from dauntlessly going ahead to develop and make available the best of the new technology. It is no good turning one's back on developments which will come about anyway." (The Danish Government 1983)

The choice of words is revealing. In spite of a verbal acceptance of the desirability of analyses of the social consequences of the technology, such analyses are rapidly transformed into 'obstacles'. Thus, those who want to consider the possible development policy alternatives — and influence the shape of things to come — are 'in the way'. And those whose discerning glances most closely scrutinize the technological developments are accused of 'turning their backs'!

Often, only minimal account is taken of the possible consequences of such technology, either with regard to industrial policy, or to communications policy, or to cultural policy. Instead, like the naïve peasant boy in the fairy-tale, one places oneself in the hands of fate, which in our time means in the hands of minutely described 'miraculous' technology. The hope is, of course, that if only one has enough good faith, then fortune will stand by the candid. In reality these are instances of a situation which is at once paradoxical and most unfortunate: even at the highest level of policy making, among such circles which are formally created precisely in order to debate value-laden long-range policy, so-called 'value-free' ('value-less', or even 'thoughtless' might be better words!) technocratic rationality prevails.

'Technocratic rationality' is a concept at once paradoxical, most unfortunate, and mendacious to boot. In purely abstract terms, the shape of the so-called 'Information Society' of the future will depend on a specific number of political choices. It is not a question of *whether* these choices will be made, but *how*, and *by whom*.

A recent futurology symposium in the United States reached the following conclusions:

- "The wristwatch video-telephone, permitting televisual communication by satellite with anyone anywhere and at any time, *will become* a reality within the next thirty years."
- "Future homes, which will be more compact and less energy consumptive, *will have* playrooms, workrooms, and sitting-rooms equipped with technical innovations, such as holographic 3 D television sets, and computers which will be operated by simple verbal commands."
- "While factories *will become* increasingly automated, the home *will become* the computerized office for an increasing number of company employees ... Here, too, an increasing amount of the demand for education and adjustment-to-industry re-training *will be met* by computers and television." (Jyllandsposten 1983)

But such forecasts are misleading. We don't *have to* put all our money on *individual* video-communications — in principle, we might just as well go all out to develop communications facilities for specific *groups* of people — neighbourhoodgroups, clubs or associations, etc. It is *not* an irrefutable matter of course that work will have to be done in the future behind a terminal within the lonely seclusion of one's own four walls: it is equally possible, for instance, to set up so-called 'neighbourhood offices' — places of work in which the advantages of long-distance communication are exploited to create new colleague fellowships within the same neighbourhoods, while at the same time avoiding the traditional daily transportation problems. It is true that in the society of the future it *will be possible* for us to revive the cottage industry life-style without the functional necessity of the traditional family unit — but it is *no less* true that we will also have the possibility of reviving a whole village type community. We shall, in other words, be able to provide frameworks embracing work, local politics, and social activities, for whole neighbourhood communities.

No, as far as their social, political and cultural implications are concerned, computerized telecommunications systems are open-ended. And that means that every decision affecting telematics development or installation policies is — consciously or unconsciously — a choice between several possible social, political or cultural futures.

Now, any choice that is made between different possible future societies will inevitably be rooted in sociological and philosophical value assignments, many of which have already been debated centuries ago: right back in classical times, for instance. This means that it becomes vitally necessary for us to examine current developments in telematics against their background of much older socio-cultural developments, together with the social routines, cycles and value systems which these developments have given rise to. We shall be able to see how the development of this new technology has brought back into play many of the earlier socio-cultural themes. We shall come to realise that many of the visions of an 'Information Society' have relatively little to do with technology and a great deal more to do with traditional utopias.

In considering the ways in which the development of the new technology is taking place in relation to historical experience and historically rooted values, one typical line of development involves thinking about the relationship between Man and Nature; the history of Man's increasing ability to gain control over Nature (at least in a limited sense). Another development trend involves the relationship between Man and Man; the way in which increasing control over Nature has played a part in the development of a mutual humanity — has shaped the history of human civilisation, in other words.

This book is an attempt to demonstrate that any attempt to comprehend the new technology is incomplete without an understanding of such major themes in the history of human civilisation as are reflected in, absorbed by — and which take on a new lease of life through — telematics technology itself. So-called 'technocratic rationality', which claims, albeit indirectly, that technology may be comprehended on its own merits, merely reflects the deliberate suppression, or purely absent-minded omission, of specific object clauses rooted in the history of human civilisation. In the worst instance, this ideology may reflect a brutal lack of regard for the main preoccupations of the humanities, involving the debasement of moral and educational aspirations. Developments in telematics may thus take place under the banner of a technocratic rationality which recommends itself in 'better', 'more', 'faster' terms, but forgets to deal with questions of quality, or is content merely to quantify such questions. One becomes, quite literally, the passive victim of an aimless determinism, the true content of which one has for ever cut oneself off from understanding.

And so we come to the problem of defining the relationship between technology and the history of human civilisation. Normally, two kinds of logic are proffered in explanation of the role of technology in social history. On the one hand it is claimed that technology is apolitical in itself, and only assumes political significance when it comes into contact with individuals or whole societies. The by now classic expression of this kind of thinking is the Marxist-Leninist version: the means of production are considered to be neutral in themselves, but they are frequently hard-pressed under dubious working conditions. Hence the battle-cry that the working conditions must be revolutionized and the means of production set free.

One often finds representatives of the opposing camp, the defenders of existing society, resting their case on the same fundamental conception — although they tend to have a very different assessment of the working conditions! Capitalist society is the best possible kind of society, they say. Any failing it has is due to the fact that it is not permitted to function freely, but has its hands tied everywhere at the mercy of powerful organisations and bureaucratic state institutions. So, from their point of view, too, the means of production must be set free — not, of course, from capitalism itself, but from all the cancerous growths which drain the freedom out of capitalism. Thus, although the assessments of the obtaining social conditions are very different, the underlying beliefs about the relationship between the means of production and the conditions of production are identical. And these underlying beliefs, which in reality cut across party lines, result in the fact that in abstract terms both political camps adopt an optimistic stance towards technological development.

An alternative way of considering the role of technology in social history is based on a hypothesis about human authenticity: Man was once unspoilt, both as regards his relationships with his fellowmen and as regards his relationship to Nature. He has since become degenerate. His relationship to his fellowmen and to Nature has been corrupted through the intervention of technology. From this point of view it is technology which is fundamentally at fault — the instrument of human decadence. And inevitably such a belief results in an abstract antipathy towards technology.

Now, in my opinion, both of these explanations of the role of technology in social history, which I have very summarily presented here, reflect the presence of purposive societal meanings immanent in technology (and by implication in telematics technology, too, of course), despite the fact that they themselves deny the existence of such immanent societal meanings.

So one of the most important functions of this book must be the development of an approach towards an understanding of the societal meanings immanent in computerized telecommunications systems; an approach which will help us to increase our awareness of the normative cultural, political and social content which they subliminally contain.

And a further consequence is that ways must be found to ensure that telematics developments are consciously brought into line with democratically chosen normative aspirations. The approach suggested in this book I have called the *social experiments with telematics* approach.

To sum up, then: what I want to argue in this book is that modern information and telecommunications technology cannot be properly understood if we persist in treating technology and society as two independent entities. But, on the other hand, another equally important aim of the book is to argue against the idea that the alternative has to be the sort of critical analysis that Marx was already propounding in the last century. In the same way as psychoanalysis has probed repressed areas of consciousness (covert remnants of past experience in the human psyche, in other words) Marxist criticism has indeed probed the covert societal content inherent in technology — covert remnants of past profit-seeking intentions, for example. But modern technical systems are not just chunks of frozen past. They also carry within them repressed future potentiality.

So I want to argue that, on the one hand, the latest telematics technology — dealing as it does with information and communications systems — is so intrinsically societal, both in form and content, that the traditional division of labour between technology (defined as the science of what is technically practicable) and sociology, or social science, is simply not able to deal with it adequately. While, on the other hand, this new technology is so future oriented, so pregnant with utopia, as it were, that the traditional critical Marxist retrospective focus is equally unable to do justice to it.

I have divided my argument into several parts: in the first two chapters I try to explore the claim that telematics cannot be comprehended as technology alone, but as a complex of ideas and meanings, both technical and social. These ideas and meanings, moreover, interact with each other dialectically: the design and development of telematics technology is significantly conditioned by its social context. In the third chapter I analyse the tendential aspects of telematics, the ways in which they reflect the artificially singled out, distorted, and dominating needs for development and economic growth, the need for profit, which is characteristic of capitalist society. So the 'past origins' of telematics are dealt with in chapter three, in other words. Chapter four deals with the 'future potentialities' inherent in telematics. For not only does this technology reflect a profit motive, as many of its critics consider, but it also derives from a yearning for social equality, individual freedom, and human dignity. In other words, telematics contains within itself many possible utopias: repressed future potentiality.

Towards the end of the book, in chapters 9-10 I explore some of the consequences of this analysis for applied research. In part, of course, as I have mentioned earlier, such an analysis points to the necessity for a fundamental change in our ways of looking at and understanding technology, but, no less importantly, it also recommends as indispensable the substitution of social experiments with telematics for traditional technology assessment. Such social experiments would permit a future-oriented evaluation of telematics, liberating the potential for free and worthy human development latent in the new technology, instead of abandoning it to the vagaries of the free market, or stunting its growth under rigid state control, which are the traditionally preferred alternatives. For instance, an examination of American and British telematics development policies reveals that deliberately uncontrolled development is both incompatible with media political goals and inconsistent with aspirations for industrial modernization, while, on the other hand, an exclusively industry-oriented state-controlled modernization program, such as the Japanese which I have summarily presented in chapter three, may all too easily nip the future potentiality of telematics in the bud. British and Danish on-line videotex development projects provide us with further illustrations of the very difficult conditions obtaining for the realisation of Information Society utopias. But in Chapter 9 I have elected to describe some promising pilot projects in France and Sweden which provide an empirical illustration of the desirability of controlled social experiments with telematics. In my final chapter I provide the theory and some practical guidelines for such experiments.

The central chapters of the book (chapters 5-8) are more speculative in character, emphasising the essential ambiguity of Information Society utopias. Brief hypotheses are offered concerning such concepts as work, democracy, power, and individual modes of perception in the Information Society. What, for example, will happen to our conceptions of space and time? What will happen to our sober estimates of causality, of the boundaries between present and future, in other words? What will happen to the so-called necessities of life, and to need-satisfaction, in a society in which the satisfaction of physical needs will be a trivial matter beside the satisfaction of cultural and educational needs? How will our moral codes develop, and, with them, the power structures in our societies?

1. THE TECHNICALITIES OF TELEMATICS

The word 'telematics' comes from the French *télématique* — a compound of two other words *télécommunication* and *informatique* —, which is thus intended to describe the growing integration between data transmission and data processing and storage.[1]

"A good communications network is basic for a country. We need fiber technology to create the transmission capability, VLSI technology for processing power and computers to exercise control."

According to Dr. Charles Kao, one of the pioneers of optical fibre technology, these three technological fields will become the cornerstones of the so-called Information Society. And he has no doubt that all three of these technological fields are already so far advanced that the technological foundation for such a society is at hand. (Kao 1982) Through the development of many different techniques, such as communications satellites, fibre optics and micro-electronics, it has become possible to increase long-distance intercourse between people, between people and computers, and between computers themselves. Possibilities have thus been created for point-to-point communication and mass communication by means of a single network, and the possibilities have been greatly enhanced for the automatic acquisition, storage, processing and retrieval of information, while the opportunities for democratic participation, for the acquisition of knowledge, and for media consumption, have reached a level which was unimaginable only a few years ago.

Developments in I.T. (information technology) and micro-electronics occur at lightning speed, so that the individual components get cheaper and cheaper at the same time as their versatility increases. Against a general background of very muted growth in western industrialized nations in recent years, the field of information technology has been characterized by dramatic expansion: it is commonly estimated that the production of E.D.P. systems displays an annual growth rate of 17%, while integrated circuit development exhibits an annual growth rate of as much as 25% (EEC Commission 1979). Obviously such developments are of enormous consequence for the future communications structures of entire nations.

Only superficially are these developments taking place 'by themselves', i.e. with technology itself as their *primus motor*. At the heart of the growth rates in I.T. lies an economic development whose most obvious connection with the I.T. explosion is the structural imbalance between industrial manufacturing sectors and so-called information sectors. The latter have exhibited above average increases in the number of people employed, but productivity increases in such sectors have been below average.[2] Just one example: the so-called 'Yankee Group' calculate that industrial productivity in the seventies grew by 90%, while office productivity in the same period only grew by 4%. (Serafini and Andrieu 1980: 19) The relatively low growth in productivity in information sectors has given rise to the need for the technical modernisation of these sectors — the technical improvement of office-work, private and public administration, communication between business, etc. And the overall growth of these sectors has meant that this need for technical improvement has been a matter of vital importance. Further elaboration of these remarks about the basis for the development of telematics technology can be found in chapter 3.

Bell Telephone Laboratories representatives in A.T. & T., the world's largest telematics business, have no doubt at all that Charles Kao is right in maintaining that the technological foundation for the so-called Information Society *is* at hand. Glass fibre technology is now so reliable that plans have been made to link up the major American cities on the East Coast from Boston to Washington in a laser-beam-conducting fibreoptic cable network. Pilot projects have proved very promising, both with regard to the *capacity* of fibreoptic cables (i.e. the amount of T.V. channels, they can carry, for example), and with regard to their *attenuation* (i.e. to what extent the signals get weakened over a given distance) which is very slight under laboratory conditions. Silicon chip technology (i.e. the construction of integrated circuits out of thousands of transistors and other electronic components packed onto tiny slivers of silicon only about a quarter of an inch square) has developed exponentially in recent years. Each year has seen a doubling of the amount of functions a single chip can hold, and we're not far from a chip with a million components. And, finally, tremendous efforts are being made to develop the so-called magnetic bubble memory, a data storage system which involves tiny magnetic areas on a thin film of magnetic silicate, where the presence or absence of a magnetic charge in a particular location represents the digital information. It has proved possible to assemble ten millions of these 'bubbles' on an area a quarter of an inch square.

But, while these techniques are being developed, work is also being done to integrate them in one vast information and communications network, the so-called Integrated Services Digital Network (I.S.D.N.). According to Wayne J. Felts, of the A.T. & T. Network Planning Group, the I.S.D.N. is the American Telephone and Telegraph Company's answer to the technical challenges involved in the realisation of the utopian 'global village'. Together with A.M. Rutkowski, the U.S. Federal Commission on Communications' expert on the legal and technical aspects of communications technology, Wayne J. Felts at a conference in Washington D.C., 1982, claimed that "development of ISDN facilities over the next two decades will foster the integration of potentially all the world's information processing, storage and transfer systems into a single, vast, interconnected and interoperable computerized network that could become the nervous system of the long heralded global village". (Rutkowski 1982: 8)

At the time of writing, the I.S.D.N. is under preparation both technologically and politically. It is already possible to 'translate' all forms of speech, music, text and pictures into common digital equivalents, and all these kinds of information can be processed and stored by computers. The task of the I.S.D.N. is to provide a common network for the transmission of the total mass of information — which incidentally means that the separation of information processing from telecommunications becomes more and more dysfunctional. Politically, the major task is to develop uniform standards throughout the world for the I.S.D.N. According to representatives of the A.T. & T., it is no longer the solution of technical problems, but the completion of this latter task, which is the crucial precondition for the enormous capital investment required to develop the system.

Communication by laser along glass fibre cables, and silicon chip data processing, are perhaps the two most significant techniques among those mentioned above. The fibre optic technique (otherwise known as the glass fibre, or light conductor, technique) has a very strong chance of influencing the creation of any society's future communications structure by means of the so-called broadband networks. While existing telephone cables have a relatively small bandwidth capacity, the new light conducting cables using digital transmission operate with much higher frequencies extending into the visible spectrum, which means that they have almost infinite bandwidth availability. This means that telephonic transmission can be integrated with the transmission of (two-way) radio and television signals, and computer information, down one and the same cable, and this, in turn, means that a single common network — an integrated broadband network — can link up a very large number of different service suppliers and users. Because these broadband networks can simultaneously transmit a very large number of two-way radio and T.V. channels, telephone and telex messages, electronic mail, divers alarm systems, and an enormous amount of electronic data, amongst other things, and because such services can be further developed and linked to each other to provide facsimile newspapers, video telephones, etc., an entirely new communications system will be created. To give just one example: functionally, the distinction between mass communication and point-to-point communication will, of course, be maintained in such a system, but technically it will be overridden by each user's dependence on the integrated network. Networks of this kind are already being tried out on a small scale in several different parts of the world.

As far as electronic data processing is concerned, the most significant technical development is the 'dedicated' microcomputer — a tiny silicon chip, with processor, memory, and a considerable amount of input and output electronic circuitry, which has a particular program of instructions 'burned' into it, so that it can be dedicated to doing a particular task. Such chips form part of a vast range of products, including many of those involved in providing the many services which a communications network, such as the one mentioned above, would interconnect. The most immediate effects of the new technology can be felt in the D.P. and W.P. (data and word processing) sectors of the business world and the public sector (office work, and private and public administration), while the influence of this new technology on our private lives (in the form of a vast range of electronic media equipment) is no less in evidence.

Nor, indeed, have these recent developments taken place without significant consequences for telematics research — the most important of which may be summarized as follows:

1. In several countries we have been witnessing structural changes in R. and D. policies rather than mere sectorial developments — the reason being, of course, that telematics embraces not one but a number of different techniques, and is, itself, a system of technical systems. An example of this might be office automation, where data is passed around for storage and processing at different points along a local area network (L.A.N.), which again has access to external networks, linking up other technical system complexes. This means that developments in any sector have consequences

for other sectors and are in turn dependent on developments in other sectors. Intersectoral R. and D. coordination is therefore requisite but not sufficient — research has to be done on the interlocking systems *per se*. In other words, structural R. and D. policies become the order of the day.

2. Technological developments in the field of telematics can affect many different aspects of our daily lives. The development of the microcomputer, for example, can affect our work situations (automation, changes in the nature of office work), our leisure time (new forms of entertainment) and our education systems (new teaching aids, different qualification requirements). Any attempt to assess the consequences of new developments in telematics must, therefore, reflect this broad spectrum of integrated effects, through a higher degree of interdisciplinary collaboration between the traditionally separate disciplines of the humanities and the social sciences.

3. The technical systems involved in telematics will have an immediate effect on any society, thanks both to their content and their form. For example, the installation of any national, or even any local, cable network, of a given type providing given services, creates sociological, as well as technological, problems. It is my firm conviction that here, too, an interdisciplinary collaboration between techno- and sociology must be established, because in this context, at least, the traditional separation of these two disciplines is no longer fruitful.

4. Finally, one witnesses increasing support for long-term telematics R. and D. — in Development Centers, 'Think Tanks', etc. — in such countries as Japan, Canada and France. Attempts are made to impart 'utopian' dimensions, hitherto the exclusive property of philosophy or the history of ideas, to this kind of academic work. This is partly due to the fact that telematics *is* in itself future-oriented — it does, in other words, contain within itself a variety of latent possibilities, possible futures.

5. In my opinion, these features of telematics are better taken into account in social experiments with telematics than they are in more traditional technology assessments, because such social experiments start with the society concerned, and with societal needs, instead of with the technology and its supposedly 'inevitable' impositions on any given society. And, no less important, the inherent flexibility of telematics is better taken into account in social experiments. Thus, instead of stagnating in its own unadventurous inhumanity, telematics technology can grow in response to the continuously

new challenges arising from discussions among those representatives of the societies concerned who are participating in the experiments.

2. THE SOCIAL SIGNIFICANCE OF TELEMATICS

2.1. *The Significance of Technology.*

> "If we only set foot in the enormous workshops, or watch the proud sailing-ships propelled by wind and currents sweeping across rivers and seas, then we have no need to have a full practical knowledge of their precise artificial construction, or to fathom the laws which they obey, in order to apprehend the true spirit of these mighty works; from their effects we comprehend not only the marvellous powers which lie concealed in speechless nature, but also those which are closest to ourselves — in our own articulate, indeed eloquent, semi-divine, Human Nature [...]."[3]

Confronted with the newest technology in England in 1830-32, the famous Danish Christian philosopher and historian, Bishop N.F.S. Grundtvig, realised at once that technology is something other than, something more than, 'speechless nature'. Technology is also the incarnation of the Mind of Man, of human nature, which you don't need to be a technician to be able to appreciate. Actually it's tempting to say that almost the reverse is true — the more you let yourself be blinded by technology as a piece of mindless matter, the more blind you become to its spiritual content, its social significance and purpose.

Telematics is a technical system. But to say that is not enough. Telematics is not just a simple tool, manipulating nature. Telematics has been created by human beings to satisfy specific human needs. Its social significance is born of the interrelationship between physical nature, tools, and human needs. Such significance is covert, and intrinsic to any form of technology.

So, if you want to analyse the significance of any technical system, what you have to analyse is the product of the interaction between human needs, tools and manipulated nature. Human needs are specific characteristics of human beings *vis-à-vis* specific things. So the 'semantics' of any form of technology, and the semantic analysis of it, means the study and analysis of the reciprocal relationship between potential use-values and potential human needs, out of which specific use-values and human needs are born. "All that is truly human, bears the impress of the human spirit — though it be the labour of our hands, without this spirit it could as little endure as it could come into being." (Grundtvig 1877: 12)

One consequence of the above is that you cannot talk about 'immanent usefulness' or about 'intrinsic human needs'. So I find it impossible to accept any evaluation of technology which takes 'genuine' or 'fundamental' human needs as its yard-stick.

It is undeniable that the existence of our species necessarily presupposes the satisfaction of its hunger and its instinct for propagation. But, in the first place, 'hunger' and 'the reproductive instinct' must thus already have been defined in relation to the means of their satisfaction. And secondly, just talking about 'hunger' doesn't define the meaning — the social significance or purpose — of hunger, and it is precisely this aspect of hunger which makes all the difference when *we* are hungry! The hunger which is satisfied with tooth and claw is quite another hunger than that which is satisfied with a knife and fork, Marx pointed out.

It is a commonplace that the more highly developed our societies become, the less important becomes the biological element. But what needs interpretation is precisely this 'biological element', because even 'the primitive', and 'the natural', acquire historically-conditioned significance. To smell 'natural', to use unscented soap, for example, is of course no better nor more natural than smelling of strawberries or Yellow Moon, though the latter is considered 'unnatural'. An example like this merely shows how complicated our semantic systems are, and that the conflict is not an objective conflict between the natural and the artificial, but a conflict between socially significant definitions — definitions which are fighting for the right to *signify* 'that which is natural'.

So I must dismiss as fallacious the notion that the criterion for the development of any form of technology is to be found in some system of authentic human needs, and that as soon as technology ceases to satisfy these 'original' needs, it becomes 'decadent' and 'unnatural'. It is a very long time since such a conception could have any degree of plausibility, and, as far as modern information technology is concerned, it is, on the contrary, frequently the case that the technology lacks needs to satisfy!

Not that I'm saying that new kinds of 'artificial' needs must promptly be developed to satisfy the technology. My point is that, while these new technical systems may deserve criticism, it could never have anything to do with the fact that they may have 'outstripped' any particular needs they might satisfy. They can only be criticised in terms of their total social significance or purpose.

Yet another consequence is, too, that I find it equally impossible to accept the idea that technological development should become the yard-stick by which societal development is to be measured. A technologico-normative conception of this kind is frequently expressed in the cliché that 'it's no use trying to go against technological development'. At its most primitive, a statement of this kind is based on the belief that there is some kind of immanent logic behind technological development which is independent of any external social factors. But, at a deeper level, it expresses an allegiance to Reason as the norm for all human endeavour: practical technological achievements become the highest manifestations of the capabilities of the human intellect, of Man's ability to reason. Yet, of course, technological development has never ever been unrelated to the identification of human needs. And secondly, technological R. and D. in the capitalist world of today is so inextricably bound up with economic considerations that it is even more difficult to take seriously such a naïve belief in the immanent rationality of technology.

Briefly, then, my point is that both of these attitudes, whether they take authentic human needs, or idealised reason, as their norm, are rooted in the mistaken divorce of technology (seen as the incarnation of reason) from human nature (regarded as the seat of authentic needs). In effect, the only 'real' difference between their respective adherents is the gratuitous one of whether they happen to prefer to bestow normative status on (human) nature or on technology. No, developments, both in technology and in human needs, *must* be analysed and evaluated as results of an interdependent process, the ongoing process of human civilisation, whose central category is, as we have said, social significance or purpose.

Finally, we must never forget that although social significance is always covertly present in technology, it is *we* who bestow it upon the technology, *we* who create the technology to fulfil our own purposes. Just as in the arts we mould form and colour and sound and taste and smell to create something more than just colour, sound, etc. — significant or meaningful colour, sound as music, for instance — so, too, in technology we mould matter to form meaningful technological systems.

In the chapters to follow, I shall be analysing the essentially ambiguous social significance of telematics. For this significance emerges from an object-need interaction, i.e. the social purpose of the technology regards an unsatisfied Now looking forward to a better Future. A Future which is the product of an unsatisfying, an imperfect Present. In order to analyse the future potentiality of telematics as it has currently been developed — in a Present which looks beyond itself, which anticipates — I must define utopian thought as 'anticipation'. And I must direct the sights of my analytical artillery so that they point forwards.

This latter strategy is, of course, to take arms against any form of pure objectivity. The future is the 'Not Yet'. So it is Man, as the change-desiring being, who possesses the future. If the future were predictable, if, in theory, it were possible to predict it in the present, then it would actually be included in the present and hence not a real future at all, not a 'Not Yet', but a false future, an 'Already'. I always find it a bit of a paradox that pure objectivity, the denial of any real future, is most strongly represented in Marxism — the one social science doctrine which ought to have taken freedom's realm — the truly New — as its banner! In fact, the rejection of pure objectivity is, in the main, a battle between Marxism and Utopianism.[4]

In contemporary society, our human needs have acquired an independent life of their own through our economic system, which has taken control of our society. So it is, of course, this economic system which has conferred on telematics technology its dominant purposive, or significant, content — its tendential content. But profit is not the only motive for the development of this new technology — the pursuit of human freedom and dignity, etc., has also played a role. And it is the felt needs behind these latter aspirations which give telematics its normally repressed content, its variety of immanent future potentialities.

2.2. *Technology: The Study of Human Ingenuity in the Pursuit of Chosen Goals.*

Technology is not just the study of things technical. It is not purely a scientific discipline beyond the concern of the humanities. Technology is the study of how to gain control of things in order to achieve given ends — of how to gain control over matter in fact, in order to satisfy human needs. Technology is thus the study of the power of Man and the satisfaction of human needs.

In the first place, this means that any criticism of the power of telematic technology, for example, must always direct itself towards the *forms* (or manifestations) of power; you cannot criticise as such the power of technology. Specific forms of (social) control may be criticised: the desire to control one's animate and inanimate environment by means of technology must not be.

That technology is the study of human need satisfaction involves, in the second place, a recognition of the fact that the technology itself is designed specifically to achieve ends formulated by human beings. The 'human needs' we are talking about here are thus defined by a complex interplay of different human considerations — amongst others, considerations of 'basic' human needs, certainly, but considerations which cannot be separated from human imagination, and social conditions. Which is why they never exist *per se* for human beings. The recognition of this fact makes it easier to understand the meaning of saying that technology is created by specific human beings in specific societies with specific regard to those societies.

A realisation of this kind has a set of analytical consequences. To start with, it is clearly misleading to divorce technology from sociology: to study technology necessarily involves studying human beings and human societies. But, secondly, it is no less misleading to regard technology and sociology as identical! Technology is indeed the study of power, of social control, but a society's control over matter depends as much on the whims of nature as on the ingenuity of those who try to tame it. Yet, thirdly, it is obviously erroneous to dream about a form of technology which is innocuous, which is devoid of power, which bends before the sophisticated ecological sway of Nature instead of seeking to break the balance and subjugate Nature — just as it would be erroneous to imagine that Nature, meekly and without any more ado, will conform itself to our man-made concept of technological rationality. 'Either/or' thinking of this kind is an example of a classic delusion which is rooted in the intrinsic duality of any capitalist society's ideological constructs, as we shall see. But, while technology is the study of how to achieve given ends (or at least attempt to achieve given ends) with the help of human ingenuity, it is also the study of *transformations*: of the transformation of *physical nature*, which technological systems — designed with the aid of human ingenuity to satisfy human ends — go to work on; of the transformation of a given *society*, with all its different life-styles which influence and are influenced by the technical systems; of the transformation of *human needs* which the technical systems were originally intended to satisfy. For the development of a new 'generation' of technology presupposes the emergence of new needs to be satisfied.

Technology, the 'study of technical systems', must therefore be redefined as the study of the whims of Nature, the ingenuity of Man, and the leashed or unleashed forces for the transformation of Nature, Man and Society, which are immanent within the technical systems themselves. Significantly, too, technology is the *integral* study of all these phenomena as mutually dependent and interactive elements — elements which are all simultaneously present within the single entity, the technical system itself. There can be no question — no fond hope — of any single one of these elements coming to prevail over the others, be it Nature or Man.

Finally, we need constantly to remind ourselves that we are not studying a steady state, an unshakeably established order, but a process of becoming: a mediation of the qualitatively new out of the interplay of *conflicting* — but *mutually dependent* — societal elements. One obviously very relevant example of this is that, in complete accord with the concrete historical situation which was created in capitalist societies as the result of what Marx called 'primitive accumulation', bourgeois ideology formulated the relationship between Man and Nature as a 'struggle' between forces which could, in turn, 'triumph' over each other and impose their own order upon each other. To talk about this 'ongoing struggle between Man and Nature' is thus to reproduce a concrete — historically specific — cliché. But unreservedly to 'take sides' in this struggle — whether one sides with Nature or with Man — is to universalize the categories of an historically specific mode of thought — to universalize a specific historical development, in fact — and to identify oneself with the ideals peculiar to that historical development.

I mentioned earlier that studying technology necessarily involves studying mutually interactive systems. Far from being harmoniously interacting systems, these systems are in fact, as the above example suggests, ongoing conflict situations, in which the conflicting tendencies rest on a mutually presuppositive foundation.

So, when we address ourselves to the *causality* of technology, we mustn't talk in terms of cause and effect. We must think in terms of 'both-and' with reference to the mutually presuppositive foundation, the foundation which inevitably generates the conflict — the 'either/or' situation. And when we think about technology in *spatial* terms, we must not think in terms of polarisation — of Man confronting Nature and *vice versa*, with technology on the outside as a distinct, mediative third-party. We must think in terms of integration. In 'good' technology the whims of nature and the logic of the human mind are in perfect unity: a fine piece of medieval craftsmanship is a utopian symbol, every bit as much as the most refined and ingenious product of capital-intensive modern technology. It bears witness to the fact that the Man/Nature dichotomy is only a thing of our (essentially transient) capitalist world. Which is precisely why, when we think about technology in terms of *time*, it is important for us to think, as I said earlier, not in terms of the present, but in terms of immanent future potentiality — not in terms of being, but in terms of becoming.

'Both-and' is the alternative to 'either/or'. Not some sort of tactical theoretical compromise, sacrificing truth on the altar of pragmatism: that of course wouldn't get us anywhere. What we need is a 'both-and' perspective which consistently maintains that, for example, within the ongoing technology debate in capitalist societies at the present time the ideological polarities are erroneous, and therefore any attempt to reconcile them can only add up to something erroneous. An acceptance of the historical existence of these categories can never be more than a necessary precondition for their rejection: 'both-and' must command a 'neither/nor' perspective.

According to Ernst Bloch, *this* sort of 'tendential' thinking is the only way to mediate that which is truly, qualitatively new. His future-oriented philosophy of the systematic, historically-specific and dynamic interaction of Mind, Matter and Machine finds expression in his post-Hegelian concept of the 'heuristic model'; for example where he maintains that "every heuristic model is methodologically a 'thesis', and every thesis involving concrete anticipation refers to a concrete experimental model which participates in the creation of the world itself and its creatures". (Bloch 1977 [1965]: 88)

2.3. *Society's Generation of Alternatives.*

In a recent article in the Danish ecological bulletin *Naturkampen*, the editors argued for the necessity and potential of I.T. on the grounds that it might enable us to design technology which would function on Nature's own 'sophisticated' premisses, replacing previous technology, which has violated Nature to suit our own 'primitive' technological rationality: technology might at last be brought into line with Nature, in other words, rather than the other way round. Thus, although the editors of *Naturkampen* clearly took the side of sophisticated Nature against primitive technological rationality, they had *already* defined a paradigmatic frame of reference within which any discussion of I.T. would have to take place: a ratiocinative paradigm, incidentally, which is something which both supporters and opponents of I.T. in Denmark and elsewhere have in common. 'Danmedia', for example, a representative organisation promoting public awareness of the aims and concerns of the Danish I.T. and telematics industry, provides us with a strikingly parallel formulation of what they consider to be a very central question: will human beings be able to control technological developments, they ask, or will the intrinsic dynamism of technology itself thrust possibly unwanted — or insufficiently pre-tested — developments upon us?

So the question arises as to why both sceptics *and* ardent supporters of new technology are so much in agreement about the *terms* of the debate. How can I.T. fertilize each of their dreams alike, whether they are politically to the left or to the right? *Why* does the I.T. debate cut right across the traditional political spectrum, so that optimistic supporters of the new technology can be found both on the left and on the right — (both of them alike strongly going in for the improved efficiency of democratic administration and the means of production in advanced industrial societies) — while pessimistic critics are similarly to be found in both political camps? Answering questions like these requires a more profound examination of the mechanisms within capitalist societies which generate 'utopias', or yearnings for some kind of alternative society.

We can start by addressing ourselves to the common misconception that capitalism produces *uniformity*. It is considered to be typical of the system that its own logic will infiltrate and gradually destroy the authenticity of 'natural' human society, and of 'natural' humanity, which was originally the foundation upon which the system itself was built. What, in other words, are commonly considered to be inevitable tendencies — and indeed inevitable goals — of social development under capitalism are such things as the dissemination of a specific rational form of control over nature; the single-minded concentration on the creation of economic wealth at whatever human or environmental cost; the demand for a disciplined labour force, and stimulation of passive consumption at the expense of the development of the more creative, aesthetic potential of the whole society's citizenry; the realisation of political and administrative process models which tend to emphasize efficiency at the expense of considerations of democratic human rights; and the destruction of those human qualities which still struggle to survive in the sanctity of private citizens' own homes. In other words, capitalism's characteristic tendency is frequently considered to be the annihilation of the essential *variety* of 'natural' human life, and the generation, instead, of a 'one-dimensional' society and citizens. And the term normally given to this generation of one-dimensionality is 'alienation'.

Significantly enough, alienation is a term which has its critics throughout the length and breadth of the political spectrum. Defining its opposite involves using such terms as 'identity', or 'authenticity'. A 'true' sense of one's own, one's authentic and original 'natural' human identity, is thus frequently contrasted with the alienating tendencies of the forces at work in advanced civilisations which 'threaten to destroy' this 'true human identity'.

Critics of alienation, however, soon find themselves confronted with the determined disciples of 'progress' — progress defined as the dissemination of reason: reason permeating technology, social control and human intercourse under the dictates of democratic law and order. Seen from this point of view, the so-called 'authenticity' which opposes progress is regarded as reaction, and the progressive aim must be to subordinate the logic of authenticity to the more advanced subtleties of rational thinking. Once again, the project reaches across traditional political boundaries, uniting left-wing 'progressives' with the most extravagant of the new technology's right-wing apologists. Representatives of both camps seem, in fact, to be united in the common belief that the single necessary precondition for the realisation of their respective millennia is the destruction of the power of the Irrational, whether through socialist reforms or a revolution which will free their society from the absurdity of capitalism's mindless and egotistical despotism, and introduce true (and efficient!) democracy, or whether through anti-strike legislation and law-and-order enforcement which will reduce the 'anarchical' element in industrial relations, and diminish the influence of 'self-appointed' grassroots movements in consumerist or environmental matters, for example — in matters on which they are 'not qualified' to speak.

There are, of course, many very powerful 'progressives' — whether on the right or on the left in capitalist societies — who are constantly working towards the realisation of their respective millennia, and their strength should by no means be underestimated. One need seek no further than the almost totally inclusive Danish trade unions, or the big American oil and electronics companies, to find examples of enormous 'progressive' power, albeit of different political observance. But the political struggle of such traditional opponents for the monopoly of the so-called 'rational society' is only *one* aspect of the ongoing development of capitalist societies. Side by side with this competition for the power to subject the inherent egoism of such societies to rational control — simultaneously and no less endemic to the system — the opposite tendency exists and flourishes. By which I mean a logic of the heart or the guts: a deep-rooted concern for Man's biological nature and for his natural environment; a concern for nature conservation in the face of the short-term ruthless pursuit of profit; a heartfelt concern for the recreational and creative dimensions of our common humanity as opposed to an exclusive morality of rational efficiency which turns its back on — and does violence to — life itself, in the interests of social survival and undiminished wealth; a concern for a concept of democracy which awards higher priority to genuine and equal individual influence than to administrative efficiency.

It is, in other words, my contention that — far from producing an all-obliterating uniformity — capitalism as we know it has actually generated a marked degree of *incongruity*, of *non-conformity*. According to this view, what is characteristic of capitalism is precisely that various kinds of logic are generated by the system which are *mutually contradictory*. Thus, if we return for a moment to the very crucial example to which I earlier referred, capitalism not only compels the exploitation and destruction of our natural resources and our environment, but, at one and the same time, it generates a concept of nature as a self-sufficient entity — as something which may be refined or processed, but which contains in itself its own essential norms. In fact, 'Nature', under capitalism, is every bit as much an historically specific societal product as is the capitalist destruction of nature itself. And similarly, capitalism does not *merely* threaten to destroy anything 'different'. It produces in itself at the same time the actual concept of something 'different', the dream of something else, of something better — of an alternative society.

Which is not to say that the critics of the inhumanity of technocratic rationality are wrong, any more than it is to say that the critics of nostalgic and technologically primitive inefficiency, superstition and greed, are wrong. It is just that neither side seems to be capable of grasping the *whole* truth. 'Alienation', on the one hand, and 'authenticity', on the other, are antonyms which *presuppose and mutually generate each other*. Thus, any criticism which devotes itself exclusively to the alienating aspects of capitalism — from environmental pollution to public sector bureaucracy — assumes, as its norm, a concept of authenticity which is a purely capitalist concept: which is why adherents of both the right and the left in politics can agree on a common attack on alienation. While any criticism of the reactionary irrationality of 'authentic', or 'primitive capitalist' spokesmen, has to measure the latter against a norm which, again, the capitalist society itself has generated: a norm of rational progress which likewise cuts across traditional party lines.

The opposition between 'rational progress' and 'natural authenticity' is intrinsic to capitalist society, which is why capitalism characteristically generates not one, but several conflicting sets of future expectations, not one but a variety of contrasting utopias. On the one hand, we have what we might call a 'Pro-Reason' normative *Weltanschauung* which seeks its consummation in the ubiquitous dissemination of that which is rational, altruistic and universal. And on the other hand, we find what might appropriately be termed a 'Pro-Nature' normative *Weltanschauung* which is acutely aware of any cost to the private interests of the individual citizen, or to his local natural environment, which may be caused by any over-hasty or narrowminded 'rationalization'. In critical contrast to the Pro-Reason adherents, the adherents of this latter *Weltanschauung* place the emphasis on the full development of the individual citizen — and on nature conservation — as their central norms. Thus, one of the historically unique features of the capitalist system is, in effect, its systematic tendency to generate self-criticism.

2.4. *The Future is Very Present.*

I mentioned earlier that it was necessary for me to define utopian thought as 'anticipation'. This is in order to make more explicit the future-content of the present. For the present is not *just* the present, i.e. that which is neither the past nor the future. Quite the reverse in fact: it is both at once! That it contains the past has long been common knowledge; take the term 'repression', in psychoanalysis, for example. But that the present also includes the future, that it also contains elements which are 'not-yet-in-being', is something which the Marxist utopian philosopher, Ernst Bloch, was the first to seriously insist upon. So it is his 'Not-yet-in-being' ontology which I want to consider more closely in the following.

"A fifteen volume history of the bovine race might be possible, but it would presumably make rather boring reading", remarked Ernst Bloch in his lecture 'Anticipated Reality: Towards a Definition of the Nature and Function of Utopian Thought'. But if the cows' history would probably be boring, human history is by contrast so much the more fascinating.

> "Mutations in animal species, which have developed over hundreds of thousands of years, are confronted by six to eight thousand years of human history, with changing forms of government, life-styles, culture, with new horizons constantly in front of us, closed, re-opened, innumerable vistas stretching away before us [...]". (Bloch 1982: 26)

Bloch is not content merely to claim that Man is an anticipative creature. He goes on to claim that our own age is especially future-laden. He even ventures to assert that we are at present *under an obligation* to anticipate, to think ahead — and, furthermore, that this obligation is *pleasurable*:

> "If we are to continue to exist, our task must be defined as the careful consideration, the anticipatory consideration of human beings as they are now in relation to their immediate, let alone their distant, future [...] This,

> however, is what makes it immeasurably pleasurable, and indeed something quite extraordinary, for human beings, who are constitutionally anticipative, to live in this present age." (Bloch 1982: 28)

This obligation to anticipate is no less relevant in our relationship towards telematics. When one understands the term as referring to something more than a mere technical system, i.e. when one thinks about such things as individual freedom and the future, then it cannot be the task of critical research to abstract, to try to minimize the social significance of telematics. Such research must, on the contrary, lend qualificatory support to the progressive urge. Qualificatory, in the sense that banality must, of course, be avoided, and guarantees provided that the enthusiasm for the future is more than a mere distraction from the present; the surge of human advance must not be exploited merely as an anodyne, rendering acceptable an unacceptable present by lending the latter a specious temporary status.

Bloch is surely right to insist that "it is the fundamental task of our time to address ourselves conceptually to the relationship of human beings to the future which will eventually become their own". (Bloch 1982: 28) But why has it taken us such a relatively long time to discover that Man is not only a reflective, but also an anticipative, creature? The future, and anticipation, have to do with the problem of *lacking* something. To lack something means that one feels a *need* for something, one wants a *change*. And the human needs problem only appears in the history of ideas once the feeling of lacking something has become primarily *historically* determined, i.e. once it has become a consequence of the prevalent modes of production at any given moment in history, instead of being a direct consequence of Nature's niggardliness.[5] It is in this light that the very considerable degree of future potentiality immanent in telematics is best understood: telematics embraces techniques and technical systems which were not created in order to liberate human beings from Nature's meanness, but which were created for people who have *already* liberated themselves from the constraints of Nature.

Our task is "to address ourselves conceptually to the relationship of human beings to the future". And, as a concept, the future is synonymous with the surprising, the unpredictable. That which may be mediated by the present, but which is not entirely contained within the present.

So, enquiring into the significance of telematics, instead of merely subsuming it under, or ascribing it to, the profit motive, our enquiry must become an enquiry into the relationship between the *predictable* (the profit motive, for instance) and the *surprising*.

> "For man, as a creature desirous of change, the utopian is always present. The world presents itself as potentiality, as that which exists only in relation to what it may become, as the great *dynamei on*. Utopian thought is a possibility in Man because he is the only creature to have a future — a true future, instead of a false future consisting of a barren sequence of eternal repetitions. Man's future is a genuine 'Not Yet', something really new, however comprehensive its mediation." (Bloch 1982: 30)

Again the word of warning, though: in dealing with the future prospects of telematics one may all too easily fall prey to *abstract* utopian thinking, i.e. to visions of the future which are totally unrelated to the present. Such visions are unable to mediate anything new out of the painful contradictions of our present age; on the contrary, they refer to the future only in order to distract our attention from the present.

If one's concern is to analyse the realisable future prospects in telematics, one has, then, to define both what telematics seems likely to do (its tendential aspects), as well as what it might conceivably be used for (its utopian elements), and how, in practice, the utopian elements in telematics can be realised. That which is predictable, tied to the present, must, in other words, be compared and contrasted with the unpredictable, the truly future-laden and progressive aspects of telematics.

As far as the academic world is concerned, the task must be to define what kind of research best can anticipate the utopian in concrete terms, how best we can keep utopian thinking alive, and make it into a real force for the future, — and we must preside over the liberation of these utopian potentialities. My own analysis in the following chapters of the tendential nature and the future potential of telematics, and of the social experiments which have already been made — and which may in the future be made — with the technology, reflects these three fundamental aims.

2.5. *Technology as Anticipation: Taking Arms against Pure Objectivity.*

"We are not here for history's sake, but history is here for ours", N.F.S. Grundtvig remarked in the introduction to his second 'Within Living Memory' lecture, which he held on June 22nd, 1838.

> "So the High Germans may say what they will about pure 'Objectivity', wherein one loses both oneself and one's audience in one's examination of historical objects, but I would just like to take the liberty to say this: it is all very fine for these High Germans if they have such an abundance of life and time and personal humility that they can daily waste them in the kingdom of the dead and still have something left; but things are quite otherwise with

me, who have so little life, time, and, indeed, personal humility, that I must administer them carefully, and have nothing at all to waste on the dead." (Grundtvig 1877: 444)

According to Grundtvig, what we have to do is to liberate ourselves from some of the fundamental fixations confined within, and confining us to, classic Enlightenment philosophy. We must try to get beyond the notion of the existent as something which is already finished and complete, and instead try to understand it as something which is not yet in being, in the sense that all 'being' is really 'becoming'. We have to try to stop appealing to a static and permanent reality, or rationality, and instead try to understand things in terms of trends and tendencies. The so-called materialistic conception of material reality must be superseded by a conception of material reality which, in Ernst Bloch's words, emphasizes the connection between reality and the Hegelian historical dialectic, between reality and utopia. In pragmatic sociological terms, the usual distinction made between existing reality and utopias must be superseded by an attempt to comprehend utopias as already existing tendentially within existing reality.

More than anyone else, Ernst Bloch has taken up the cudgels — most constructively — against classic Enlightenment philosophy on this ground, with his theories of the Not-Yet-in-Being (*Noch-Nicht-Seiende*) and the Not-Yet-Realized (*Noch-Nicht-Bewusste*). He has thus found a way of superseding 18th century notions, which he makes full use of in his works in his critical accounts of the antinomies of bourgeois thought. (Bloch 1977 [1975]: 115-132)

One of Bloch's most fundamental and germinative assumptions is that the abundance of contradictions immanent in any society generates tensions which, in turn, produce ideas about the future, and fantasies: hopes about what has not yet come into being. Significantly, Bloch insists on the fact that these ideas and fantasies about the future do not amount to fully-fledged positive utopias, for those would of themselves be already rigidly established affairs — or to put it in grammatical terms, they would be like presuppositive subjects with a foreknowledge of their own not-yet-in-being predicates. No, these future inklings find expression in the desire and urge to experiment with the future, not with any particular purpose in mind, but enthusiastically, in the awareness of the possibility of 'something else'. They arise out of a felt *lack*, an *emptiness*, which, in Western society, capitalism itself is primarily responsible for engendering, in that it generates ideas about, and demands for, human dignity and happiness, which in itself it can neither honour nor extirpate. These speculations about the future arise, then, from a Present

Nothingness — but, of course, a Nothingness which, in that it is experienced as a yearning, or lack, is steered, by those who feel it as such, towards a something — the Not-Yet-in-Being — which is formed out of the resolution of the contradictions which produced the initial dissatisfaction. The contradictions immanent in capitalist society ensure both that the existent is never already finished and complete but always incomplete, and that the incomplete constantly aspires to completion. The nature of the existent is such that it generates and maintains an ongoing process in the present which points towards its own consummation.

All this is true of technology, too, of course. The significance of any given technology at any particular moment in history is characterized both by what people say it can do, and by what they say it can't do. Besides, the social significance of technology is partly a function of other social systems' significance — the state's, for example.

The true significance of a T.V. broadcasting satellite, for instance, actually comes very close to the ideals of power and equality within the state. The purpose of a T.V. satellite is to ensure that an exceedingly large number of people may be supplied with the same program channels. Which means that, when people say that the *technical* advantage of a T.V. satellite is that it can cover a large geographical area and reach a large number of people, they are mistaking technology for its social significance. Technology in itself cannot be evaluated on the grounds of the number of people it can reach, but the true *social significance* of the technology *can* be: a T.V. satellite is *socially significant* because it broadcasts over such large geographical areas. In another social context it would be possible to imagine that the ideal were not power, but *powerlessness*. In that kind of a society, if the social significance of the satellite were again to be fallaciously expressed in terms of its technical excellence, the T.V. satellite would be considered 'bad' technology. Bad, because it doesn't reach a few, but many, people. Bad, because it doesn't differentiate, but is neutral. In fact, it may well be the social significance of T.V. satellite technology which provides the fundamental explanation for the existence of European (high power, DBS) T.V. satellite projects, for it is apparently easier, cheaper, and more appropriate to the communications requirements of the European nations to cable the territory. Still, in a few years' time, they're sending high power satellites up. Why? Perhaps because they have 'grander' social significance!

There's another sense, too, in which these T.V. satellites are artificial satellite states: they are not what they ought to be. They *ought to* ensure individual liberty, just as the state ought to be synonymous with individual liberty (but is not). They *ought to* facilitate intercommunication, because, in our society, the truth ought not to be the monopoly of the state but ought to be freely established through the continuous interchange of opinions among its members, subsequently mediated through the state. So the T.V. satellites stand not only for the virtues of their states — their ideals of power and equality — but also for their vices, their lack of liberty and intercommunication among their members. For, at the present time at any rate, T.V. satellite technology precludes receivers of programmes from transmitting programmes themselves. In short, it is truly remarkable that the technical reasons for the construction of the T.V. satellite should, to such a degree, recall reasons of state. T.V. satellites are socially significant!

With his 'Not-Yet-in-Being' and 'Not-Yet-Possessing' (*Noch-Nicht-Haben*) concepts, Bloch broke up the intrinsic inertia in more traditional thinking, and we see him do this again with his concept of the 'Not-Yet-Realised', a phenomenological concept parallel to the ontological 'Not-Yet-in-Being'. This notion of the 'Not-Yet-Realised' is best understood in contrast to the concept of repression in psychoanalysis, in that, while the latter concept refers to something already in being which has been conveniently 'forgotten', or displaced, Bloch's concept refers to the vague intimations, or inklings, of something New and Different, which the ongoing Not-Yet-in-Being process generates out of the sparks which fly between societal contradictions as they are perceived in the individual mind. This inversion of more traditional Enlightenment theories runs through all that Bloch wrote. Referring to the subject-object antinomy in his *Subjekt-Objekt-Erläuterungen zu Hegel*, he writes, for instance, that Hegel "is an instructor in living movement instead of dead existence. His theme was the self becoming aware, the subject dialectically penetrating the object, the object the subject, the true the real. And truth itself is not some static, fully-developed fact, any more than Hegel's thinking was ever static or fully-developed in itself. The fusion of the true and the real is far more the result of a process: truth must be perceived clearly and it must be won." (Bloch 1977 [1949]: 12) The subject and the object are not static, discrete entities, but parts of each other in their ongoing process of formation; truth is not a term dissociated from reality, truth, on the contrary, is reality in motion.

This, again, has critical implications for the deadlocked distinction made by more traditional philosophers between mind and matter. Matter is not dead and inert, our minds are not unaffected by the external world, Bloch says, thereby resolving the conflict between vulgar materialism and idealism within the notion in which matter may be defined thus:

> "it is not just a millstone around our necks, burdening us with all the weight of the past, but, on the contrary, and in accordance with the notion implicit in Aristotle's definition of matter, it is *both* that which *post-possibly* exists [...], i.e. that which is conditionally, historically-materialistically, determined by that which has been possible at any given historical moment, *and* it is that which exists *within the realm of possibility* [...], i.e. that which is objectively really possible or actually existent: the substratum of possibility which serves as the basis of the dialectical process." (Bloch 1977 [1949]: 12)

And this, in turn, has critical implications for the static definition of self-repetitive causal relations in more traditional philosophy. These must be superseded by concepts of reality's tendentiality and latent future potentiality. In the product of his old age, *Experimentum Mundi*, Bloch summarises this by saying that "whereas the establishment of laws renders permanent that which repeats itself, the concept of the tendential leaves room for the New." (Bloch 1977 [1975]) Our hopes for the future must not be pinned on that which has already come into being and demonstrated its obedience to established laws, but on the questing, experimental Not-Yet-in-Being.

Bloch helps to put us on the trail of this perspective by recommending 'magnetic needle-type cricitism'; criticism which sensitively turns its attention towards those areas of society which focus, in a potentially explosive way, the abundance of contradictions contained within it. Telematics is a case in point. It is an explosive focus of societal contradictions because its social significance is so complex. Thus, on the one hand, I.T. systems are the incarnations of dreams of prosperity — of a society whose industry functions faster, and more efficiently, thanks to a modern, streamlined, symbol-transporting infrastructure. They are the incarnations of dreams about universal education and democracy: dreams of education, because possibilities exist to make large bodies of information freely available to all; dreams of democracy, because the enlightened opinions thus formed may the more easily be expressed. They are the incarnations of hopes for a greater measure of freedom from work and a reduction of commuting-time — dreams of more free time for voluntary personal relationships. But, at the same time, they are the incarnations of fears about the oppression of the individual and the trivialization of work, fears about police surveillance and thought control; fears, too, about increasingly longer periods of undifferentiated free time, with more and more passive entertainment and electronically mediated human relationships. Focussing such fundamental contradictions, telematics is a typically explosive area: an area in which hope and anxiety exist side by side within a large variety of mediatory phenomena.

3. THE TENDENTIAL CONTENT OF TELEMATICS

3.1. *Technology or Economics?*

In any capitalist society, the economy has a life of its own and is not a true representation of the complex of human needs present in that society. Economically, we tighten our belts in Europe not because agricultural productivity has decreased, nor because the food supplies in the E.E.C. have been exhausted, but because our balance of payments deficit demands it. We sacrifice ourselves to the abstract Moloch of our economy.

But the economy is only one of several such fateful abstractions. Technology is another. And the situation becomes truly absurd when social science provides the arena for these unfortunate — but indeed momentous — abstractions' struggle for predominance. Some maintain that technology and technological innovations are the *primus motor* in societal development; others, that the economy and economic developments are in reality of greater importance. So the controversy is about which abstraction is the most oppressive; and when the public at large is encouraged to discuss which *form* of oppression is the most crucial, then the oppression itself is conveniently left out of account!

In this chapter I want to take a closer look at these Molochs. Nothing is more naïve than not to take them seriously, but nothing is more paralysing than the acceptance of them as absolutes. For what is peculiar to these forms of oppression is that they are socially instituted: they do exist, they are powerful, they do in effect exercise their power with no uncertain consequence. But, at the same time, they only exist by virtue of the oppressed's acceptance of them — an acceptance which is not only in the mind, but which is also societally mediated. This means, in effect, that when we discuss them, we have to keep two trains of thought going at once. We can think *in terms* of them and discuss the differences *between* them, but we have also, at the same time, to stand back from them and discuss them critically from without.

In the first place, I want to introduce the reader to the kind of historicism which gives pride of place to *technological* developments. Subsequently, I shall be examining some of the features of I.T. industrial policy in Japan, the one country in the world which has most single-mindedly tried to live up to demands for *economic* growth. And, finally, I shall be analysing the most important features of the way in which economic factors have acted as incentives in the development of telematics technology.

Technology as the Engine of Change.

"Behind such prodigious economic facts lies that great, growling engine of change — technology", Alvin Toffler wrote in his book *Future Shock* (1970: 25). Whether one takes an optimistic or a critical view of the results of technological development, one is more or less likely to follow one particular model in one's attempts to write a history of technology. In the first place, of course, one will probably make technology a central, if not the only, cause of social evolution. And, secondly, there will be a temptation to divide the evolution of the societies concerned into rigidly defined 'ages' — and frequently in such a way that the 'age' which the society or societies concerned is about to enter any moment now, just happens to be one whose characteristic features fully confirm one's underlying optimistic or critical opinions about technology.

I believe it was Daniel Bell who first coined the phrases the 'Information Society', or the 'Post-Industrial Society' — most influentially in his book *The Coming of Post-Industrial Society* in 1973, (Bell 1973) although he had published an article entitled 'The Post-Industrial Society' as early as 1964.

Since then, a spate of such books has appeared, including Christopher Lasch's *The Culture of Narcissism*, which is a classic exposition of the view that I.T. and the mass media generally destroy our natural humanity, making us passive, superficial, unnatural. Alvin Toffler is another example. He, too, sees technology as a decisive factor in social evolution, but he distinguishes himself from the majority of such writers in that he combines cultural criticism with an optimistic attitude to technology. That technology should threaten our natural humanity is, in his opinion, only a feature of *industrial* society. In our *post*-industrial society technology has been transformed, and it is now 'on our side':

> "[...] the most revolutionary feature of the new means of communication is that many of them are interactive — permitting each individual user to make or send images as well as merely to receive them from outside. Two-way cable, video cassettes, cheap copiers and tape recorders, all place the means of communication into the hands of the individual." (1980: 406)

The kind of historicism which sees technology as the cause of everything (and — no less importantly — predicts a rosy future for us) has today become very big business. Alvin Toffler is now the star of 'The Toffler Show' — and another rising star on the horizon in the United States is Marc Uri Porat. In books, in lectures, and on the screen, he proclaims that the history of the world may be divided into three ages: the Agricultural Age, created by the invention of the plough; the Industrial Age, created by James Watt's invention of the steam-engine; and, finally, the Information Society, which the development of I.T. has created. The three ages are further differentiated from each other by some superstructural characteristics, such as changes in the composition of the labour force and in their power structures. With regard to the former, over 90% of the labour force in the U.S.A. was engaged in agriculture or in extractive industries as late as 1790. By the turn of the present century, the industrial labour force had gained so much ground that, in 1920, it made up 53% of the total labour force. It was at this time, around 1920, that the information sector began to make its mark numerically. Defined as a sector to include academic and educational as well as I.T. occupations, it made up over 50% of the U.S. labour force in 1976, and it is estimated that it will exceed 60% of the labour force by the year 2,000. As for the power structures prevalent in his three ages, Marc Porat claims that one can trace a development from power based on land ownership to power based on capital, and further, in our own age, to power based on information.[6]

There are a large number of writers who indulge in this kind of historicism, but let me mention only two others here: Robert D. Hamrin, Senior Policy Economist at the U.S. Environmental Protection Agency, and Graham T.T. Molitor, President of Public Policy Forecasting, Inc. in Potomac, Maryland. Hamrin defines the so-called Information Economy in terms of the composition of the labour force and also in terms of the global market for industrial goods. "By the mid-1970s, America's working population was predominantly engaged in information handling: more people were involved in the manipulation of information than were employed in mining, agriculture, manufacturing, and personal services combined", and sales figures are expected to confirm this tendency: "By the late 1980s, the widest information market, the world electronics industry, is expected to grow from about $100 billion (1977 dollars) to about $325-400 billion. In 10 years, electronics will be the world's fourth largest industry, surpassed only by automobiles, steel, and chemicals, which will all total about $500 billion." (Hamrin 1982: 66f)

As I suggested at the beginning of this chapter, I would find it irrelevant to query figures like these (although one might expect considerably more precision in the definition of the various categories used), but I would merely raise the objection that such figures in themselves do not give us any grounds for talking about a qualitative jump from one kind of economy to another. If that were the case it would seem to be more appropriate to call our own age the Automobile Age, or the Steel Age, or the Chemical Age!

According to Hamrin, significant characteristics of the so-called Information Economy include the fact that it is economical in its consumption of natural resources (the entire software sector involves work on non-physical raw materials, and, if one accepts that mental raw materials cannot be polluted or destroyed, the observation is self-evident); and the fact that the information handling capacity of the hardware has increased exponentially (the reader will recall my mention of the fact, in chapter 1, that it is now virtually possible to pack a million electronic components onto a single chip); as well as the fact that we have witnessed a dramatic fall in price per unit of effective computing power ("Computer circuitry that in 1955 cost about $1 million can be bought today for about one 1955 dollar.") (Hamrin 1982: 66)

In like manner, Molitor maintains that "... agriculture and manufacturing no longer constitute the foundation of the economy. A new economic order has emerged — one based not on material goods but on information". Again, in an attempt to characterize the so-called Information Economy, the usefulness of the information sector is stressed:

> "By 1976, only 4% were engaged in agriculture, 29% were in manufacturing, 50% — fully one-half — were in information, and 17% were in other service occupations. [...] in postindustrial society, the major resource is knowledge. [...] The production, understanding, and control of knowledge have become essential, especially in the advanced nations. Knowledge and information industries are fast becoming the decisive factors in the growth of the productive forces of nations."

And again much is made of the fall in the cost of hardware products:

> "During 1980, microprocessor costs declined at an annual rate of 22%, information storage costs fell by a 40% rate, and communications equipment dropped at an 11% clip." (Molitor 1982: 84ff)

As I said at the outset of this chapter, I find this kind of historicism suspect. In the first place it is, to an unreasonable degree, the advocate of a technological determinism; it panders too much to the belief that it is the invention and development of tools which, to the exclusion of all other factors, condition the development of societies as a whole. And, secondly, it is frequently characterized by an unreasonable tendency to oversimplify. Thus, an historical perspective which neatly divides history up into 'ages' is insufficiently sensitive towards the contradictions immanent in the technical, social, political and ideological systems at any given moment in the history of the societies described. And, in particular, it means that one is ill-equipped today to confront the welter of contradictory phenomena and opinions which are only too apparent to the watchful observer of the emergence of the so-called 'Information Society' and the debates which accompany its birth.

3.2. *Japan: I.T. Development Policy with Material Wealth as its Premiss.*

In any capitalist society, human needs acquire a distorted and independent life of their own through the economic system, which takes control of the entire society — subsuming, too, of course, an emergent electronic symbol-transporting infrastructure — subsuming telematics.

A basic tendency behind the development of telematics has been, as we have seen, a movement away from traditional industrial production towards the processing and transmission of information. The needs which have acquired an independent life of their own are, in this instance, 'needs' for the furtherance of this development, together with the 'need' to increase productivity in the information sector. First and foremost, what is 'needed' is the creation of a system as ubiquitous as the telephone network which will enable information to be *communicated* rapidly and efficiently, which will provide unrestricted *access* to information, and which will permit the efficient and rapid *processing* of information. This system is the integrated broadband network, so-called because all sorts of different services, from traditional telephone and telegraph services to interactive videotex, can be 'integrated' within such a network, and the virtually infinite bandwidth availability, provided by the digital transmission of laser light down the very thin flexible fibres of pure glass over relays of 50 kilometers or more, means that the optical cable has room for the simultaneous transmission of even the most data-intensive services. 'Ideally', of course, such a system should have national coverage (at least).

But let me just return to my former remarks about the artificial 'need' for such a system. It is true that the economic system in a capitalist society assumes a life of its own, and dominates the entire society with its own laws, which must be obeyed if it is not to take horrible revenge upon us in the form of stagnation or recession. But, while the artificial needs of a capitalist economy are certainly tendentially present in the growth of telematics, it is, I would maintain, still possible to *combine* an 'economic realism' which takes such laws into account, with a social enthusiasm, i.e. with a respect for other societal needs, such as the gratification of the need for equality (of socialisation, and reward — not merely of opportunity!); the need for (fully participative) democracy; and the need for respect for — and for the realisation of — one's own and others' true human worth. On the other hand, however, it is no less possible to give full rein to the artificial 'need' for indiscriminate growth inherent in capitalism, while at the same time deliberately disregarding any other societal needs.

An example of this latter pure and unadulterated I.T. industrial policy can be found in Japan, where the state-controlled policy has, as its only goals, the creation of the most efficient electronic symbol-transporting infrastructure, and the provision of optimum conditions for the development of the nation's electronics industry. The social costs of such a policy are reduced to insignificance. The keynote is, in other words, the belief that the true end of civilisation is the consolidation of material prosperity, and that, in relation to this, any other human needs are of minor importance.

3.2.1. *Japan's Integrated Cable Network.*

At the present moment, national and international communications networks are under preparation all over the world. Based to a greater or lesser extent on laser and glass fibre technology, they are, at all events, faced with demands for a data transmission capacity which would have been impossible to meet only a few years ago. In Britain, government commissions have drawn up reports on the desirability of a nation-wide cable system, and in France and Germany, too — though with different political objectives — plans have been presented concerning such cable-systems and their development and diffusion. In the United States, as I mentioned in chapter 1, A.T.&T. representatives have drafted a global cable network — the I.S.D.N. And in Canada, France, Holland, and in many other countries, experiments are being carried out with Local Area Networks integrating a variety of different services. But Japan is perhaps the one nation which has come closest to realising such plans.

The Nippon Telegraph and Telephone Public Corporation (N.T.T.) is responsible for the plans to build Japan's integrated cable network. (Murata 1982: 157) The aim is as far as possible to integrate all those services which have previously been on offer separately, so that all kinds of information, from telephone messages and television programmes to large quantities of data from computers, may be transmitted along a common cable. The word 'integration' has a purely technical reference, here, of course; at the same time, the Ministry of International Trade and Industry has in effect expressed a desire to counteract the N.T.T.'s dominance of the market for equipment which could be coupled onto the network.

Digital transmission is to be gradually introduced into the system. In purely economic terms, two principles are to be upheld: in the first place, the new system must not raise the subscription costs of existing services — it mustn't become more expensive to make telephone calls, for example; and, secondly, the difference in the cost of making calls over shorter or larger distances must be evened out — a consequence of the introduction of digital transmission techniques which will make cable length and relaying a relatively insignificant cost factor.

The basic principle underlying the future cable network's attractiveness for the subscriber is that the latter will be able to choose between a variety of different services: telephone services, facsimile document delivery, data transmission, video communication, etc. Part of the aim is that all the users and providers of services will be able to interact along a single common cable to which they jointly subscribe, and it is further intended that each subscriber will be able to make simultaneous use of more than one service — such that one will be able to receive computer-based information on one's visual display unit at the same time as one will be able to converse with someone on the other side of the country on the telephone, for example. A further goal is the development of terminals which will enable inexperienced users to track down the information they want by means of relatively simple procedures, so that all the subscribers will be able to make full use of the databases to which the cable network will provide access.

The strategy for the implementation of the project starts with the gradual transformation of the existing telephone network through extension and modification. The entire project should take twenty years to complete, at an estimated cost of between 80 and 120 billion U.S. dollars.

By 1985 the gradual installation of modems — (MODulator/DEModulators, digitalising the analogue soundwaves of the human voice, or reconstructing them after digital transmission) — should have commenced, and existing data transmission and facsimile document delivery networks will be extended.

The digitalisation of telephone conversations should be more or less complete by 1990, and existing Local Area Networks fully combined within a single integrated network. By the year 2000 the digitalised telephone network and the integrated L.A.N.s should be combined to form a totally integrated network. And by now the advantages of the system should already be making themselves felt: today's complicated tangle of many independent parallel communication lines will have been superseded by a single common broadband network — with the one exception of video communication. One and the same computerized telecommunications technology will be used to make a variety of different services available to subscribers, with the possibility always open for the further integration of familiar, or previously unknown, services. And finally, some time in the beginning of the 21st century, the entire integration will be completed, including the data-intensive video communication, which, like the entire mass of computer data, will become available along the unified cable network.

But what will this technological triumph be used for? Representing the N.T.T. at the IDATE conference on *L'expérimentation sociale en télématique*, held at Montpellier in October 1982, Masatoshi Murata replied that the system would, of course, be used for all the 'usual' things — above all for the high quality transmission of telephone conversations. But, beyond such uses, he was also able to mention a number of other functions specifically presupposing the integration of a number of services which are provided independently today.

One example of these integrated services is actually already available in Japan, namely electronic shopping. CAPTAIN, the Japanese viewdata system, permits customers to call up lists of available goods on their screens and records their orders. In the future, of course, the only real difference would be the extension of the service to cover a much larger range of shops, together with the fact that the increased bandwidth availability of the connecting cable would permit the integration of video communication with the shopping service.

Electronic banking would be another possibility. Over the integrated communications network, customers would be able to get information about their bank balances either on their visual display units or on their home facsimile copiers. Actual bank transactions could be undertaken along the network and, in combination with electronic shopping, would thus make it possible for customers to order their goods and pay for them simultaneously.

The future communications network is also intended to include local authority information centres, with details of available public facilities, so that citizens can obtain instant information about office opening hours, social security rights and benefits, etc. Video conferencing studios are to be built, too, linking local politicians with various public assembly halls and cultural centres in their constituencies.

And, finally, the authorities — (and, not least, the local authorities) — have stressed the desirability of providing local business communities with better access to data storage and processing facilities, together with other built-in network services, such as centrally monitored burglar alarm systems.

The immediate advantages of the telematics project for Japanese industry are obvious. The actual construction of the integrated cable network creates a new home market: the system has to be developed; components have to be manufactured for it; the installation process will generate a demand for a large number of services. And the home market thus created is not without export relevance, since the product development and expertise required to realise thc project will improve the subsequent competitiveness of Japan's telematics industries abroad.

But no less important interests are at stake in the longer term for Japan's manufacturing industries, retail trade and business administration. The manufacturing industries look forward to the improved coordination and control of production in geographically distant sub-branches. Manufacturing, transport and sales are eventually expected to become integrated in a single centrally controlled system. The retail trade will benefit from the electronic banking and shopping facilities mentioned above. But the most far-reaching consequences will no doubt be felt in business administration, where integrated sales figures, stock delivery orders, and book-keeping, on a central computer of the kind referred to above, will cut down the numbers of supporting staff. There will, for example, be no need for elaborate accounts departments with lots of typists producing and filing invoices — and that, in turn, will cut down the number of managers. And further, text and information processing will no longer have to take place in vast office blocks owned or leased by the companies. Instead, the administrative staff will be able to work at home, using the integrated cable network to send information to each other. Or, again, centralization and specialization may permit a large number of smaller concerns to have their administration done by a handful of giant bureaucratic service companies.

So, if all goes according to the N.T.T.'s plan, the total information traffic in Japan in the 21st C. will be able to travel along the single integrated cable network. But the N.T.T. is fully aware of the fact that there are major problems connected with the project which will have to be overcome if the planned advantages of the system are not to be lost along the way. In their opinion, the only way to tackle this situation is to carry out pilot projects in limited areas, in the hope that they will cast some light on both the technical and the social aspects of the new communications system under realistic working conditions. The main reason for N.T.T.'s representative Masatoshi Murata's attendance at the Montpellier conference, in 1982, was precisely in order to present plans for a pilot project of this kind. Actually, he admitted that the main purpose behind the pilot project was to demonstrate the advantages of the future communications system to the public: "If the public understands what the idea behind the system is, and what benefits it will give them, then the actual introduction of the system will go much more smoothly", he said. But of course he did mention that there were other reasons for undertaking an experiment of this kind. An integrated system on such a large scale requires testing, if technical problems arising not from the malfunction of individual components, but from their interaction within the complex common network, are to be pinpointed. And the extent to which the future communications system will be used must be measured in practice with regard to the information traffic load at given times of the day; with regard to the optimum interaction modes for the various services supplied; and with regard to the tariff structure. Finally, too, the social consequences have to be assessed.

Construction work has already begun on the pilot project, which is intended to come into operation in September 1984. In the first instance, the network is intended to serve 10,000 subscribers in the West Tokyo suburbs of Musashino and Mitaka, but a further system is eventually to be built in Tokyo itself, which will link up with the ring in the suburbs.

The project's integrated cable network will make a substantial range of services available to the public, including private and public digital phones (which will simultaneously visually register the number from which calls are made, and provide current information on telephone rates); the digital transmission of handwritten characters, drawings, and photographs; a Japanese and English teletex word-processor link, with facsimile print-outs; a high speed facsimile document delivery service, providing for the scanning, transmission, and reproduction of a standard size full-colour document in under 30 seconds; video conferencing facilities and an ordinary video telephone service; a computer-to-computer data-exchange system; electronic mail facilities, permitting the simultaneous and virtually instantaneous delivery of facsimile circulars to a large number of addresses; and multimedia communication, permitting the simultaneous transmission of voices and videotex information from several different terminals.

So much for the pilot project which, as I mentioned earlier, is partly intended to demonstrate the many advantages of the future integrated information network, but is also prompted by an awareness of substantial problems which must be tackled along the way.

Typical problems include the potential dangers to personal security and privacy which may arise from the combination of so many different databases within the integrated communal network. Such problems must be solved, but without sacrificing the advantages of the integrated system at the same time. Personal code systems, for example, will presumably be necessary, and, while they will have to be unbreakable, they will at the same time have to be sufficiently user-friendly both to avoid intimidating their owners and to avoid substantial increases in communication time.

The increased centralisation of information storage also makes possible concentrations of power both within central government offices and in larger private business. Again, this is a problem which is engendered by precisely those aspects of the system which constitute its advantages.

The extension of access to information technology beyond the range of people accustomed to data processing methods creates so-called 'man-machine interface' problems, which are far from being solved, particularly if voice recognition is to replace manual entry methods in an effort to cut down the search time for information. Present suppliers of Local Area Networks naturally claim user-friendliness for all their products, but while some systems are user-friendly to a degree, others stop just short of requiring the skills and instincts of a programmer! Yet, if top priority is not given to research into this kind of problem, the integrated cable system's terminals will make available more information, and award more influence, to a new élite of D.P.-trained subscribers, while the great majority will be relatively worse off than before.

Nor, finally, should it be forgotten that the technical integration of so many services in a single network has the disadvantage that major technical faults will — if only temporarily — affect many different social sectors at once.

Problems like these are, in other words, difficult to solve precisely because they are inextricably bound up with the advantages of the system. Yet, now that the system itself has been approved, and its advantages widely proclaimed, the general public are virtually unaware of the reverse of the medal. (Jeppesen et al. 1982; Yokoi 1982: 285ff)

In Japan, telematics development policy is primarily under the jurisdiction of the Ministry for International Trade and Industry, M.I.T.I., which has major political power in the life of the nation. This is partly because it comprehends so many different functions, dealing with areas of society which, in Denmark, for example, would belong under the Home Office, the Department for Trade and Industry, the Education Department and the Foreign Office - and partly because its staff is reputedly very highly qualified. And, to judge by Western standards, there are unusually close links between the Ministry and private industry. The Japanese Ministry of Post and Telecommunications, M.P.T., does also have some influence on telematics policy, but it is mainly concerned with the regulation of existing internal and external telecommunications services.

R.I.T.E., the Research Institute for Telecommunications and Economics, is a private institution which both undertakes pure research in telematics and applied research with regard to legislation and industrial policy. One might expect this institute to play a modificatory role in relation to a purely industry-oriented telematics development policy, but although such policy is, as we have seen, at least formally in the hands of several independent institutions, the results reflect a remarkable degree of unanimity: for all its different shades, telematics development policy in Japan is informed by a concerted belief in a Rational Society.

3.2.2. *The Ideology: the Vision of a Rational Society.*

In September, 1981, the M.I.T.I. published a report on I.T. development policy which provides an excellent summary of the predominant attitudes in Japan.[7] The report lists some general goals for I.T. development policy as a whole. With regard to production and distribution, R. and D. is to be staked on the development of 'intelligent industrial robots' which, at least in principle, are to totally supersede the human labour force in the production sector. At the same time, management and administration functions are to be rendered more efficient through the construction of 'rational, intelligent office automation systems'. And the market is to be rationalised, too. The end product is a rational society in which production, administration and distribution are linked together in a single smoothly-running system:

> "An important aim for the future is to create a distribution-information system, which will link production, transport, financing, and wholesale and retail trading in an efficient way, and will increase the number of businesses

> over a broad front. This will make it possible for users of the system to obtain immediate, precise, and detailed information about sales, stocks, sales promotion, orders received and dispatched, etc."

Public administration and private life are not to escape rationalisation either. The national executive is to become a rational communication and decision-making system with "comprehensive administrative information systems, including data links between the ministries and between central and local authorities". And the interaction between the ordinary citizen and the administrative bureaucracy is to be made more efficient by means of 'computerized counter service'. Private life is to be made more comfortable: "household appliances and equipment can come under central remote control. Telephone operation will permit the improved automation of domestic affairs, and thus further rationalize everyday life." And the resulting increased leisure time might profitably be used for citizenship training, for example by means of "a picture service promoting the consolidation of a friendly and stable society, which will perhaps lead to an improvement in contact among more responsive human beings".

All in all, then, we are presented with a complex of ideals for the development of Japanese society which unreservedly point to efficiency, material wealth and the absence of civil conflict as political goals, and which render these goals beyond discussion, such that the State, on behalf of its citizens, sees it as its task merely to provide incentives for their realisation, and to promote their acceptance.

So the directives for I.T. development policy become the following: social considerations are to be taken into account inasmuch as it pays to do so — I.T. initiatives are described as a kind of '*investment* in a social infrastructure' — an investment which, however, is only subject to very long-term cost-benefit analysis, since "If, owing to present-day economic difficulties, preparations for this social investment are postponed, difficulties will probably arise later"; a combination of state-control and free competition is to be effectuated, involving rational I.T. development planning by central government authorities, on the one hand, and incitements to the toughest form for competition, on the other, under which consumer safeguards are to be reduced to a minimum: "Any possible applications for the technology are permissible except for those which are directly forbidden"; and an efficient public information service is to be established to remove any doubts about the rosy prospects offered by the State's I.T. development policy:

> "Just at the moment when information technology is getting off the ground, a negative attitude towards it has grown up, frequently characterized by such expressions as 'information pollution', and by rumours that such 'devilry' is an 'instrument for social control'. Suitable initiatives must be taken to vanquish such objections and to further the population's acceptance of information technology".

The independent R.I.T.E. scarcely represents a threat to government industrial policy, as was mentioned earlier, and it in fact provides a good illustration of the very limited amount of criticism with which prevailing industrial policy in Japan has to contend. In 1982 a three-volume R.I.T.E. report was published (*A Vision of Telecommunications Policy in the '80s*) which came out in full agreement with the M.I.T.I.'s guiding principles: the dramatic increase in productivity, due to the extensive rationalisation of production lines in the '70s, necessitated a corresponding upgrading of office productivity in the '80s; the previously unchallenged sovereignty of human intelligence and creativity in research and development areas was now to be complemented by more efficient data communications, and such artificial intelligence expert systems as a 'Computer Aided Design' service, in the interests of increasing R. and D. productivity; marketing was to be made more efficient, in that, amongst other things, the instant analysis of consumption patterns would accelerate feedback-based modifications in the supply of goods and services; political participation was to be increased, in that local residents were to be linked to a community center with a computer from which they could get information, and by means of which they could conduct 'interactive dialogues' with each other, and achieve 'consensus systems' through electronic voting, while sitting in their own homes; and, finally, private life was to be rationalised by means of fully-automated telephone-controlled household appliances, and 'teleshopping' with automatic bank account transfers ("payment reliability will [...] be easily confirmed at the store"). (R.I.T.E. 1982: Pt.II, 30ff)

Taken altogether, the R.I.T.E. proposals for I.T. development policy may be summarized as follows: I.T. development policy must be universal, i.e. it must embrace hitherto separate societal areas; it must be flexible, in order to accommodate technical and industrial policy innovation; it must provide incentives for private enterprise and commercial initiative; it must promote the development of a national telecommunications network integrating telephone services with data exchange and televisual services; it must provide at least minimal protection for consumers; and it must contribute to the maintenance of a national consensus about I.T. development policy:

"[...] special heed must be paid to harmonizing the interests of those receiving services and those providing them." (R.I.T.E. 1982: Pt.I, 15)

The most important difference between the R.I.T.E. contribution to the public debate about I.T. development policy and the 'official line' from the M.I.T.I. is, however, that the R.I.T.E. report does draw readers' attention to some problems in connection with the proposed integrated cable network. Thus, something must be done about the security problems surrounding the future database availability, so that reliable information may be obtained without any danger of misuse; personal freedom in private life must be safeguarded against the threat of insufficiently confidential centralized archives with detailed information about individual citizens; and efforts must be made to develop interactive services with due consideration for the wishes of the population at large — so that viewdata services, for instance, should be extended to include communicative and mutual information exchange functions, and local communications systems should generally be elaborated.

3.2.3. *R. and D. to the Greater Glory of the Japanese Economy.*

Telematics development policy is to a large extent a function of a nation's R. and D. policy, and on this point Japan has staked a great deal, investing heavily in research on a broad front while at the same time making no compromises over demands for efficiency.

The Economist has repeatedly drawn its readers' attention to the fact that the Japanese are gaining ground in the international market for information technology, not least on account of their effective superiority in R. and D. For example, according to an article of June 19th, 1982: "Japan has progressively taken a larger share of world markets as new electronic consumer goods have come along." (The Economist 1982, June 19) At that time, Japan's share of the global market for radio equipment stood at 10%, while its share of the V.T.R. video equipment market was over 85%. According to the *Economist* article, the explanation was to be found in the fact that "Japan's universities train 10 times as many engineers as Britain's. Its industry spends as high a proportion of the country's GNP on R. and D. as almost any western nation. It employs more people in R. and D. than Britain, France and West Germany put together."

Microchip technology provides a further illustration of this:

> "Until recently, microchip technology was dominated by America. Now Japan is closing in fast on the American lead. Its most spectacular success

> has been in chips called random-access memories (rams). If microchips are the flagship of American technology, rams are the flagship of the microchip industry. The current generation of rams are called 64k rams because they pack roughly 64,000 minute memory cells into a tiny sliver of silicon 50 thousandths of an inch square. Each of these memory cells can store one bit of computer information. Last year Japan obtained 70% of the world market for 64k rams".

And the explanation is said to lie in an efficiently-organized state-supported development programme:

> "Japan decided on a big push into microchips in 1975. A government-backed development programme began the follow-year. In late 1978, four Japanese companies entered the American market for the then state-of-the-art chips, 16k rams (with about 16,000 memory cells)".

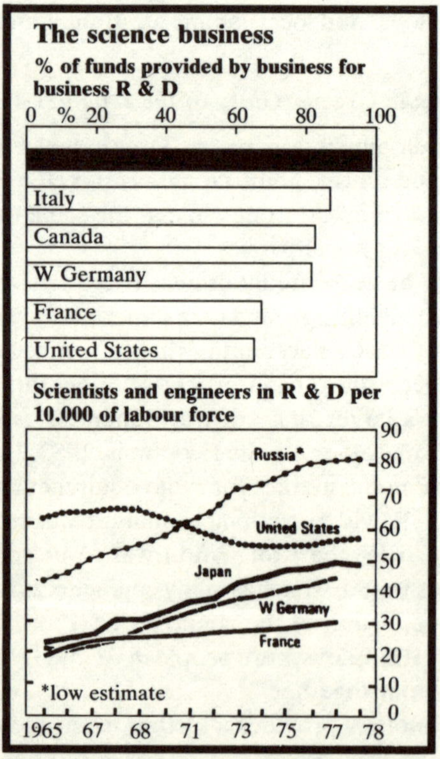

Sources Science Indicators. 1980: OECD

Yet *The Economist* maintains that it is not just a question of the *size* of the investment made in R. and D. — it is also a question of the *structure* of the investment. As one can see from this table, reprinted from *The Economist* July 18th, 1981, companies, with an eye on their earnings, supply a bigger share of what Japan spends on research, and universities less, than in western countries. And this aspect was taken up again in detail in the later *Economist* article (June 19th, 1982). That R. and D. in Japan should receive such massive government aid is said to be a myth:

> "In America and Britain, over half of all R. and D. is paid for by the governments. In Japan, the figure is much smaller. This is sensible of the Japanese. Studies of innovation in America show that R. and D. is much more likely to lead to commercial products if it is done by, and paid for by, industry. Projects backed by governments tend to be big schemes with small commercial prospects: ones that industry should be sensible enough to stay clear of. [...] Even in fields like electronics where Japanese government support has been most publicised, the sums of money tend to be small. The governments of Britain, France and West Germany each spend more to support electronics technology than their counterparts in Tokyo".

But even facts like these are not sufficient in themselves to explain the Japanese phenomenon. For, again, it is not so much a question of *where* the money comes from — from the state or from private companies — but *how* the money is invested. In the first place, there is a considerable difference in defence expenditure between Japan and the other Western industrialized nations. This naturally goes some of the way towards explaining the differences in the figures for state-financed R. and D., but it also has some bearing on the apparently different degree of cost effectiveness associated with this research, since "in big Western countries, defence tends to swallow about half of government spending on R. and D. This encourages the development by industry of low-volume products for which high cost is no barrier — exactly the opposite of what is needed in the civilian market-place". Secondly, there is a much closer link between research and industrial production in Japan, irrespective of whether the research is publicly or privately funded. The Japanese government "sees its role as acting as a catalyst to get industry to undertake most of the development. A national plan is agreed only when industry has made a moral commitment to commercialise the technology". And a similar coordination of resources is reputedly to be found on the individual business level: "In Western companies, the departments for R. & D., for production and for marketing are distinct empires, sometimes fighting each other as much as the competition. In Japan, links between departments are much closer."

3.2.4. *Japan's Significance in the Technology versus Economics Debate.*

What sort of relevance does this — somewhat daunting — picture of I.T. development policy in Japan have for the rest of the world? First let me emphasize that the picture given here is *not* a picture of a technologically created 'Information Society': what I have been trying to convey is what N.F.S. Grundtvig would have called 'the true spirit of these majestic works', if I may remind the reader of the quotation at the beginning of my second chapter — the social significance, in other words, which the Japanese have assigned to telematics technology — its *raison d'être* in *their* eyes, and the significance which it may eventually come to have in Japanese society.

The Japanese phenomenon, as I have described it above, is not, then, in my belief, an inevitable result of technological development. And I would even go so far as to say that I don't believe that Japan's example is sufficiently tempting to inspire any serious imitation among policy-makers outside Japan (*pace 'The Japanese Challenge'*!), though unquestionably the most interesting aspect of *The Economist*'s coverage of Japanese R. and D. policies was the liberal British magazine's undeniable infatuation with Japan's ideals of rationality and efficiency.

Nevertheless, the Japanese experience does seem to me to be relevant on two counts: firstly, because this nation's I.T. policy furnishes us with a clear illustration of the exclusively optimistic equation of civilisation with the growth and consolidation of material wealth. And, secondly, because, to a large extent, Japan is the nation which dictates levels of competition within the international market for information technology — and, as such (and only as such), it is of enormous consequence for the rest of the world. This was what made *The Economist*'s reaction so interesting — Japan is fascinating because it is the realisation of a stereotypic manager's dream of a 'good' society; it is alarming because its competitive capability can constrain a certain degree of imitation. "Although the U.S. now leads, some indicators suggest that the country's competitors are rapidly catching up. In a knowledge-based economy, research and development are especially important and can be indicators of coming innovations and future economic progress. In the U.S., the funds spent on research and development have declined in the last few years. West Germany increased R. & D. expenditure as a percentage of gross national product by approximately 50% from 1964 to 1978.

During the same period, Japan's increased by 30%. The U.S. underwent a 23% *decline*", writes, somewhat anxiously, the otherwise optimistic historicist whom we met earlier, Graham T.T. Molitor. (Molitor 1982)

Even so, the Japanese challenge has to be interpreted with due respect to its specific social context. Any critics of social change designed to promote an 'Information Society' of the future are not likely to be taken seriously if they start to confuse Japan with Western Europe or North America, and adherents of such a policy would be asking for trouble if they were to fall into the same trap.

3.3. *The Tendential Content of Telematics.*

In spite of my reservations the Japanese case illustrates only too clearly, then, the way in which telematics technology is subsumed under the artificial 'needs' problem in capitalist society which I mentioned earlier at the outset of the second section of this chapter; the way in which the tendential content of telematics is the pursuit of profit, which is seen to be 'necessary' at the historical moment of production. In fact, as we have seen, the economy in Japan is so sacrosanct that it virtually assumes the authority of a law of nature, transforming other phenomena into random infringements, into obstacles, into irritatingly human 'disorder'.

That specifically telematics has been considered to be a profitable field for investment at this particular moment in history undoubtedly has to do with (at least) two very significant factors. On the one hand, there is the structural change in advanced industrial societies brought about by the increasing substitution of capital-intensive production techniques for labour-intensive production techniques, which, in turn, has led to the increasing substitution of administrative and information workers for manual workers. And on the other hand there is the below-average productivity growth in the so-called 'information sector'. The dramatic growth of this sector as a whole, coupled with its noticeably slow growth in productivity, has meant that the sector has increasingly burdened the entire economies of advanced industrial nations, which in turn has meant that attempts to revolutionize activities within the information sector by means of I.T. and telematics have been welcomed with open arms.

Such, at any rate, would be the explanation offered for the latest turn of events by adherents of an economic determinism. Technological determinists point to technological developments whose existence is undeniable, but if they go on to explain social developments in terms of technological innovations, economic determinists will accuse them of distortion: technology cannot bear causality within itself; the cause of the technological developments we have been witnessing in recent years is sooner to be found within the logic of capitalist economics.

The growth of the information sector in the post-war period is a fact of which we are all very well aware, but for a detailed analysis of it we ought, perhaps, to start with the figures provided by the most recently acclaimed optimistic historicist mentioned earlier, Marc Uri Porat: his conclusions may be dubious, but his figures would seem to be undeniably of central significance. (Porat 1977) Right back in 1967, only three years after the invention of the laser, Porat was compiling input-output matrices in the U.S.A., at the Department of Commerce's Office of Telecommunications, in the hope of finding documentation within the economy of the United States for his 'Post-Industrial Age', or 'Information Eonomy'. He came to the result (which has subsequently been even more fully documented) that, as the table shows, agriculture absorbed the largest proportion of the U.S. labour force until 1905, when it was overtaken by industry. But, since 1955, information occupations have taken over the largest share of the total labour force.

Changes in the U.S. labor force 1860 - 1980

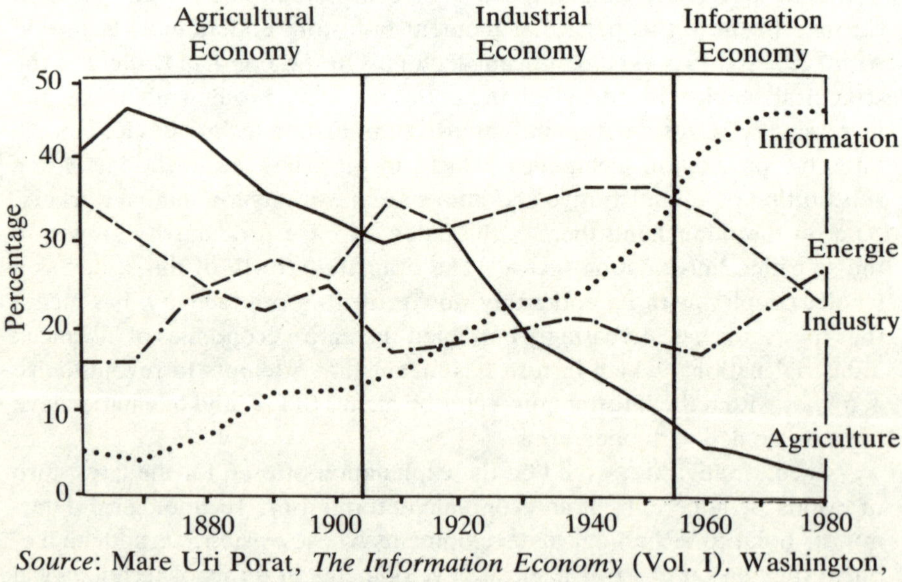

Source: Mare Uri Porat, *The Information Economy* (Vol. I). Washington, DC: U.S. Department of Commerce. 1977.

Only a few years ago, in 1981, the O.E.C.D. complemented Porat's research with a survey of recent changes in the composition of the labour forces in Canada, England, Sweden, France, West Germany, Austria and Japan. (O.E.C.D. 1981) Although there were different levels of employment in the information sectors in these countries, they did all exhibit the same tendency: the information occupations' share of the total amount of workers in each country over the period 1950-1975 presents remarkably parallel growth rates.

I mentioned earlier that Porat's figures, though not sufficient to justify his conclusions, were of central significance, and I do in fact believe this to be the case, in spite of the problem, which I hinted at earlier, concerning the difficulty of defining an 'information occupation'. Under those occupied in the information sector, the O.E.C.D. includes, for instance, as 'information producers': scientific and technical workers, information gatherers, market research and co-ordination specialists, and consultants. As 'information processors', the O.E.C.D. includes administrative and managerial staff, process controllers and supervisors, and clerical and engineering staff; as 'information distributors', educators and media personnel; and, as 'information infrastructure workers', information mechanics and P.T.T. employees.

Obviously there are problems concerning the criteria for classification here: workers who build computers are included, but what about workers who produce pencils or other writing equipment? — Or automobile workers who make mail vans? And the so-called 'scientific and technical workers' could equally well be involved in the thinking and planning behind a number of other totally unrelated products — ships, toothpaste, etc.!

Even if one accepts the classifications at face value, the resultant group of workers in 'information occupations' will be very much a mixed bag, coming, as they do, from different sectors of the economy (both public and private), employed, as they are, in traditional forms of industrial production as well as in advanced software production, working, as they do, in totally different fields, and undoubtedly representing very different trends in job definition, productivity, etc. One cannot escape the conclusion that the growth of the information occupations' share of the total amount of workers active in any economy — thus defined — may be indicative of a number of different social and economic trends rather than just one unambiguous one.

Whatever the validity of the figures, I must remind the reader of the point I made earlier in the second section of this chapter: they are not necessarily sufficient to justify the conclusion that we are on the brink of a qualitatively new 'Information Society' or 'Information Economy'. The mere reclassification of a mass of workers into so-called 'information workers' is not enough by itself to call into being such a qualitative change. To argue *for* something *with* itself always runs the risk of tautology, and, worse still in this case, tempts one's audience to conclude that the new is not the new at all, but merely the old in a new guise: the 'Information Society' becomes no more than capitalism with a larger number of wage-earners in information occupations — a relief for the cautious, perhaps, but a disappointing prospect for enthusiasts.

In the light of the above objections, one is tempted to ask whether the apparently scientific arguments and statistics really do prove irrefutably that a new society is on its way, or whether, on the other hand, the arguments and statistics are the products of wishful thinking, dreams of a new and better 'Information Society'. If Porat's figures are to have central significance, it can only be if they are understood in relation to the variety of different trends in the development of industrial societies, which produced them. In their book *The Information Revolution and Its Implications for Canada*, Serafini and Andrieu list seven such trends: changed production techniques in manufacturing have led to a substitution of information workers and capital (such as computers) for non-information workers; the increased complexity of modern life in urbanised industrial societies has given rise to a growing number of consultative services which are informational in nature; the increasing role of government has contributed to the growth of public bureaucracies; the increased size of firms and government has brought about the growth of private bureaucracies with more administrative and managerial personnel; urban growth has contributed to an increased commitment to educational services; R. and D. activities have been given greater priority by governments and private business alike; and the trend towards more and more public services, such as health and unemployment insurance, has necessitated substantial increases in the number of administrative personnel. (Serafini and Andrieu 1980: 18f)

Taken together, these seven trends illustrate two basic structural developments in the growth of capitalist society: firstly, the increase in productivity through the refinement of the means of production, which substitutes fewer and fewer machines for more and more production workers. The result is that, relative to this, production work itself consists more and more of control functions and planning and administration, i.e. of functions involving the transmission and processing of information. A further result is that relatively more educational activity is created, for the retraining of workers on adjustment-to-industry courses.

The second major structural development reflected in the trends listed above is the growth of the public sector. The state gains more extensive control and planning functions, and greater demands are made on it to take care of redundant or retrained workers by creating employment for them within the public sector, or by supporting them financially in the form of pensions, unemployment benefits, etc., or by putting them into various institutions — hospitals, homes, etc.

To return to Porat's figures, then, it would seem that they are in themselves not insignificant symptoms of fundamental developments in the growth of capitalist societies. But, even on Serafini and Andrieu's deeper level, we cannot maintain that the increased automation of production coupled with the expanding public sector's absorption of the redundant labour force can adequately explain what has happened to the *nature* of information work; quantitative increases will always be inadequate explanations of qualitative changes. No, an adequate explanation of the way in which information work has been so strikingly revolutionized in the '70s and '80s necessitates the inclusion of the further factor which I mentioned at the outset of this section, namely the below-average productivity growth in information work.

Not until recent years has administrative work — both in private and in public sectors — undergone its own form of 'industrial revolution'. As the International Data Corporation takes pains to point out to potential managerial customers, the distinction must be made between office mechanization and office automation. (International Data Corporation 1983: 40) The former process has been going on for many years, and often deals with a single function — examples would be the installation of type-writers, electronic type-writers, calculators, etc. But office automation involves the linking together of all aspects of the office and allows for interaction between them. This means, in effect, that office work becomes subjugated to machinery in the same way as so much blue-collar work already is.

In the United States, the so-called Yankee Group maintain that, while industrial productivity grew by as much as 90% in the period 1960-1970, office work productivity was increased by as little as 4%. (Serafini and Andrieu 1980: 19) And, in their weighty monograph from 1979 entitled *The Office of the Future*, Uhlig, Farber and Bair operate with similar figures, as the adjacent table confirms. (Uhlig, Farber & Bair 1979: 12)

Nor has the educational sector displayed the same phenomenal growth

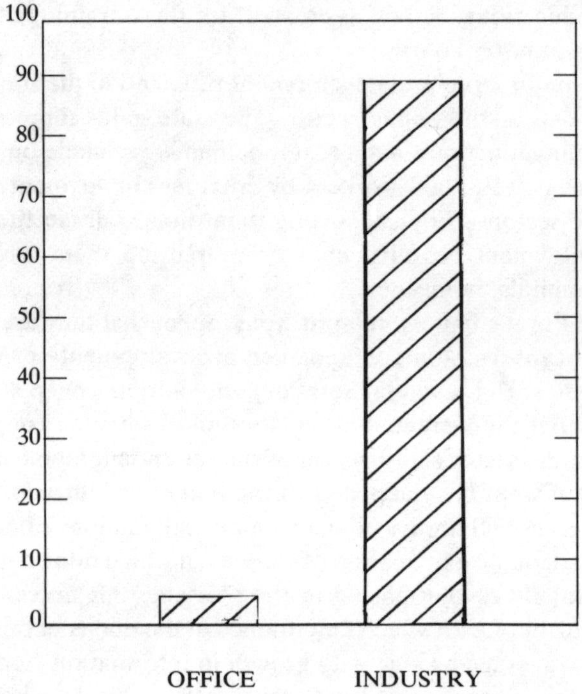

(a) AVERAGE 10 YEAR PRODUCTIVITY INCREASE

in productivity which has characterized so many other sectors of the U.S. economy. In spite of the installation of overhead projectors, copying machines and video cassette recorders, not much has really happened qualitatively to change the classroom collaboration of pupils and teachers. Nor, indeed, can such change be expected until the 'next generation' of electronic teaching aids has been installed, i.e. the generation of small (desk top) micro-computers, which, it is claimed, will be able to take over the teacher's role.

But will information work become increasingly automated? Generally speaking, expectations are high with regard to the replacement of workers by machines in the office of the future. Though there are those who argue, on the basis of analyses of secretarial work, that the routine jobs (type-writing included) only make up a minor part of office work taken as a whole. And, in the educational sector, sceptical voices are heard as to whether it really will be possible to cut down on the number of teachers employed, and, should that prove to be the case, doubts are expressed as to whether the quality of the teaching will not be adversely affected.

It is, however, important to remember that it is not the mere growth of the information sector which necessitates the 'revolutionizing' of information work, but as I mentioned earlier, a *combination* of this factor plus the no less important factor of the relatively sluggish productivity growth in the sector. These two factors together comprise a fundamental contradiction in capitalist society, which, in the face of all opposition, must, and assuredly will, precipitate a second 'Industrial Revolution', a transformation of this steadily growing twofold burden on the economy.

If this second Industrial Revolution does not take place, we might, in the company of Ernest Mandel and others, foresee the disintegration of the capitalist system. If it does take place, we may assume that the capitalist system will continue undisputed. Either way, however, no real qualitative change is anticipated. Whether capitalism goes on or not tells us nothing about an eventual alternative to it. The possibility of something qualitatively new happening is left out of account. But, in fact, something qualitatively new might very well happen.

In my own view, this kind of 'either/or' explanation is thus inadequate if we are to analyse and fully comprehend the phenomena with which we are confronted. What we need is a 'both/and' explanation which subsumes elements from both the above apparent alternatives: a 'both/and' explanation with a 'neither/nor' perspective.

In 1972, in his classic work *Der Spätkapitalismus*, Ernest Mandel documented that capitalism had passed through two phases: the first of which saw productivity growth mainly in sectors producing consumer goods, while in the second phase productivity growth was concentrated in sectors producing machines. The two phases reflected, in other words, a transition from the manual to the mechanical production of production tools. Observing the trend towards the increasing automation of both of these production processes in our time, Mandel concluded that, for this reason, we are witnessing the final phase of capitalism. Capitalism's fundamental aim, the maximization of profit — (in Marxist terminology 'the augmentation of surplus value') — can no longer be pursued because human labour has been entirely superseded — or is, at least, in danger of being superseded. (Mandel 1972)

To my mind, Mandel was essentially right in his analysis, but in his conclusions he underestimated capitalism's capacity for survival. It would seem undeniably to be correct that a trend towards increasing automation can be observed within the sectors producing both consumer goods and production tools. It would also seem to be correct that, other things being equal, a continued trend in this direction is irreconcilable with capitalism's fundamental principle concerning the creation of surplus value, i.e. the extortion of surplus labour from the labour force: you cannot exploit a labour force you have superseded. But, instead of the capitalist system disintegrating, it is equally conceivable that capitalism will find a new outlet, for example in the transition from what one might call 'internal' to 'external' productivity growth.

Internal productivity growth is an increase in productivity capability *within* a given business — or, to be more precise, an increase in productivity capability with regard to the immediate processing of goods, whatever they may be. External productivity growth is an increase in productivity capability in areas which lie *outside* the immediate business of processing goods: i.e. in offices, in administrative functions, in communication between businesses, in education, and in labour management, etc. — above all, an increase in productivity capability in the informational infrastructure linking individual businesses.

The transition from internal to external productivity growth illustrates one way in which capitalism may survive and develop in the future. The I.T. revolution is a manifestation of this trend, which will become a reality insofar as productivity is increased in (at least) four different areas: in business administration (office work, etc.); in information processing and communication between individual businesses; in government bureaucracy (for example by increasing the 'efficiency' of democracy in the way in which Daniel Bell and others consider desirable); and in marketing, with particular regard to forecasting, because the fully automated production of large batches of goods presupposes long-term planning and stable, or at any rate predictable, markets. It is precisely for this reason that telematics technology and I.T., and their related occupations, have attained such importance: not because they usher in a new, qualitatively different, non-capitalist society, but because they mark the birth of a new phase *within* capitalist development.

But, again, irrespective of whether you find *my* predictions of capitalism's undismayed continuance (through the cultivation of new opportunities for profit) more — or less — convincing than Mandel's doomsday prophecy (based on the fact that you can't get surplus value out of robots), the fact remains that the qualitatively new, and any genuine alternative, is inconceivable in terms of such explanations. They are too closely tied to the present and to the past, to that which is already in existence: they suffer from excessive sober-mindedness and rationality.

In marked contrast to the pertinacious rationality of the economic determinists, whether they are optimistic, like the M.I.T.I. and the R.I.T.E., or pessimistic, like Mandel, we are tempted to turn back again to the more extravagant analyses of the technological determinists, whether pessimistic, like Lasch, or optimistic like Molitor, Hamrin, Toffler and Daniel Bell. The reader will, however, remembering my earlier comments about optimistic historicism and abstract utopianism, scarcely expect me to offer the latter group's enthusiasm as a viable alternative to the excessive rationality of the devotees of that rival abstract Moloch, the Economy. Their analyses are too facile: correctly perceived quantitative tendencies in existing industrial societies undergo a sea change, and the old is suddenly replaced by the new — with a wave of the wand, capitalism becomes Something Else. Or so they would have us believe.

Daniel Bell has furnished us with the classical analysis in this vein. It is his 'basic premise' that "[...] knowledge and information are becoming the strategic resource and transforming agent of the postindustrial society."[8] In the 'Information Society', the two central factors in present-day Western industrial societies — capital and labour — are superseded by information and knowledge, according to Bell. Information processing is the means of production in post-industrial society, while knowledge is the unprocessed raw material; so it is no longer labour but knowledge which is the source of value and profit. Consequently, knowledge must be the most fundamental factor in the post-industrial society. And yet we find Daniel Bell writing for instance that "Increases in productivity depend increasingly on the more efficient distribution of necessary knowledge [...]". (Bell 1979: 197)

Only too characteristically, increases in productivity and efficiency appear still to be central factors in Bell's post-industrial society, factors in relation to which knowledge — and the distribution of knowledge — apparently play a purely subsidiary role. And, of course, if this is the case, knowledge and information occupations have nothing at all to do with a new kind of society but are no more than appendages to the old. Bell — and many others — have let themselves be fooled by the increase in the number of information occupations into mistaking advanced capitalist society for a qualitatively different 'Information Society'.

But, as I remarked earlier, the inflexible rationality of the economic determinists is, to my mind, at least as dubious as the mistaken enthusiasm of technological determinists like Bell. Whichever fateful, oppressive, societally-mediated abstraction they put their faith in, neither group has the monopoly of the truth. An analysis of capitalism, whether optimistic or pessimistic, would be unsystematic if it started to contemplate alternatives to capitalism. But technological determinism, obsessed as it is with the quantifiable aspects of the newest and latest technology, is no less able to put its finger on that which is qualitatively new in this technology. In fact, in its naïvety, it tends to see something new everywhere around in abstract utopian fashion, and is utterly unable to distinguish between the truly new and the oldest of Man's technological and social achievements — between the pencil and the computer!

Taken together, however, both of these lines of thought about technology and society can help us to comprehend the emergence of the truly new as recognizable trends within the old, rather than as an abstract ahistorical gift from the gods, whoever and wherever they may be.

Furthermore, each of these lines of thought can usefully function as a corrective to the other: we can avoid the pitfalls of a too rigid materialistic determinism without rushing into the arms of a too idealistic voluntarism: utopias don't have to be any more — nor less — metaphysical than principles of societal evolution.

And both trains of thought are necessary to help us to get to grips with the complexity of our present-day situation. It would indeed seem to be the case that capitalism is about to enter a new phase, a phase characterized by 'external' productivity growth. But I believe it would be equally correct to assume that this struggle for the survival and continuity of the capitalist system may release forces for the qualitative transformation of social systems which are already tendentially present within the latest products of existing capitalist societies. A failure to realise this may lead to fatally inadequate responses to the challenges before us. It cannot be repeated often enough: our destinies are *not* predetermined — but if we throw away our chances now we could very easily end up in a situation painfully resembling the *status quo* — a *status quo* which, however, we do, at present, have the chance to liberate ourselves from. What is needed is practical policy-making which combines utopian enthusiasm with socio-economic sober-mindedness; policy-making with lofty aims for the future which, however, does not belie the tenacity of the *status quo*. These are heavy demands to make on any policy-maker: his dreams must be potent; his patience infinite. But they cannot be made lighter. As Ernst Bloch so rightly remarked: "In matters of such moment you have to aim beyond your mark if you are to have any hope of attaining it." (Bloch 1982)

4. THE LATENT FUTURE POTENTIAL INHERENT IN TELEMATICS

4.1. *Technology: Salvation or Perdition?*

> "As far as mankind is concerned, I suppose we are nearly all familiar with speed produced by steam; we have tested it either on railways or in a ship crossing the ocean. Yet a rate such as that is like the ambling of a sloth or the crawling of a snail compared with the speed of light, which travels 19 million times faster than the swiftest runner; and the speed of electricity is even greater. Death is an electric shock that our heart receives; on the wings of electricity the soul, now free, flies upward. The light of the sun takes eight minutes and a few seconds to travel over 92 million miles. With the help of electricity's 'express delivery' the soul requires even shorter time to travel the same distance. The space between the planets is for the soul no greater than it is for us between the houses of our friends living in the same town, even when these are fairly near each other". (This and the following quotations are from Andersen 1958: 7-63 [1838])

As far as mankind is concerned, I suppose we are nearly all familiar with this same fascination with the wonders of technology that Hans Christian Andersen so vividly described over a century ago: technology triumphs over the boundaries of space and time — it liberates us. But does it make us happy? Not according to Andersen, a determined critic of mid-nineteenth century civilisation. Technology deceives us: it makes its entrance on a strident note of hope with the promise of happiness to come, but in its wake it leaves only sorrow and grief. It claims to liberate us, but in reality it only sets new and still more restrictive limits to our freedom.

The technical system which Andersen imagined could triumph over space and time consisted of a pair of goloshes, goloshes deceptively called 'the goloshes of fortune'. "The point about these goloshes", says one of Fortune's lady's-maids, who, as a birthday honour, has been entrusted with the goloshes to bring to mankind, "is that whoever puts them on will at once find himself at the place or time where he would most like to be; every wish as to time or place will immmediately be granted, and so for once man will at last be happy here below".

But, contrary to her expectations, unhappiness is the result whenever anyone puts on the goloshes. Councillor Knapp, a medieval enthusiast, suddenly finds himself back in the Middle Ages — dark, dirty, primitive, superstitious, frightening, surrounded by company at an ale-house which he considers coarse and vulgar — a very far cry from the 'modern' Copenhagen evening party he has just left. A watchman, who finds the goloshes in the street where the Councillor had left them, wishes that he could change places with a handsome young lieutenant — only to find himself love-sick, lonely and beset by financial problems! Instead, he wishes that he could visit the moon, but no sooner has he arrived than he finds that it is inhabited by frighteningly superior creatures.

Next, a young house doctor shirking night-duty finds the goloshes, and tries to squeeze through the railings around his hospital without waking the porter; he wishes that his head could get through the railings, only to find that the rest of his body can't! Later, having wished himself free again, after enduring anguish in the expectation of being made fun of by schoolboys the next day, he wishes that he could see into the hearts of his fellow-men — and receives some rather nasty shocks!

The by now unwanted goloshes are turned in, but the police clerk who checks them in puts them on himself by mistake. He becomes a poet, complete with rejection slips and cosmic melancholy — which drives him to wish that he was a lark, only to end up in a cage, of course! Home again at last, after evading the clutches of a hungry cat with glittering green eyes, he takes off the goloshes and leaves them outside the door, where his neighbour, a theology student, finds them and borrows them. The latter's search for happiness takes him first to Switzerland, where the discomforts of travelling in a crowded coach, and his anxiety about losing his money and travel documents, combine with the cold to spoil his enjoyment of the scenery. Hoping and longing for something better on the other side of the Alps, he finds himself surrounded by ragged, blind, crippled and fingerless beggars and by thousands of poisonous flies and gnats. Hungrily he sits down to some inedible food in a malodorous inn with bats flying about under the ceiling. Unable to appreciate the beautiful landscape outside he wishes for 'the happiest goal of all' and promptly finds himself at home again sleeping 'the quiet sleep of death' in a large black coffin!

We need not dwell on the moral of the story: if technology can take you to Switzerland, then all you want to do is go to Italy. Technology is always but an instrument for the restless aspirations of humanity, already so powerfully registered in Goethe's *Faust*: "Wherever I go", sighs Andersen's theology student, "there is a something lacking that weighs me down. Something better than the present is what I want". Technology merely aggravates this perpetual dissatisfaction.

While it was indeed the ambassadress of Fortune who brought the goloshes to mankind, it is the fairy of Sorrow who claims them as her own at the end of the story: "Sorrow disappeared — and so did the goloshes. No doubt she felt that they belonged to her."

Another 19th C. Danish celebrity no less relevant for our purposes, N.F.S. Grundtvig, also had doubts about the ability of technology to render mankind happy. A dozen or so years before Engels produced his famous report on the condition of the working class in England in 1844, the otherwise enthusiastic Grundtvig had visited the country and had no doubt found the latest enormous factories somewhat daunting, as my next quotation indicates:

> "Our sensibility need not be in the slightest bit poetical, — but merely human, to instil a certain horror into our minds in the presence of vast machines, which not only make such a din that nobody can hear themselves speak, and which blacken and roast anything in their immediate vicinity, but which also transform thousands of people of all ages into mere supernumeraries, mere appendages to the machinery itself, the fundamental driving-force in their midst". (This and the following quotations are from Grundtvig 1877: 446f)

Machinery, however, is deceptive. Only superficially can we mistake it for 'speechless nature', the incarnation of pure objectivity. Actually, as was pointed out in chapter 2, it is the product of our hands and, as such, bears the imprint of our minds, which compels Grundtvig (eagerly assuring his readers that such a conclusion is all the more true because it goes against his original conviction):

> "On the contrary, to admire the mighty spirit which, even in the desert, can create a Paradise, and which can make mathematics, by itself the emptiest and deadest of all the branches of our knowledge, into an unparallelled incentive to human industry and a lever for the elevation of such things as are too heavy even for the united hands of mighty spirits themselves".

But N.F.S. Grundtvig was much too acute a thinker to give way to naïve enthusiasm. Already in the early days of the Industrial Revolution he was aware of the fact that technology has both a tendential content — in the England of his day it bore the unmistakable traces of the pursuit of private profit — and a content of latent future potential — aspects inherent within it which could bring us closer to the ultimate liberation of mankind from material considerations. For example we find Grundtvig regretting that

> "industry in England seems more and more to have taken so-called net gain as its end without regard to the means — it serves the present moment without giving a thought to the future; but every day I see more clearly that the reason for this has as little to do with the human industry itself as with the freedom it procures us, but rather with something utterly different which would be all the more deplorable if one sat there with one's hands in one's pockets and did nothing at all with ardour or commitment. For it is a fact that, as long as the spirit of the people is making mighty strides forward, then it is undeniably on its feet, and, as long as it performs feats which can only be considered monumental in human terms, it is full of vitality; so that even if all these mighty strides were strides in the wrong direction, and all the momumental feats were the most dangerous and rash of undertakings, life would still be far better than death, vitality ineffably more valuable than impotence. As long as there is life, there is hope for the best that life can achieve; and, as long as there is vitality, then a more enlightened population can correct its own past mistakes and prolong its days."

Not surprisingly, then, we find Grundtvig hoping that

> "England will soon realise that it is on the wrong road, inasmuch as it is sacrificing hundreds of thousands of human beings to machinery, and sapping its own spiritual vitality by exclusively devoting it to that which is arithmetically and mathematically quantifiable; and then the same mighty spirit which has created these machines will understand what to do with them — either destroy them, or place them in a subservient and serviceable relationship to human industry and human good fortune."

The dissemination of education, literacy, enlightenment, was the cause for which Grundtvig became famous in Denmark — but, to my mind, he was no less importantly one of the first to strike a blow for the true understanding of the social significance of technology.

4.1.1. *The Deceptive Nature of Technology.*

Irrespective of their differences of opinion about the significance of technology, Grundtvig and Hans Christian Andersen were at least in agreement on one point which is a necessary precondition for the recognition of such significance — namely on the fact that technology is deceptive. It seems at first glance to be a purely physical phenomenon, a lifeless objective entity. But it is in reality the incarnation of an entire social system, or, as Grundtvig would have put it, an incarnation of the 'mighty spirit' of an age or a nation. And thus these two 19th C. thinkers were also in agreement on the fact that technology can only be fully comprehended when it is comprehended as something more than an assemblage of physical or mechanical equipment. The awe-inspiring and hazardous forces latent in the 'speechless nature' of machinery require other minds than the technician's or the mechanic's if they are to be properly understood.

A further consequence of the above is, of course, that whether technology increases or narrows down the limits of human freedom, whether it helps us to realise to the full our own human potential or whether it represses us, it is — strictly speaking — no fault of its own. The fault, if fault there is, lies in the social content of the technology, in the original purpose behind its creation and the subsequent significance which it acquires. Every technical system, from a factory to a Local Area Information Network, has been shaped by a specific societal content, and cannot but retain the unmistakable mould of its original social significance.

Where Andersen and Grundtvig disagreed was on the question of whether in actual fact technology would lead to human liberation or to human bondage. But their very disagreement contains a paradigmatic symmetry: Grundtvig believes in progress — he is not unaware of the considerable dangers lying ahead, but he has, all the same, the unshakeable conviction that Reason will prevail in the end. Andersen emphasizes the costs — the human and environmental costs for each and every one of us — if we fall for the allure of unbounded progress. It is in this way that — as we shall discover in relation to Kant and Rousseau later — Grundtvig and Andersen together carve out a paradigmatic symmetry in their disagreement: they represent the two opposing sides within a traditional normative philosophical debate which has broken out time and time again.

Finally, it is worth noting that the significance of technology is by no means a cut-and-dried affair for either of these men, and most certainly not for Grundtvig. The superstitious denigration of technology which has beset later periods of history has not yet started to petrify 19th C. Danes. They have not yet fallen for the temptation of believing that the significance of technology is merely a function of its speechless nature. Only 'High German' objectivity enthusiasts can afford to waste their lives on the lifeless past. The development of technology, i.e. the determination and fabrication of its social significance, takes place as the result of an ongoing struggle between its tendential content and its latent future potential, between its overt and apparently irreducible and ever-present past and its covert capacity to liberate the future.

4.1.2. *The Anticipative Task Ahead.*

These 19th C. thinkers, then, were aware of the importance of thinking ahead, of adopting a long-term future perspective in our attempts to evaluate technology. Ernst Bloch, as the reader will recall from chapter 2, would have agreed with them. And when he reminds us of the "six to eight thousand years of human history, with changing forms of government, life-styles, culture, with new horizons constantly in front of us, closed, re-opened, innumerable vistas stretching away before us" (Bloch 1982), he is confronting us with the best evidence for the claim that the human race does have a future, if what we mean by that is that our race, at any given point in time, has before it a broad spectrum of possibilities. Defined as "a being constantly desirous of change", human beings are surrounded, then, by a variety of utopias.

But unfortunately the future which may be mediated by the present, the as yet incomplete but anticipated future, hardly enjoys the most favourable conditions. Freud used the term 'repression' to refer to the latent past whose suppression is ever present and partially determines the future of the human psyche. Capitalism, as a social system, confronts us with an enormous dead weight of repression, bringing the past heavily to bear both on the present and on the future. The current misconception of technology as 'speechless Nature' is an example of how past criticism has been suppressed, so that what was already dubious in our past has become an accepted (mis)guiding assumption for our future.

With critics of capitalism, then, we must agree that the past cannot be — and indeed must not be — denied, when we contemplate the limited sphere of action which capitalism would seem to leave us for the future. But how constructive *is* the kind of criticism which merely goes along with the assumption held by apologists of capitalism that our past *is* our future — with their belief in the immutability of the system? Surely it is preferable to insist on a better future — and to make that better future the object of scientific analysis, with the aim of revealing grains of the future in the pores of the present, in the contradictions which currently surround us. Call such a science 'utopian thinking', 'preemptive science', 'futurology', what you will, the name is unimportant, the enterprise itself is surely of value.

As far as telematics technology is concerned, the task is to disclose the abundance of (possibly contradictory) potential futures which are latent in the technology; to exhibit them; and to put them to the test. The aim must be to keep as many options open as possible for posterity. The name of such an approach, incorporating all three of the operations mentioned above, is of little importance in itself, but, for the sake of convenience, I would suggest calling it the 'social experiments with telematics' approach, as I mentioned in my introduction.

4.2. *Against Oversimplification: Towards the Structural Analysis of the Latent Future Potential Inherent in Telematics.*

If one is asked to explain what is understood by the concept of a future 'Information Society', a technical run-down along the lines I followed in my first chapter would seem to be necessary. Necessary, but not sufficient to answer the question. For, however lucid the technical explanations, there will still be room left for fundamental disagreement about what is meant by the 'Information Society' itself: confronted by the same technical data, two different people can easily take the concept of the information society to mean totally different things in terms of its content. Any analysis of the significance of technology has, in other words, to be a more comprehensive analysis, an analysis going beyond technology's own terms of reference.

The reason for this is twofold. In the first place, technology is not 'just' technology: technology is purposive, and it exists within a specific context. Broadly speaking, technology is an incarnation of the relationships of human beings to their natural environment and to each other at any given moment in their history. Which is why any attempt to explain what is understood by the concept of a future 'Information Society' must include the analysis of the notions, prevalent in existing societies, about the kinds of aim which technology is supposed to help them to achieve, and about the (un)acceptability of certain forms of technology. The analysis of technology must thus be both comprehensive and richly suggestive and thought-provoking: comprehensive, because part of the significance of technology is its *social* significance; thought-provoking and open-ended, because part of the significance of technology is *anticipative*. Moreover, I believe it is possible — and indeed desirable — to systematize the findings of an analysis of this kind, and to place them in their proper contexts in the history of ideas.

In the second place, even if one accepts the fact that technology has a social significance as well as a purely technological significance, our analysis has to be all the more comprehensive because these very significances are intrinsically ambiguous. Technology is rarely in itself an exclusively defined and unambiguously specific means to an exclusively defined and unambiguous end. This is why I find it impossible to share in the widespread belief that all societies go through clearly defined and universally valid phases, or 'ages', progressing from one specific set of beliefs about means and ends in relation to technology in an 'Industrial Society', to another in an 'Information Society', for instance. On the contrary, what seems to occur is an ongoing development of contemporaneous but totally different — indeed mutually contradictory — technological and ideological bodies of thought, which oppose each other, supplement each other, modify each other.

4.2.1. *Tackling the Ideological Confusion Surrounding Telematics.*

Two such bodies of thought about means and ends in relation to technology are what one might call, in the company of historians of ideas, the pro- and anti-civilisation ideologies. Personally, I prefer to call them Pro-Reason as distinct from Pro-Nature ideologies, because the difference between them does not reside in the fact that one 'goes in for' something while the other doesn't, but rather in the fact that different social categories — Reason or Nature — are selected as the basis for two different, but equally normative, systems. Common to both of these belief systems is the fact that they are born of an antinomical *Weltanschauung*, a fact which makes it very tempting to deal with them together, since, in consequence, they relate very closely to each other, supplement each other, generate each other, as it were.[9]

Pro-civilisation ideologies side with technology and progress, labelling them *rational*. They are contrasted with an irrational human element, which, in the worst instance, can retard rational progress through untimely interference. This kind of ideology can be traced back to late Renaissance and Enlightenment philosophers (in a Baconian tradition, Immanuel Kant is the example *par excellence*). It is 'pro-civilisation' in the sense that civilisation itself, understood as the highest level of the most elaborately technologically developed society in the world at any point in time, is taken to be the incarnation of what is most rational, and is awarded normative status.

Anti-civilisation ideologies side with human beings, labelling them *natural*. They are contrasted with technology and progress, which are seen to be unnatural and threatening factors, threatening nature and human nature even to the point of extinction. Such ideologies can similarly be traced back to late-Renaissance and Enlightenment thinkers — (Montaigne and Rousseau are the obvious examples). The 'anti-civilisation' designation is due to the fact that civilisation, again understood as the highest level of the most elaborately technologically developed society in the world at any point in time, is considered to be unnatural, and therefore suspect.

As I see it, the point on which both these ideologies are most clearly vulnerable to criticism is precisely that point on which they both agree: the distinction, which they insist on, between technology and progress, on the one hand, and (human) nature, on the other. It is because they both start from this same misconception that both their conclusions necessarily involve exaggeration and oversimplification. Worst of all, for our purposes, both ideologies obstruct any attempt to make an adequately detailed analysis of the social significance of technology in general, and telematics technology in particular. Pro-civilisation supporters reject such an analysis as a waste of time, unnecessarily impeding the necessary and inevitable march of rational progress. Anti-civilisation supporters reject such an analysis as unnecessary intercourse with 'the enemy'. But underlying both these dismissals of a thorough analysis of the social significance of the latest technology is a fundamental inability to conceive of such an analysis. How *can* one subject something to analysis which is, in itself, either supremely rational or repellently unnatural? And if such an inconceivable analysis is nevertheless effected, it is effected in an atmosphere of marked mutual distrust, with pro-civilisation adherents muttering accusations of procrastination and sabotage, while anti-civilisation adherents consider such analysis to be a disreputable attempt to legitimate technological developments of dubious value. 'Give the devil an inch and he will take an ell', they remind us. And, of course, new technology, such as telematics technology, does seem to be the work of the devil when one only examines it in the gloomy light of a blinkered and absurdly oversimplified conception of causality.

The chaos of public attitudes and opinions surrounding the birth and growth of I.T. is, of course, partly due to the fact that its social significance is derived from its capacity to affect so many different areas of society at once, everywhere blowing new life into the smouldering embers of age-old debates, of varying magnitude and sensitivity, about politics and ethics, means and ends. The pattern of argumentation is always the same: I.T. is the premiss, but the conclusions are diametrically opposed to each other, and seem to have more to do with the quality of life than the quality of the technology. What, it is asked, will be the effect of this technology on human beings in general and on given societies in particular? Will it be emancipatory or repressive? Will it lead to democracy or totalitarian control? Will it make our societies more rational or more chaotic? Will the freedom of the press pass away with the passing of traditional printed newspapers — or will a new equally free electronic press arise? Will the mass media become even more standardized and less adventurous, or will the enormously increased availability of information ensure much greater diversity? Will the enormous flood of information drown out our faculties of discrimination, or will we at last get a truly enlightened and well-informed breed of man? To understand the point I am trying to make about the nature and quality of this sort of speculation about the consequences of telematics technology, it may be helpful to look at some of the ongoing debates in more detail.

4.2.2. *More Information Equals Spiritual Wealth or Spiritual Impoverishment?*

We could start with the question of whether more information will lead to spiritual wealth or to spiritual impoverishment. The familiar optimistic argument is that the improvement of data processing, storage and transmission techniques will create a society which is in fact characterized by its wealth of information. "The introduction of microelectronic capabilities into the home, classroom, and office is initiating a period of explosive innovation and is changing our perceptions of the world around us", writes Alan P. Hald, President of the P.G.I. Corporation and Chairman of MicroAge Computer Stores, Inc. (1982: 9)

> "In essence, a New Renaissance is taking place. Microelectronic technology is dramatically increasing our ability to recall information, communicate, create knowledge, and understand complex relationships. We are moving from a society perceived as resource-constrained to one that is "information rich". We are entering a new era in which economic growth is derived from the exchange of information and the creation of knowledge rather than from the accelerated consumption of natural resources."

"Oh, no, it won't be!" his opponents maintain. The further development of I.T. will not mean that we are spiritually or materially any the richer for all the information which will become available to us. On the contrary, we shall be so inundated by information that we shall drown in a welter of disparate and disjointed data. The editor of *Future Survey*, Michael Marien's predictions are pessimistic: "The computerized society is becoming increasingly complex, and with complexity comes the real potential for breakdown. Paradoxically, as more information is made available to us, we become less well-informed and decisions become harder to make. [...] Therefore", Marien concludes, "as a matter of caution, as well as truthfulness, I think it far more appropriate to label our era the Age of Infoglut, rather than an Information Era or Information Society." (1982: 62-68) Marien mentions four types of non-communication: 'failed' communication, in which important messages either do not get sent, or do not get received because they are drowned out in the enormous daily welter of information; 'flawed' communication, in which incorrect messages are sent intentionally or unintentionally; 'miscommunication', in which messages are received but are not understood or are misunderstood; and 'junk' communication, which includes the vast bulk of messages which are sent and received, but which are irrelevant to the receiver and prevent him from participating in more meaningful activities, or devoting more time to more important communication.

It is, however, not for me to select the winner in any kind of credibility competition, here. What interests me is the symmetrical pattern of the conflicting arguments: on the basis of a single common factor, I.T. development, conclusions are drawn about far-reaching and all-embracing social changes. The strategy is a familiar ingredient in traditional technology assessment. It admits a plethora of disparate results, and all too often the assessor's expectations are self-fulfilling: his own hopes and fears are more crucial for his results than the technology under investigation. My own conclusion has to be that the two predictions about telematics say less about the possible consequences of the technology than they do about specific social expectations in relation to future societies. As expressions of such specific social expectations, the opinions presented here are, however, of the utmost relevance and demand interpretation.

4.2.3. *The Greater Efficiency of I.T. will Produce a More or Less Human Society?*

Other conflicting predictions, of perhaps even greater significance than the above, concern the rational, emancipatory effects of the new technology as opposed to its hypothesized repressive, totalitarian encroachment on the sanctity of private life and human relationships.

In many of his studies of the 'Information Society', Joseph P. Martino, senior scientist at the Dayton Research Institute in Ohio, and one of the editors of the journal *Technological Forecasting and Social Change*, foresees a society characterized by greater efficiency, better information, and more enjoyable spare time. In the first place, work will become gradually more decentralized, as more and more people are enabled to work at home behind their domestic V.D.U.s. For employees, this would permit more flexible working hours and more comfortable working conditions. Employers would only have to pay for the actual work done: all other overheads would be substantially reduced, while work force discipline would become a thing of the past. The only problem Martino foresees is the problem of maintaining the workers' loyalty to an office they so seldom visit!

Spare time, according to Martino, will become more enjoyable as routine chores disappear and the selection of computer games and video entertainment becomes larger. Electronic shopping and banking will save a great deal of time and trouble, leaving us with all the more time to enjoy our high-definition stereophonic visual display units.

Better information will produce better-educated populations, a consequence both of the improved accessibility of information and of the increased efficiency and flexibility of the educational system. (Martino 1982: 30-36)

Frank W. Schiff, Vice-President and Chief Economist on the Committee for Economic Development in Washington D.C., has expressed views similar to Martino's on several occasions. Decentralized places of work will mean a lot in terms of efficiency, job satisfaction, savings in relation to time and fuel consumption, etc. Naturally, new solutions of this kind will produce new problems, but none that will not be soluble in a rational and systematic way, if we reduce friction — (=potential opposition) — to zero, as it were!

Schiff points out that problems regarding the management of work done domestically, or at least outside the central office, have already been solved. Work done on a remote V.D.U. is actually much easier to check up on than work done in a traditional office — any remaining worries on that score cannot be put down to anything other than die-hard conservative thinking or anachronistic notions about office discipline.

The isolation of the future information workers could cause problems, Schiff admits, but presumably none which sophisticated telematics systems will not easily surmount. The 'missing-the-comradery' problem and the 'honey-do-that' problem are two possible exceptions, however, but Schiff has suggested on several occasions that all that is required is an adaptation to one's new circumstances. The need for social fellowship can be satisfied in other places than at work, and spouses must learn not to distract each other when they are 'on the job' in front of their terminals. (Schiff: 1982)

Not surprisingly, views of this kind frequently encounter a good deal of opposition. John Wicklein, author of *The Electronic Nightmare*, fervently maintains that the increased efficiency and decentralization of the society of the future will be introduced at the expense of fundamental human qualities. The efficient society will be a society full of control systems. Authorities and large private concerns have an interest in monitoring individual activities, and the new technology provides them with the means to do it. Our private lives will be threatened, because our political attitudes, financial transactions, selection of information or entertainment, etc., will be automatically registered. (Wicklein 1981)

Somewhat more surprising, perhaps, is the fact that such attitudes receive considerable conservative political support at grassroots level in the U.S.A. There are a large number of popular conservative organizations which, though making little impression on the conservative academic or administrative circles geographically centred around Washington D.C., nevertheless enjoy considerable popular support: Conservative societies, Back-to-Basics groups, Fundamentalists, religious sects, the Moral Majority. Many of these groups and popular movements see the latest developments in media technology as constituting one of the most dangerous of the potentially corrupting influences on human nature. George Ainsworth-Land, author of *Grow or Die* and *Forward to Basics*, and Burton Pines, author of *Back to Basics*, are typical representatives of such attitudes. According to them, telematics is a threat to all that is authentically human. On the other hand, though, it is worth noting that there are religious spokesmen who welcome the new media technology as a powerful potential ally. Ben Armstrong, for instance, author of *The Electronic Church*, and Jeffrey Hadden, who wrote *Prime Time Preachers*, are both enthusiastic about the new technology, and both expect a lot from it in terms of broadening the scope of their missionary activities.

Reactions like these are more than entertaining curiosities, in that they constitute an interesting proof of the fact that both the criticism and the defence of telematics tend to cross traditional political boundaries. Neither the criticism nor the defence may be neatly classified as traditionally left or right wing. The ongoing debate about telematics (to mention just one example of late 20th C. technology), whose parameters are defined by views such as those I have outlined above, is a logically coherent and independent battleground for conflicting values and beliefs, and not a mere appendix to the traditional spectrum of political values.

4.2.4. *Other Ongoing Debates about Telematics.*

The controversies I have examined above concerning the spiritual wealth or impoverishment of the 'Information Society', and the repressive as opposed to the emancipatory effects of the new technology, are only two of many such ongoing debates. Others concern the effect of telematics on financial transactions and, as I mentioned earlier, its effects on the press and on the mass media generally, with particular reference to socialisation and education. And also, as we have seen, the effects of the new technology on our entire life-style with regard to the traditional work/leisure dichotomy.

We could start with the debates concerning the future of the press. Evolving from the latest developments in interactive videotex systems one might expect that the traditional newspaper will be superseded by massive continually updated databases, containing news and news commentary, which may be searched on an individual access basis, so that appropriate items are printed out which correspond to the individual reader's interests. The question of how such a development would alter the traditional function of the press in the society of the future is again a question which provokes strong emotions and conflicting answers. Not least because recent developments in computer graphics systems will enable interactive videotex services to finance themselves with advertising revenues, presumably at the expense of traditional newspapers, whose financial basis is heavily dependent on such revenues.

Again, if domestic V.D.U.s really do enable more and more of us to stay at home and work instead of having to work in an office, will the traditional social fabric of our lives consisting of work and leisure, office and homelife, disintegrate catastrophically or heuristically together with our traditional work ethic? — And how will our children be influenced by the similar problem of the dissolution of the traditional boundaries between work and leisure, when they are as often in front of a screen at school as they are at home? They may be saved from the fate of being 'corrupted' — as passive, innocent victims of the ever more freely available but often ethically dubious broadcast films and entertainments — by the growing popularity of interactive computer games. But, as such games penetrate schools and other places of education as learning devices, and learning becomes more and more heuristic and less and less didactic and preceptive, what will be the effect on socialisation, for instance?

The incalculability of the answers to such questions may make some of the other questions appear to be of lesser importance. While I would advise the reader to be very wary of the temptation to jump at any such fallacious conclusion, I would like to round off this detailed account of some of the typical controversies aroused by telematics with perhaps the biggest question of all. In the words of William E. Halal, Professor of Management at the George Washington University in Washington, D.C., "[...] the revolution now underway toward an information society is transforming business into a more mature, enlightened institution that should transcend the original vision that Adam Smith and others saw only dimly." Halal foresees "[...] a growth of large numbers of small, innovative, constantly changing enterprises", "an endless variety of sophisticated goods and services", and corporations "governed in a fairly democratic manner." (1982: 39) The question is, then, will I.T. land us back with Adam Smith — or rather with his vindicated, freely-competing capitalist utopia which 'necessarily' produces a more enlightened and rational population; or will the result be a spiritually impoverished population living in an information-saturated technocratic dystopia? Or are there any grounds for believing that there may be a way out of this dilemma, involving democratic intervention under the auspices of the state, so that, despite the pessimists' well-grounded scepticism, the positive aspects of telematics may be promoted, and the negative aspects checked throughout the gradual transformation of our societies, so that I.T. really can become a tool to help us to build up a better future for ourselves?[10]

4.2.5. *The Necessity for the Systematic Structural Analysis of Telematics in Relation to the Life of the Individual in Society.*

At the outset of this section I wrote of the confusion of public attitudes and opinions surrounding the birth of I.T., which has little to do with party politics but rather more to do with traditional and quasi-superstitious cultural optimism or pessimism. And now that the reader has been presented with some of the ongoing controversies in detail, the necessity for — and desirability of — systematic analyses of the effects of telematics on everyday life (understood as the temporal and social context of the technology) will have become apparent.

We have to get away from the isolated contemplation of specific problems connected with the introduction of the new technology, whether they are purely technical in nature, or whether they concern only a few arbitrarily selected aspects of I.T.'s comprehensive social content. For what is so characteristic of telematics technology is precisely the fact that it constitutes a ubiquitous technical system which reaches into every corner of our societies. Not content with affecting our working lives alone, or our leisure activities alone, it soaks into every pore of our existences, affecting both our working lives and our private lives and our political lives as well. I suppose, really, this is the most important aspect of telematics: the fact that it doesn't 'merely' re-open time-hallowed debates about the nature of work, the meaning of democracy, etc., but the fact that it does this through its creation of an all-inclusive social synthesis, through its theatre producer's control of each individual's enactment of every scene in his life, from the cradle to the grave, at work, at political meetings, in bed, etc. In fact the three basic questions with which we have to confront this new technology, in its capacity of (far-from-divine!) social synthesizer, concern the *total* effect it will have on *each individual's* working life, political life, and private life, respectively.

If we start by looking at each individual's *working life* — as I do in Chapter 5 — we have to assess the consequences of the introduction of telematics against the fact that an integrated broadband network would permit the comprehensive interlinking of private and public sector institutions and firms together with computer service centres. This fact would have considerable consequences for the development of automated information exchange, revolutionizing office work (the advantages or disadvantages of domestic office terminals have already been discussed) and public and private administration. With regard to the composition of the labour force, the new technology will undoubtedly ring the changes. As I mentioned in the last chapter, trends have already been observed in such countries as Canada, Sweden, and Austria, as well as in Japan, the U.S.A., West Germany and the U.K., involving a growth in the percentage of the total labour force employed in so-called 'information occupations' in post-war years. And there has been an accompanying change in the actual composition of those employed in such occupations (more software and hardware experts, and fewer typists and clerks). Worthy of note, too, is the fact that 'information workers' have infiltrated different industrial sectors at different rates and in varying quantities.

If we go on to examine the effects of telematics on each individual's *political life* — as I do in Chapter 6 —, surveys and experience around the world indicate that the laying of cables for an integrated broadband network may lead to improvements in both vertical and horizontal information and communication structures. As far as the former is concerned, one would need to take into account the results of experiments with so-called 'instant democracy', in which voters participate in political decision-making by means of relatively frequent electronically effected referenda. Such systems are already on trial in miniature in experimental districts around the world, provoking serious discussion about whether they really do constitute an improvement in democratic political processes, or whether they produce the opposite effect, by increasing the isolation of the individual voter, and by reducing his influence over his own affairs in denying him the possibility of a truly independent grassroots evaluation of the issues in question. In such instances, it would seem, the time-honoured maxim that the essence of democracy is not the referendum but the gradual achievement of consensus by means of a public dialogue among free and equal citizens has been forgotten.

On the other hand, as far as the horizontal information and communication structure is concerned, one must not overlook the possibility of increased political participation as a result of the increased point-to-point and inter-group communication. A complete, fully integrated broadband network would not only facilitate the transmission of locally produced television programmes, but ultimately, too, audio-visual communication between private homes. Teleconferencing systems are at present being developed which will enable large groups of people (members of an association, for example) to participate in continuous and lengthy debates on particular topics, thus transcending the physical limitations normally associated with meetings of restricted duration in buildings of limited size. With regard to each individual's political life, then, the open question is whether such new modes of interaction can supplement, or supplant, the physical togetherness and comradeship which frequently play a part in each individual's decision to join political associations, or take part in other political activities. The consequences of such developments would, in other words, have to be assessed in relation to their effect on truly democratic popular participation in political decision-making, on both national and local levels.

Finally, in assessing the effects of telematics on each individual's *private life* — as I do in Chapter 7 —, we would have to take into account the widespread fear that the introduction of the new technology would mean a general impoverishment of the quality of our leisure time activities. The actual leisure time at our disposal will doubtless be increased, but the amount of available activities and challenges may well be reduced. We would have more time at home with our families if domestic terminals could shorten the average working day, if teleconferencing facilities could cut down on transport time to and from political meetings, if the video telephone's replacement of the traditional telephone rendered private visiting less popular, and thus, again, saved us transport time. But the activities on which we would tend to spend all this increased free time could well be increasingly trivial and stupefying. In that a broadband network would be capable of supplying us with a large number of T.V. channels, one might expect an increase in the amount of time spent passively in front of 'the box', and a corresponding decline in the quality of the programmes broadcast, since they would have to be mass-produced. Not that this decline in quality would in any way apply to the formal packaging of such programmes, which rather represents the ultimate refinement of one-way communication techniques. But, faced by more, and more sophisticatedly packaged low-quality programmes, local T.V. stations on a less commercial and more actively democratic basis, and video cassette libraries containing higher quality programmes, would presumably be unable to compete for anything more than minority audiences, since the attractiveness of much mass-produced trivia is a carefully calculated function of its ability to avoid making any notable demands on the intellect.

In short, as far as each individual's private life is concerned, the danger is that, in endeavouring to realise the very attractive utopia of more private life and time together with our families, with the enhanced sense of security and happiness which that would entail, we will systematically be made to forget what actually was the attraction of the utopia. More time with the family at home may paradoxically mean less home- and family-life in any real functional sense.

To sum up, then, our task consists in assessing the actual *structural* consequences of telematics for the social and temporal context of each individual's entire life in his or her society. One of the basic structural constituents of existing democratic societies is the political sphere, within which general political activities take place under the auspices of clubs, associations and societies. The question is to what extent these political activities will be superseded, or altered, by telematics' potential for effecting electronic intercourse and political opinion polls. Another basic structural constituent in existing societies is the division of each person's life into private life, and time spent on socially productive, or reproductive, work. If the latter are increasingly to be based on domestically confined labour, what will happen to this fundamental structural dichotomy? Will its erosion simply mean 'more time for the family', or will the traditional concepts of 'private life' and 'working life' take on completely new meanings? Considerations like these render a structural analysis of the consequences of telematics necessary not merely because of the growth and qualitative changes in the pattern of media consumption.

4.3. *Traditional Normative Thinking and Its Limitations.*

The indispensability of the systematic structural analysis of telematics in its social context thus becomes apparent. But such analysis must take into account — and, where possible, try to free itself from — the underlying prejudices which have their origins in the antiquated Pro-Reason v. Pro-

Nature polemic mentioned earlier. Too often, unsystematic assessments of telematics in relation to a varying amount of specific social aspects are informed by one of two — (or, at most, of three) — basic attitudes. There are those who go in for the new technology at all costs, those who go against it at all costs, and those who tend to sympathise with these latter-day Luddites but nevertheless believe that it may be possible for the technology to proceed under new colours.

A speech by the American director of a computer firm, Walter F. Bauer, serves rather well to illustrate the traditional élitist optimistic attitudes about the future — though admittedly in a rather exaggerated form. At a managerial conference in Copenhagen for 500 I.T. representatives from all over the world, Bauer prefaced his speech thus:

> "Ladies and gentlemen, we meet as leaders in the computing services industry. We *are* the leaders of this industry, but we are more than that. I see each of you as a leader of a new society. I see standing behind each of you a growing population of leading citizens in this new society. [...] Information has [...] replaced industrial society's criteria for social stratification. During the industrial revolution the power shifted from ownership of property to ownership of production. In the last few decades those with ownership of production — the money rich — are giving way to the information rich, the knowledge rich, the wise. The power base can be described by the simple words of Francis Bacon, 'Knowledge is power'." (Bauer 1982: 1 and 6)

However much innovation and novelty these words are intended to proclaim, they are in effect an echo, or indeed a mirror image, of the industrial society to which they purport to bid farewell. In the world of his fancy, Bauer is still postulating a society based on power concentrated in the hands of an élite, a one-(or at most two-!)dimensional world, the development of which is myopically ascribed to the single factor of technological progress. In spite of the replacement of Industrial Revolution technology by computer technology, it is the maintenance of the old order which informs Bauer's attitude; an old order which, primitively and pathetically, elevates considerations relating to efficiency and G.N.P. growth above considerations of the multiplicity and equivalue of the genuine needs of individual human beings. Bauer's attitude is by no means uncommon. Vice-President Frank Schiff, whom I mentioned in my last section above, is in line with a lot of other people when he declares that the revolution in I.T. is to bring about increased productivity, to introduce 'electronic' (i.e. more efficient and centralized) democracy, and to extend the amount of time spent on passive relaxation.

According to Schiff, the greatest advantages of I.T. and telematics technology is that they can reduce the costs of office work. Workers in 'information occupations' will be able to work at home behind V.D.U.s linked to central offices by public networks, permitting economies in office space and reductions in transport costs, and creating more possibilities for flexible working hours and for job flexibility generally and for temporary contractual employment, while reducing distracting physical contact among employees and misconceived shop-floor solidarity. Employers will also find it much easier to keep a check on the amount of work which actually gets done. Democracy will become a sort of opinion-poll democracy, with issues periodically put up for electronic voting. Inevitably, the presentation of the issues will increasingly be centralized, but wasteful and unproductive communication among voters at meetings, etc., will be minimized. And, finally, the amount of entertainment on offer in our spare time will also be increased, with T.V. games and many more channels available, while time wastage on shopping, banking, etc., will be reduced. (Schiff 1982)

In contrast to the above, an abundance of pessimistic attitudes to the technology is also to be found. In fact, opposition to the optimists seems to be growing all over the world. In their report to the Canadian Department of Communications in 1980, Shirley Serafini and Michael Andrieu, for instance, took a very different view of the possible consequences of telematics with regard to decentralisation. Their fear was that the new technology would further promote the growth and influence of monopolistic concerns like the multinationals. Improvements in communication between computers could permit increases in the scale of these firms' activities because the cost of running such enormous and complex organisations would thus be dramatically reduced. Centralized computer resources could increase the control of the headquarters of such firms over their geographically distant branches, and one result of this might be a corresponding loss of control over domestic economic activities experienced by the governments of their host countries. An apparent decentralization over a vast geographical area would, if the worst came to the worst, in fact amount to an increased *centralization* of power and management. (Serafini and Andrieu 1980)

Anxiety is also expressed about the possible undesirable consequences of developments in telematics in Japan, in relation to their broadband network plans, as the reader will recall from my presentation of them in the last chapter. The interlinkage of many different databases may constitute a threat to personal privacy and security; centralized information storage may permit unhealthy concentrations of power within central government offices or in larger private businesses; the extension of access to data beyond the range of people accustomed to working with I.T. may result in a widening gulf between the initiated and the general public, unless R. and D. is concentrated on the solution of man-machine interface problems, both with regard to software and to hardware. And finally, anxiety is expressed about the vulnerability of the integrated network as regards 'technical hitches' — a vulnerability which presumably varies in proportion to the size and complexity of the network.

In many of the critical predictions concerning the developments in the mass media which telematics will render possible, however, the scepticism of the Canadian and Japanese researchers referred to above — a scepticism which derives from ideals concerning decentralization and small-scale private enterprise as opposed to large corporations or government interference — this scepticism is replaced by a more deep-seated mistrust of the technology, or of the mass media, *per se*. Such more fundamentally conservative and unreservedly negative attitudes are based on a purported opposition between technology and human needs. Judgements are thus passed on the technology, or on the mass media, in accordance with normative divisions of human needs into the 'genuine' and the 'artificial', the 'good' and the 'bad', the 'fundamental' and the 'superficial'. Thus categorized, human needs are considered to be static. That which is historically mutable is the technology, which, for one reason or another, has changed from being in harmony with our 'genuine' and 'fundamental' needs at some earlier stage in our history, to being in harmony with the 'artificial' and 'superficial' needs of the present age.

A critical paradigm of this kind will result in criticism which is healthily sceptical and deeply concerned, but which is, at the same time, unhealthily defensive, and restrictive, with regard to the formulation of any constructive policy concerning the mass media, or the new technology. This is regrettable since, for this reason, such criticism is inclined to overlook any truly progressive prospects offered by recent technical developments.

The third fundamental attitude which can be prejudicial to assessments of the social significance of telematics, is the attitude which shares much of the optimism of the first attitude with regard to the inherent advantages of the new technology, but which also shares the ideals concerning decentralization, and small-scale private initiative, which, as we saw, inform some of the more pessimistic attitudes to telematics. From this third point of view, the new telematics technology is considered to be a possible tool for decentralization, democratization, and the promotion of respect for individual needs.

Toffler, in *The Third Wave*, is, of course, the most famous proponent of such expectations concerning I.T.'s ability to assist in the creation of a decentralized and enlightened, free, equal, and democratic society — a 'de-massified' society, as Toffler himself calls it. Professor William E. Halal would seem to be clearly in line with Toffler. Industry will indeed become decentralized, he claims, because software production is gaining more and more ground, and software production is less capital-intensive than hardware production. Rigidly hierarchical management structures will gradually become more flexible and democratic, because I.T. renders such a development possible, and because competition with other firms, making more intensive use of their human resources, will make such transformations imperative. In the political sphere, Halal expects that, thanks to viewdata systems, etc., the increased volume and accessibility of information will have a stimulating effect on democratic processes, which will become more fully developed because of the growing network of horizontal communication channels, i.e. lines of communication among individual voters, rather than between the individual voter and central legislative or executive authorities. (Halal 1982)

But perhaps the most extreme representative of a Toffleresque optimism is the Japanese Yoneji Masuda. According to Masuda, his own country (at least) is on its way towards a post-Capitalist society in which the economy, which is at present based on money and commodity exchange, will be superseded by an economy based on the collective production of basic necessities. The centralized hierarchical authority of the present Japanese State and the major private companies will be superseded by a free multicentral society. (Masuda 1981)

In Denmark, Toffler's optimism is shared by the so-called P.U.M.A.-group, a team of production researchers dedicated to the creation of new jobs for Metal Union workers. Far from being representatives of the old order, like Walter Bauer above, they have taken as the central inspiration for their work some collective millenarian hopes for a radically new order. Thus, one member of the group proclaimed that

> "in its basic structure, the microcomputer is in fact a piece of decentralizing equipment. Its utilization in the creation of centralized systems is more problematic than in the creation of decentralized systems. So this technology has enormous potential. It may be used to effect a kind of mass production, as it were, on an individual craftsman basis [...]. A decentralized society really becomes feasible." (Nørretranders 1982)

In the work of the P.U.M.A.-group the new telematics technology thus has an integral role to play in the cultural revolution which they envisage. According to them there is "a substantial need for new political approaches, for a new popular spiritual awakening, like the folk high school and cooperative agricultural movements seen at the end of the last century. We are standing on the brink of a new popular revival [...]."

Enlightenment Utopian Thinking: The Cradle of Today's Deadlocked Debates.

In the final instance, it would be tempting to content oneself with a division of the above-mentioned attitudes into those which go in for, and those which go against telematics, in the same way as there have always been friends and enemies of technology throughout the course of history. If, however, we are to make an adequate analysis of the social significance of telematics we have to go further — we have to get beyond the popular appeal of such facile conclusions, and get to grips with an analysis of the *content* of the optimistic or pessimistic conceptions of technology: we have, as our most fundamental task, to analyse the whole polemical structure of the ongoing debate, with its full societal content. Which is where, it seems to me, the traditional Enlightenment philosophers can help us. They can help us to get our present complex of problems into perspective — a perspective which is as free of prejudice as it must be.

Between the English Revolution and the French, between the collapse of the Spanish and Portuguese Empires and the birth of the United States of America, 'rational' philosophers, revolutionary in their thinking because of their membership of the burgeoning bourgeoisie, were engaged in an international endeavour — in France, in Germany, in Britain — to comprehend the societies which were coming into being all around them. And the interesting thing about these philosophers is that — already then — they succeeded in producing an unusually clear picture of the sort of thinking which is fundamental to industrial societies.

Political and social dilemmas which today confront us as absolutely central challenges were in essence defined for the first time by these philosophers. Free, as they were in those days, from the apologetic urge which was to cramp the style of later defendants of industrial society, they were able to express the central problems and contradictions confronting them with a lucidity which constitutes a very reasonable justification for returning to them in the search for a comprehensive picture of the major outlines of industrial society. Theirs was not to defend an already established society of this kind, with all the temptations to embellish, or to pass over in silence, which might accompany such a task. Theirs was to prepare, with the utmost rational clarity, the coming of a new order.

Kant and Rousseau, pioneer thinkers of and for the emergent industrial societies, agreed on the fundamental proposition that human beings are, at least 'originally', free and autonomous. "Man was born free", Rousseau declares in the famous opening sentence of *Le Contrat Social* (1977: 1), while Kant, in his little manifesto 'Was ist Aufklärung?' (1975: 39 and 55) writes similarly, "sapere aude!". "Dare to rely on your own reason" is the motto of the Enlightenment. But, while Kant confidently proceeds to discuss the uses of reason for the public good, Rousseau, still struggling with his opening sentence quoted above, ends it with the no less famous statement: "And everywhere he is in chains."

Kant's optimism about the future, though, is unambiguous. The general application of reason for the common good will lead to a general increase in material wealth, to political democracy, and to the highest level of happiness obtainable for each individual. The attitude is summarised in his famous categorical imperative: "Act only on that maxim whereby thou canst at the same time will that it should become a universal law." (Kant 1973) A statement, in other words, in crystalline form, of the belief that only that which is rational and universally valid has ethical value and warrants further development. Anything which is not in accord with this, whether it be individual human characteristics or specific natural features, has no validity, and therefore cannot serve as a foundation for the future.

Kant is thus the exponent of a classical educational ideal, in which grandiloquent phrases about justice and morality apparently exist in perfect harmony with quantitative utilitarian considerations. It is his voice we can hear whispering in the wings of history when the Walter Bauers of this world take the stage to say, without any apparent illogicality, that the developments they outline will produce a much more democratic and civilized society in which "[...] personal convenience increases, menial tasks are removed from human hands, public policy becomes more responsive to perceived needs". (1982: 3) That, in other words, the revolution in welfare and in information processing leads society "[...] to a revolution in wisdom". (Ibid.)

But Rousseau is ready to confront them with his critique. In indignant tones he proclaims that it is money, power, and private property rights which corrupt the natural moral instincts of free individuals. In *Emile* he writes that civilisation as a whole is 'in bad taste': "All the true models of taste are to be found in nature. The further we get from the master, the worse are our pictures." Denying ourselves "every beauty that is found in the works of man", we subject ourselves to the lavish bad taste of those in power over us:

> "Those leaders are the artists, the wealthy, and the great, and they themselves follow the lead of self-interest or pride. Some to display their wealth, others to profit by it, they seek eagerly for new ways of spending it. This is how luxury acquires its power and makes us love what is rare and costly; this so-called beauty consists, not in following nature, but in disobeying her." (Rousseau 1911: 306)

Thus, while Kant's teleology of Nature was fully in harmony with his ascription of supremacy to Reason and his celebration of Reason as the guiding principle for Civilisation, Rousseau saw Civilisation and Nature as irreconcilably antagonistic. Unlike Kant, who premised his utopias on rationalism and universality, Rousseau does the reverse: he emphasizes the singularity of individual human nature and of specific natural phenomena as that which above all else must be considered central — partly for its own sake, and partly because, through its resultant elevation, it can serve as a norm against which the critical analyst can measure the fraudulence of unjust and corrupting civilisation.

In contrast to Kant's, the ideals deriving from Rousseau's interpretation of the relationship between Civilisation and Nature include respect for the complex individual soul, for creativity and imaginative play, for decentralization rather than centralization. Where Kant formally represents the classical cultivation of reason as the norm, Rousseau represents what some have called critical humanism and others Romantic delirium.

However you prefer to label them, there is no doubt at all that Rousseauesque attitudes have made a remarkable come-back in recent years, and not least in discussions about technology. The novel element in the on-going debate consists in the attempt made by the P.U.M.A.-group and others of the same ilk to soft-pedal the classical relationship between reason and technology in an attempt to 'get back to nature' in an air-conditioned Cadillac, as it were.

Obviously, an elegant and supremely simple move of this kind can give critical humanism a new and optimistic lease of life. But it is equally understandable that it is met with a certain amount of scepticism from time to time. Isn't technology after all an incarnation of Reason, of a normative belief in a rational future, in other words? Isn't it a confidence trick, then, to start talking about microcomputers as 'decentralizing', 'handy', even 'natural' technology? Small is not necessarily natural, let alone beautiful in any ideological sense!

The scepticism is understandable, but it is in the last resort of dubious validity, proceeding as it does from too superficial an identification of a Bauer-type ideology with Kant and a P.U.M.A.-group ideology with Rousseau, without realising that in spite of the fact that the two Enlightenment thinkers' visions of the future would seem to be so diametrically opposed to each other, they were in effect remarkably similar — inextricably bound up with each other, as it were.

The common denominator of the two so radically different philosophers' work is nowhere so much in evidence as in those pages where Rousseau has to grapple with a social framework for the realisation of his ideals concerning the cultivation of the naturally moral individual. If one was expecting that Rousseau's critical attitude towards civilisation would produce a utopia fundamentally different from Kant's, one is in for a shock — his utopia is described in words which might have been taken directly out of Kant's own mouth! At the end of *Emile*, we find him endeavouring to persuade his now grown-up protégé of the benefits of submitting himself to the laws of his 'sovereign', defined as "a moral and collective body, consisting of as many members as there are votes in the Assembly": "Individuals having only submitted themselves to the sovereign, and the sovereign power being only the general will, we shall see", he maintains hopefully, "that every man in obeying the sovereign only obeys himself, and how much freer are we under the social pact than in the state of nature". (Rousseau 1911: 424f)

The idea is, of course, fundamental to *Le Contrat Social*, where we find Rousseau writing that, by entering into the social compact, the individual "gives up his natural liberty, or unlimited right to every thing which he is desirous of, and can attain", gaining in return "social liberty, and an exclusive property in all those things of which he is possessed". What is more, if he fails to recognize that the resultant society is synonymous with the highest form of freedom, "Whosoever refuses to pay obedience to the general will, shall be liable to be compelled to it by the force of the whole body", which, according to this supposedly anti-civilisation spokesman, "is in effect nothing more, than that they may be *compelled to be free*". (Abraham 1973: 75)

So, in spite of Kant's and Rousseau's very different starting points in terms of universal and societally-oriented Reason, on the one hand, and in terms of individually-oriented Nature, on the other, there is a fundamental congruity with regard to the bearing principles on which their visions of society are constructed. In effect, the social contracts based either on Reason or on Nature are not antagonistic but complementary: their existence is mutually conditioned — they are two sides of the same medal, as it were. The utopias have equal validity, and have coexisted side by side and in mutual conflict (the strength of their attraction varying respectively from time to time) as long as capitalist society has existed.

In the light of the above, when we find people arguing for something or other on the basis of the postulate that it is 'rational' or 'natural', it is salutary to remind ourselves that the apparently universal and eternally valid concepts of 'Reason' or 'Nature' are in fact historically specific — and systematic — socially-conditioned abstractions, for all their pretensions to universality. Far from being an academic exercise, this realisation has very real political consequences in the assessment of the latent future potential of telematics.

As far as the rationalists are concerned, any crises or side-effects produced by the introduction of the new technology are ascribed to external irrationality of one kind or another. While those who make 'Nature' their norm — irrespective of whether they are fundamentally sceptical about all forms of technological progress, or whether they regard them with a grain of optimism — have to realise that they are fighting for an ideal which is itself the product of capitalist society, and, as such, has little to do with any concrete reality. Generated, as it is, by the society which it opposes, this kind of ideal will never be totally suppressed — but neither will it be capable of realization within the confines of that society. Both optimism and pessimism of this kind are thus ill-founded, in that they are based on an inadequate understanding of the significant forces behind, and mechanisms within, the sort of progress from which they expect so much.

Rational optimists, with their steadfast faith in the future, tend to overlook and neglect the enormous influence of the very real and deeply felt opposition which the society which they wish to perpetuate has generated. They forget that the latent future potential of telematics has no less validity than its tendential content. But, on the other hand, those who criticize the tendency to take the highest form of existing civilisation as the norm, tend to forget that their 'alternative' ideals cannot pretend to have any real authenticity.

So, what we have produced together with our Enlightenment philosophers in their laboratory is a paradigm for debate in which one bunch of enthusiasts claim to have the monopoly of Reason, and accuse their opponents of wanting to sabotage any form of progress, while the other lot put all their faith in Nature and accuse the self-styled rationalists of window-dressing for ruthless pursuers of profit.

This sort of misguided on-going social debate has been analysed here not because I cherish any illusions of being able to get rid ot it very easily, but in order to increase our awareness of its short-comings. Getting rid of it would actually be very difficult, since, I would maintain, this kind of social debate is endemic to the kind of society we are dealing with. Its basic postulates inform so many fundamental discussions regarding aspects of the latent future potential of telematics — discussions involving concepts such as work, education, power, democracy. The chapters to follow deal in varying degrees of detail with such discussions, enabling the reader to see how the advent of the new technology has reopened long-forgotten debates, sharpened their tone, and sometimes even altered the relative strengths of the arguments adduced.

4.4. *Anticipative Normative Thinking.*

Before we leave the present chapter, though, I would like to stress the importance of the points I have been making about how best we can endeavour to liberate the latent future potential of telematics. For, in spite of the strength and persistence of the all-too-apparent tendential content of the new technology, which I analysed in the preceding chapter, I do believe that it is possible to share the 'naïve' belief of Hans Christian Andersen and N.F.S. Grundtvig in our democratic ability to shape our own future societies — at least to some significant degree.

I believe, moreover, that we *must* act on the good advice of these 'pioneers': we *must* think ahead, critically and constructively, and we *must* experiment with the new technology — continuously subjecting our ideas and the results of our experiments to stringent analysis.

Finding out how, in practice, the utopian elements in our available future-making technology can be realised is the subject of the last two chapters of this book, where I deal with my 'Social Experiments with Telematics' approach in greater detail. But the present chapter on the latent future potential of telematics would be incomplete without a precise definition of what these utopian elements of the technology actually are. Which specific aspects of what particular long-cherished dream of a 'better' society is the new technology actually capable of realising?

The dream of a 'better' society has — in my opinion very aptly — been called the dream of a 'global village'. Like all mythical or utopian dreams, it consists in a resolution of hitherto apparently irreconcilable contradictions.

As a dream of 'global proximity', it involves freedom from a claustrophobic provincialism, on the one hand, and yet at the same time a return, on the other hand, to the security and straightforward simplicity and manageability of traditional village and home life. I.T. and telematics systems can actually open doors and windows onto a world full of possibilities which have hitherto only been available in the metropolis — while at the same time enabling one to remain in one's own familiar and manageable provincial world with its traditional forms of neighbourhood fellowship and time-hallowed morality.

It is a dream, too, of the transcendence of the rigid distinction between work and free time. The new technology actually can render unacceptable any equation of work with compulsion, or of leisure with meaningless time-killing activity. Necessary routine work can be substantially reduced, and work processes can be adapted to suit individual workers' capabilities. Leisure time mediaviewing need not any longer be subject to the remote, centralized programme-scheduling of broadcasting networks, but can be liberated for 'fractionation' — private scheduling on a time-shift videorecording basis, which will enable each individual to exercise greater freedom of choice both with regard to *what* he wants to watch, and *when* he wants to watch it. This, in turn, should release viewers from the tyranny of pacifying pulp so that they can devote more time to creative and interactive communicative activities outside their armchairs. The annihilation of space, too, is another aspect of the 'global village' concept which plays a role in the erosion of the work/free time dichotomy: the domestic office effectively banishes for ever the soul-destroying tedium, stress, and discomfort of daily commuting.

If it is a dream of 'going back home', it is not a dream of a return to a claustrophobic little nuclear-family container, made of concrete, timber and glass, but rather to an *extended* home base. The ergonomics of the new out-of-the-office work and the new interactive and creative leisure time will probably imply neighbourhood offices rather than home offices, and the neighbourhood offices will probably be more economically situated in neighbourhood cultural and recreation centres, since I.T. entertainment can be based on the same machines and cables as I.T. office work.

A further consequence of this expansion of 'cottage industry' into communal 'village industry', of passive armchair box-watching into active neighbourhood participation, is that politics can actually become, at last, a truly democratic grass-roots phenomenon, instead of a private ballot reaction to deceptively packaged moves by remote and powerful central authorities. Increased neighbourhood interaction should permit the free exchange of opinion which is necessary both for the generation and perpetuation of a healthy cultural climate, and for the generation and perpetuation of a healthy political climate.

Such, then, is the dream — which now seems stronger, more vital, and closer to realisation, than at any previous time in our history. But the very same future-making tools — now in our possession — which can make this dream come true, constitute, at one and the same time, a threat to the dream, of a potency the like of which has never been known before. The outcome of the battle raging around us between the forces of human oppression and the forces of human liberation has never been so crucial, so decisive, so irrevocably final.

The new technology does indeed make it possible for us to transcend the boundaries of (commuting) space, and (office-clock) time. The new methods of production do enable us all to determine the content of our own jobs. Private and public bureaucracies are not any longer technically necessary. Information *can* become public property. Decision-making need no longer be the privilege of an élite.

But the very same technology threatens this dream of an increasingly open, democratic, and interactive society, in a way which seems, at first glance, to be far more difficult to do anything about than any traditional physical threats or resource shortages. The threat is the threat of the socially isolated, televisually pacified, intimately observed, remotely controlled and comprehensively registered impotent individual: Orwell's Winston Smith, hypnotized by the inanities of a telescreen he can't turn off, secretly or openly watched by 'Big Brother' — the cover used by omnipotent bank-managers, mail order firm and supermarket owners, advertisers, politicians, and employers — his every action monitored, disciplined if necessary, and registered in vast impenetrable computerized bureaucratic archives.

Tendentially present in the new technology side by side with its opposite, the latent utopia outlined before pales into insignificance beside this ubiquitously threatening dystopia. If the latent utopia is to be liberated, if it is not to remain illusory, we must create a practical and workmanlike framework for its potential realisation. But a framework which is open-ended — not one which claims to know all the answers beforehand.

Known throughout the world as 'a social laboratory', Denmark has a long tradition of social experimentation which we are hoping to build on in the creation of communal workshops for the development and testing of democratically selected 'utopias'. What we envisage are limited regional experiments, on the basis of democratically-expressed local desires and needs, whose broader perspective is the evolution of new ways of living together in the future with telematics as one of several fundamental tools. As I said earlier, I shall be returning to projects like this in greater detail in the last two chapters of this book.

5. IDLENESS DOESN'T PAY!

Nowhere is the paradoxical nature of the conflicting tendential content of I.T. and telematics so apparent as in the question of their influence on work in the society of the future. On the one hand, the new technology holds out the brightest prospects to us of liberation from the bondage of hard and/or routine labour, while, on the other hand, this very prospect of liberation from the bondage of toil seems to constitute one of the greatest problems which the new technology confronts us with.

James Martin, author of *Telematic Society: a Challenge for Tomorrow*, foresees a 3½-day week as the result of the development of the new technology. The machines will be working continuously, but the wage-earning machine-minders will relieve each other, working on half-weekly shifts. The machines will in effect have become our slaves, and our leisure time will have been substantially increased. (1981: 170ff)

But, for W. Dostal, this glowing prospect presents itself as a problem of alarming dimensions. In a 1981 O.E.C.D. report entitled *Microelectronics, Productivity and Employment* he predicted that at least 30-40% of our present office jobs will disappear as a long-term result of the introduction of I.T. and telematics. The prospect is indeed alarming when one considers the fact that virtually 50% of the total labour force in a country like West Germany, for instance, is employed in clerical or administrative occupations. (O.E.C.D. 1981b: 46)

In the same year, another O.E.C.D. publication was released in an attempt to pour oil on troubled waters. Predictions concerning so-called 'technological redundancy' are not as easy to make as is commonly assumed, the report said. Unemployment of this kind is dependent on at least three factors: on whether the development of the new technology really *is* labour-saving; on whether redundant workers are not absorbed by other sectors of the labour market; and, finally, on whether capital accumulation resulting from the reduced labour costs is not ploughed back into industry in the form of an expansion of activities which are at least as labour intensive. (O.E.C.D. 1981a: 82ff) We have to remember that productivity increases, due to the installation of labour-saving technology, don't take place in a vacuum: their effects need not necessarily include reductions in a nation's total labour force.

Even so, one must understand workers' and unions' scepticism. For, whereas it is as yet unclear to what extent the new technology will reduce the size of the total labour force, or (if we can swing it that way!) to what extent it will reduce the amount of time we all spend at work, there is no doubt at all that the introduction of this technology will involve structural changes in the labour force — changes which may be positive or negative for the individual worker, depending on such variables as sex, qualifications, and geography. It has already become only too apparent that, just as the automation of production has thrown an increasing number of unskilled routine manual workers and labourers onto the job market, with little prospect of further employment, so, too, the automation of office work will turn large numbers of unskilled or virtually unskilled workers out of their routine manual/clerical jobs.

And this time it will be the women's turn. For women make up a very substantial proportion of those employed in information occupations, and especially of those engaged in more routine information work. Since it is precisely this kind of work which is expected to be hardest hit by the installation of I.T. and telematics systems, the result will be a remarkable above-average increase in the availability of unskilled female labour on the job market. Without any foreseeable prospects of immediate re-employment, this category of the unemployed represents a sizable potential burden on welfare state economies, unless women can be coerced into a return to unpaid socially-reproductive labour as old people's nurses, kindergarten teachers, and child-minders, in privately rented or owned and privately financed familiar institutions! In the same O.E.C.D. report in which Dostal made his gloomy predictions about the alarming prospects of 'technological redundancy', J.S. Smith mentioned an Australian survey revealing that over half the total number of female wage-earners are occupied in only five sectors of the Australian economy — namely office work (30% of all women employed), the retail trade (12% of all women employed), domestic work, education and nursing. (O.E.C.D. 1981b) I need hardly remind the reader that office work and the retail trade are central targets for I.T. automation.

The introduction of the new technology will affect the labour force structurally, then, in that an increasing number of women will be released onto the labour market, while, in general, the total amount of unskilled jobs available will be reduced. Competition for skilled jobs, too, should become tougher as a consequence of geographical factors. Remote domestic (or local) terminal office work may have the advantage of cutting commuting time and costs, but it is hardly likely to make for worker solidarity in any traditional sense.

In that they represent limited and rigidly defined sectors of the labour force, with their memberships based to a worrying extent on anachronistic qualifications, it is, then, scarcely surprising that the unions are very sceptical about the structural consequences of the new technology for the composition of the labour force. But it is by no means certain that individual women, or individual unskilled workers of either sex, exclusively regard the new technology and its consequences as a threat. It may also bring a promise of liberation. Liberation from the bondage of routine manual work, which would enable the individual worker to improve his or her qualifications so as to become a skilled worker at last, on an equal footing with the others — or to devote more of his or her time to voluntary private or political activities. Freedom from toil, as I said at the outset of this chapter, is both a utopia and a threat.

The dream of liberation from the need to work is a very old one. Way back in ancient times, Plato's pupil, Aristotle, Alexander the Great's tutor, toyed with the idea of a life free from toil. In the famous passage from the opening of his *Politics* he wrote:

> "[...] a possession is an instrument for maintaining life. And so, in the arrangement of the family, a slave is a living possession, and property a number of such instruments [...]. For if every instrument could accomplish its own work, obeying or anticipating the will of others [...] if the shuttle would weave and the plectrum touch the lyre without a hand to guide them, chief workmen would not want servants, nor masters slaves". (Bierstedt 1959: 26)

Robots not yet having been invented, however, Aristotle had to leave material production in the hands of servants and slaves, so that the 'natural rulers' could attend to the affairs of government and state. Alexander the Great would seem to have taken his point.

Years later, when new empires were producing slaves for new generations of 'natural rulers', the invention of the flying shuttle — not to mention the steam engine and the spinning Jenny — caused the dream of liberation from the need to work to reappear with renewed potency. Adam Smith, who was one of the new industrial technology's earliest enthusiasts, mentions with approval the spirit of technological invention demonstrated by a youthful fire-fighter:

> "In the first fire engines, a boy was constantly employed to open and shut alternately the communication between the boiler and the cylinder, according as the piston either ascended or descended. One of those boys, *who loved to play with his companions*, observed that, by tying a string from the handle of the valve which opened this communication to another part of the machine, the valve would open and shut without his assistance, *and leave him at liberty to divert himself with his play fellows* (my emphases). One of the greatest improvements that has been made upon this machine, since it was first invented, was in this manner the discovery of a boy who wanted to save his own labor". (Bierstedt 1956: 145f)

Yet, even in those days, Adam Smith was aware that being chained to a machine in a factory was to cut oneself off from any chance of fully realising one's worth as a free human being:

> "The man whose whole life is spent in performing a few simple operations, of which the effects too are, perhaps, always the same, or very nearly the same, has no occasion to exert his understanding, or to exercise his invention in finding out expedients for removing difficulties which never occur. He naturally loses, therefore, the habit of such exertion, and generally becomes as stupid and ignorant as it is possible for a human creature to become. The torpor of his mind renders him, not only incapable of relishing or bearing a part in any rational conversation, but of conceiving any generous, noble, or tender sentiment, and consequently of forming any just judgment concerning many even of the ordinary duties of private life. Of the great and extensive interests of his country, he is altogether incapable of judging [...]." (Smith 1976: 782)

From words like these it is not such a far cry to Marx's son-in-law's plea for *The Right to Be Idle*. Towards the end of the prosperous Victorian era which Adam Smith foresaw, indeed in the early days of the gramophone (of Aristotle's lyre touched by the plectrum without a hand to guide it!), Paul Lafargue was writing — in the work which was to become his own chief claim to fame — that, if society could be released from the pursuit of profit, the number of hours spent on necessary work could be substantially reduced. Unnecessary production could be abolished, and, freed from the extortion of surplus value from their long overworked bodies, workers would at last have the time to 'grow' and realise their own true selves. (Lafargue 1883)

One has, however, to remember that over a hundred years had gone by since Adam Smith's enthusiastic dreams had been interred with his bones. In Smith's day, just as in Aristotle's, *Le Droit à la Paresse* for factory workers and slaves would have dealt a fatal blow to his own *Wealth of Nations*, just as it would have done to Aristotle's freedom to indulge in his *Politics*. The boy who wanted to save his own labour in order to 'divert himself with his play fellows' is a utopian figure. Elsewhere, for instance in his praise of the efficiency of the factory system in contrast to the inefficiency of cottage industry, Adam Smith is the first to criticise 'the habit of sauntering and of indolent careless application' which, in his eyes, rendered the country workman 'almost always slothful and lazy'. (Bierstedt 1959: 144f)

In fact Adam Smith's attitude to workers is generally much more in line with his more reactionary Christian successors. Thomas Carlyle, to whom Dickens dedicated *Hard Times*, formulated the *locus classicus* on the Christian work ethic in *Sartor Resartus* in 1838:

> "For us was thy back so bent, for us thy straight limbs and fingers so deformed; thou wert our conscript on whom the lot fell [...]. Yet toil on, toil on: *thou* art in thy duty, be out of it who may". (Ford 1969: 43)

The veiled threat of immortal punishment for the idle exploiting rich derives its strength from what Nietzsche was to call an (age-old) *Sklavenmoral* — the Genesis myth of paradisaical freedom from toil, with expulsion and the duty of hard labour as the subsequent punishment for Adam and Eve's disobedience against God. This myth, even older than Aristotle's and Plato's philosophizing, was an attempt to dramatize the dreams and the realities of the life of slavery for the Jews in Babylonian captivity. It came in handy for the Victorian mill-owners, especially since there was a widespread fear that 'ordinary workers' might start to get some unfortunate ideas into their heads if they chanced to read any Adam Smith-like reservations about the spiritual healthiness of factory work, for instance — as this early anonymous pamphlet from 1770 illustrates:

> "The factory-working plebs in Britain have got it firmly into their heads that all British citizens, just because they are British, have as their birthright the privilege to be more free and independent than the workers in any other country in Europe. This idea may have some utility for soldiers, whose bravery it may rouse; but as for factory workers, the less they are imbued with notions like these, the better both for themselves and for the state. Workers should never think themselves independent of their superiors. It is extremely dangerous to encourage any such fatuous nonsense in a commercial state like ours, where perhaps seven eighths of the population possess little or no property. The cure will not be complete as long as our indigent industrial workers will not resign themselves to working six days a week for the same amount of money as they now earn in four". (Anonymous 1770; quotation from Lafargue 1970: 107)

Incredible though it may seem, this employer's hope of being able to pressure wages down may not, after all, have been so unrealistic. For misconceived Luddite attacks on machinery, or more rationally argued Lafarguian attempts to shorten the working day have seldom received support comparable to that which is given to the struggle for 'the right to work' — to ward off the 'threat' of being released from work, even at the cost of much tougher working conditions.

In fact, though, it would appear that the sharp contrast between the Judaeo-Christian work ethic and the 'right to idleness' is more apparent than real. They are but two sides of the same coin, as it were. Work has hitherto always been regarded as a necessary evil — *as* necessary as it is (or may on occasion be felt to be) evil. One might dream of being liberated from its bondage, but one returned dutifully to its bondage of one's own free will. In a sense, then, the utopian dreams of freedom from the need to work are reminiscent of the masochist's fantasies — their very attractiveness residing in the fact that the freedom is relative, bounded by the necessity of continually returning to work. The right to 'grow', and realise one's true worth as a free human being, turns out to have been no more than the right to do *less* work — quantitatively negotiable along a sliding-scale; merely another form of wage bargaining.

The real, *qualitative* contrast is between work and total liberation from work. The ruling classes, no doubt from way before Aristotle until well beyond the present day, have always managed to handle this — (and may continue to do so) — better than the working classes, for whom total liberation from work is synonymous with 'unemployment', and thus is morally and psychologically problematic.

Today, however, I.T. and telematics technology do confront a far larger section of the population than ever before with a real contrast, a real challenge. The robots have released — and will increasingly release — Aristotle's slaves from their bondage. Now, at last, they really do have the chance to grow and realise their potential as free human beings. Yet, paradoxically, the liberating aspects of the technology are still regarded as threats. In Denmark, political science professor Bengt-Åke Lundvall supplied us with a typical example of this kind of 'doublethink' in a recent newspaper article: "Characteristic of I.T. is the fact that it paves the way for extensive rationalisation [...]. This includes every kind of routine work, whether in offices, in the retail trade, or in service industries", he writes. But, before very long, we find him referring to this long overdue automation of a number of boring routine jobs as "the technological threat"! (Lundvall 1983)

Why, then, do the former slaves regard their freedom as a threat? In England in 1978 Chris Freeman came up with a possible answer:

> "The psychological as well as the economic consequences of unemployment can be devastating for individuals and for societies, because work, both formal and informal, is the main means by which people in most different cultures relate to each other and to the world, and acquire a sense of dignity and purpose, *even though many jobs are boring and hard*." (Freeman 1981: 311; my emphasis)

There is undoubtedly a large element of truth in this, but it is not the whole truth, and it in fact misses out the most crucial point of all. For work is not just the fashioning of objects designed to satisfy one's own and others' needs, through the play of the worker's imagination, knowledge and skill. Work is also a way to make money, and as such it is closely bound up with power and status. To have a job is to have power — to be unemployed is to be powerless.

Which is why the 'false' contrast of a shorter working day, or a shorter working week, is preferred to the 'true' contrast which telematics has at last actually made possible for many more people by replacing the age-old necessity for human workers: the true contrast between, on the one hand, routine toil, and, on the other, the dream of full self-realisation, the right to be idle as a real, meaningful right. For, as long as work and power are inseparably connected, work, far from being regarded as a realisation of each individual's spiritual and physical potential, will be regarded as a burden: as the sale of the minimum amount of the worker's resources which he can get away with, in order not to lose his wages.

This, too, is why the right to be idle is rejected. Unemployment is synonymous with powerlessness and with the loss of self-respect. Powerlessness, because the unemployed are, at least temporarily, debarred from access to the social power which a wage represents. Powerlessness, too, because the worker is debarred from any fellowship with his workmates, either on the job or in related social situations. And loss of self-respect, because the worker's reduced wage is now no longer received as an — ostensibly fair — due payment for services rendered, but as alms from all the other more powerful people in the community.

The latent future potential of I.T. and telematics technology would seem, then, to consist in the realistic possibility of realising an age-old dream of freedom from hard, and/or routine, labour, without the hitherto unavoidable, and morally unacceptable, premiss of simultaneously condemning large numbers of one's fellow human beings to a life-sentence of hard, and/or routine, labour. But no less tendentially present in the new technology is the prospect, which is actually antagonistic to its introduction, of large numbers of people — unskilled workers in general, and women in particular — losing their former access to paid labour.

But a true future, as we have learnt, is by definition qualitatively different from the present. If we are to anticipate it, we must not make the mistake of merely extrapolating tendencies from the *status quo*. So it would be wrong to suppose that the new technology merely offers us the traditional choices: choices producing either more and more powerless people in our midst, if we introduce the technology, or an unchanged number of frustrated people, if we don't.

No, the new technology does carry the seeds of qualitative change latent within it — it is both a product of a frustrating present *and* a real tool for shaping a liberating future. Existing within the technology, and realisable by means of it, is, amongst others, a utopian possibility of individual freedom to decide for oneself the content and scope of the work one wants to do; a revitalized utopia of self-realisation and personal need-satisfaction, which is premissed on the separation of work and power, of work and wages, in such a way as to transcend the limited possibilities which the existing relationship between work and power and work and wages dictates.

A tentative first step in the direction of releasing the latent potential of the technology would have to involve an attempted qualitative resolution of the problematic connection between work and wages which the technology itself cries out for, as it were — perhaps by the introduction of a fixed social benefit for all the members of a given society, which would cover the basic costs of clothes, food and lodging, so that work itself could become a luxury instead of a necessity. (A suggestion put forward in Meyer, Petersen & Sørensen 1978)

It would hardly be necessary for me to go into further details, here, for the reader to grasp my point, which concerns the necessity of establishing a suitable social foundation on which to base experiments designed to liberate the latent future potential of the technology: experiments working towards the fulfilment of its promises of shorter working hours, of an end to exclusively meaningless routine work, and of the birth of new collaborative neighbourhood fellowships.

Such experiments would be all the more necessary because the technology as we know it today has an all-too-obvious tendential content which is

— and would continue to be — at odds with the sort of utopian content which the experiments would be attempting to realise. In itself the technology bears the impress of past and present social conflicts which, in a number of ways, might make it inappropriate for a genuine, qualitatively alternative future. I'm thinking, for instance, of the fact that office automation technology is not just designed to increase productivity in technically neutral terms, but to increase productivity through the simultaneous imposition of a stricter and more efficient managerial discipline on information workers. Of course the unfortunate connection between work and wages in the present scheme of things justifies this 'suspicious' managerial approach. It is, as we have seen, in the nature of things that the worker will try to sell as little as possible of his labour for the highest possible price. But truly anticipative utopian technology would have to be designed to increase productivity through its flexible ability to allow individual workers to set themselves their own targets and monitor their own performances to their own satisfaction.

For I.T. is not 'neutral'. At the moment, according to the Director of Olivetti, Franco de Benedetti (*not* just some 'radical socialist', as Vincent Mosco and Andrew Herman emphasize), I.T. "[...] is in fact an organizational technology and, like the organization of labor, has a dual function: as a productive force and a control tool for capital". (1980) And in a recently published report, the Swedish National Data Union has aptly drawn attention to three fundamental tendencies in the technical design of I.T.: improved facilities for monitoring worker efficiency (one thinks of the technical ease with which the relative speeds of cash-registering supermarket personnel, or word-processing personnel, can be monitored); improved facilities for checking the quality of the work done (the automatically registered error percentages of work-processing personnel would be a case in point); and improved facilities for maintaining general office discipline (one thinks of the automatic registration of all out-going electronic communication from any office, for instance).

The same report furnishes us with other examples of how the *status quo* tendentially informs the new technology, jeopardizing the possible release of its utopian potential. I.T. may have a negative effect on social relations, the Swedish union claims. Personal contacts, and meetings, both informal and formal, are typical areas where there is much to be gained from potential rationalization. Office automation may threaten these last oases of human freedom, which have hitherto evaded the tyranny of machines.

Video conferencing, for example, (or, more particularly, computer conferencing, which, with digital transmission of data as well as digitalized interactive audio-visual communication will no doubt prove to be much the most efficient means of teleconferencing), will almost certainly have a formalizing effect on the conduct of meetings, cutting out the 'covert agenda' in the interests of efficiency. Whether such meetings will be qualitatively improved, though, would seem to be an open question: the report draws attention to the dangers of 'over-stimulation', where participants' judgements may be impaired by the bombardment of too much relevant information at once, as well as by the pressure of having to distinguish rapidly between relevant and irrelevant information. Computer conferencing would also no doubt be dogged by the 'dual dialogue' problem familiar to managers in banking, travel agencies, and the retail trade generally. This refers to the impaired judgement of staff who are in simultaneous dialogue with customers and machines. The two dialogues have their own often very different rhythms, fulfil different needs, and require different qualifications on the part of the staff. (Persson et al. 1980: 101ff)

I opened the present chapter with the statement that nowhere is the paradoxical nature of the conflicting tendential content of I.T. and telematics so apparent as in the question of their influence on work in the society of the future. In their present shape and form they bear the impress of the societies which produced them. To realise the utopia which is latent within these instruments of managerial discipline, and which necessitates comprehensive social reforms, a lot of progressive and imaginative technological modifications and improvements will have to be initiated.

6. PARTICIPATIVE GRASSROOTS DEMOCRACY AT THE PUSH OF A BUTTON?

"The three basic questions with which we have to confront this new technology in its capacity of (far-from-divine!) social synthesizer, concern the total effect it will have on each individual's working life, political life, and private life, respectively", I wrote in my fourth chapter, in the section entitled 'Against Oversimplification: Towards the Structural Analysis of the Latent Future Potential Inherent in Telematics'. In my previous chapter, I offered an assessment of the social significance of telematics for the individual's *working life*, and now it is time to consider in greater detail some of the problems connected with the social significance of the technology in the individual's *political life* which I mentioned briefly in chapter four. (A useful longer discussion of the questions dealt with in this chapter may be found in Druet, Thill and Kemp 1980)

Is telematics the ally of democracy, or is it its worst enemy? This is *not* a question to be resolved at the push of a button! The question is not capable of technological resolution, if only we find the right mathematical formula, or design a smaller chip. The distinction between grassroots politics and rigged referenda is *not* primarily a technological matter: it is first and foremost a matter of *social* concern, and only because it is a social dilemma is it also a dilemma for, and within, telematics technology.

Again in chapter four, in the section entitled 'Enlightenment Utopian Thinking: the Cradle of Today's Deadlocked Debates', I stressed the relevance of Rousseau's and Kant's seemingly interminable wrangling about nature, reason and society, for an enlightened analysis of the polemical structure of on-going debates about telematics, in relation to their full societal significance. Understanding *how* our situation is dead-locked — both philosophically and technologically — is a necessary precondition for breaking out of it. In the following, I want to return to the primitive laboratory of those Enlightenment philosophers in an attempt to convince the reader of the justice of that earlier claim — and I make no apologies for doing so to the impatiently waiting technocratic rationalists, itching to get on with their business of designing a meaningless tomorrow for us. It would seem that philosophers always have the last laugh, especially when sales-talking technicians — true to their form — dismiss philosophy as 'superfluous acrobatics'!

6.1. *Vertical and Horizontal Communication.*

Ever since Rousseau and Kant published *Le Contrat Social* and *Metaphysische Anfangsgründe der Rechtslehre* respectively, controversy has raged between 'natural' and 'rational' jurisprudence. Developments in I.T. and telematics technology have fuelled the flames of this controversy, awarding higher or lower priority to the one or the other normative conception of legalized societal collaboration in accordance with the respective priorities awarded to *vertical* information and communications channels (satellite broadcasting between central legislative, executive, and judiciary bodies and peripheral citizens, for instance) and *horizontal* communication (video-conferencing between and among broadband-network-linked individual citizens, for instance, and between and among themselves and their presumably more responsive and responsible representatives in local and central government).

A number of experiments have already been carried out with regard to vertical communication. Specifically relating to central *legislative* activity we have seen the so-called QUBE two-way cable T.V. experiment in Columbus, Ohio, for instance, with 'instant democracy', 'electronic polling', or whatever other names it may have been dignified with. (Neustadt 1982: 252ff) Essentially what is involved here is a push-button response from viewers to programmes watched, or to persuasively presented political issues, within the framework of an opinion poll. Within seconds of pushing the buttons on the little black boxes connected to their T.V. sets, viewers can see the results flash onto their screens of instantaneously computed yes/no answers, or degrees of popularity in terms of quantified popular support. Rabble rousers of Jim Jones' ilk, who are not too concerned about whether the results of such polls merely reflect the arbitrary decisions of the bored pre-school offspring of parents rich enough to install the equipment, may welcome the innovation — and indeed Dallas, Omaha, Pittsburgh and several other cities are already installing, or have already installed, similar systems. One remembers, with a wry smile, de Tocqueville's predictions almost a century and a half ago:

> "It is vain to summon a people, which has been rendered so dependent on the central power, to choose from time to time the representatives of that power; this [...] exercise of their free choice, however important it may be,

> will not prevent them from gradually losing the faculties of thinking, feeling, and acting for themselves, and thus gradually falling below the level of humanity." (quoted from Ford 1969: 45)

In describing, in chapter four, the chaos of public attitudes and opinions surrounding the birth and growth of I.T., I mentioned an influential spokesman for the rational, emancipatory effects of the new technology working at the Dayton Research Institute in Ohio, Joseph P. Martino, co-editor of the journal *Technological Forecasting and Social Change*. To the electronic polling facilities supposedly improving the efficiency of central legislative activity, Martino would want to add a limited amount of point-to-point communication via satellite in the interests of improving central executive activities, such as those of the police, fire, ambulance, and other emergency services — while judiciary activities could be streamlined by means of vertical 'remote testimony'. The idea would be that witnesses could testify in District Courts or Circuit Courts of Appeal without leaving their home towns. They would go to their local courthouse, be sworn in, and have their testimony televised via satellite to the state capital, for instance.

While it is true that Martino is typical of those I.T. and telematics enthusiasts whose emphasis is primarily on one- or two-way vertical communication between individual citizens and central or local government and services, believing that the democratic process will be significantly improved by "permitting the public at large easier access to state and federal legislators and regulatory agencies", he is, of course, not unaware of the technology's potential for horizontal communication: "Tomorrow's CATV systems", he writes, "which will make extensive use of optical fibers in place of the wires and coaxial cables currently employed, will be able to offer two-way communication and even multi-way communication both between the subscriber and the 'head end' and among individual subscribers". (This and the following quotations are from Martino 1982: 30-36)

As with point-to-point satellite communication, however, Martino tends to reserve horizontal communication for élites of businessmen or government workers (still firmly anchoring them to central computers, though!). With regard to 'private citizens', on the other hand, very little reference is made to the possibility of planning joint participation in various activities — the emphasis being placed on innocuous activities like computer games and 'postal' chess tournaments, though even here the reader is left in no doubt that Martino himself would prefer to play alone against a superior centralized computer any day rather than against another 'private citizen' of mere flesh and blood!

While Martino would be happy to see an end to government restrictions on the new technology, so that a 'fair' free-for-all fight for market shares would ensure the competitive development of the technology in all its forms, which, in turn, in his opinion, would automatically produce cheaper improvements in the efficiency of every aspect of our corporate lives in his hierarchically structured and functionally disciplined societal model, ex-President Carter's former policy adviser, Richard M. Neustadt, is into the restrictions business. He is currently practising communications law in Washington, and an article he wrote two years ago, on 'Politics and the New Media', reveals that — with an eye to presidential elections in the 1990s — he is more concerned about what he considers to be revolutionary developments in *horizontal* communications.

Today's nationwide news broadcasting, for all its superficiality, provides "a homogenous information base for the most diverse society in the West", writes Neustadt, adding that this homogeneity is now under threat from what he calls 'narrowcasting', the proliferation of cable T.V. networks dedicated to minority interests:

> "Some channels will provide only news about their particular themes, and many — such as the movie and sports networks — will offer no news at all. Narrowcasting may fragment Americans' perception of events, and the vast menu of entertainment channels may draw some people away from the news altogether. An electorate awash in video information may end up less informed. One result is that when the president goes on television in 1990, he may be carried on six networks, but he will not be on two dozen others. For the first time since F.D.R.'s fireside chats, the mass audience that presidents have automatically commanded will begin to erode." (Neustadt 1982: 248-254)

In particular, of course, Neustadt is worried about Martino's business élites taking advantage of the present confusion surrounding the application of the Communications Act to cable and satellite-to-home broadcasting. This act requires regular T.V. and radio broadcasters to sell time to candidates at minimum rates, to treat all candidates equally, and to provide balanced coverage of controversial issues. What worries Neustadt is an initiative taken by the U.S. Chamber of Commerce to launch its own television network.

> "'BizNet' will use a satellite to broadcast six hours per day of business news, interviews, and — of course — lobbying messages, directly to receivers placed at corporate headquarters around the country. The Chamber has spent $5 million on studios and will spend several millions more each year to run the operation. [...] The new technology will touch off a new scramble

> for money to buy teleconferencing studios, satellite transmitters, and fancy computers, and only the well-heeled interest groups will have the money to use all the new machines. Few liberal groups can match BizNet's millions."

Traditionally in America the Republicans have preferred minimal government regulation, while the Democrats have considered it their task to strengthen the central government in an effort to democratize the dictatorial power of industry — only to find that they themselves are accused of dictatorship by the threatened dictators, of course![11] For Neustadt, restrictive legislation on the new technology is a logical step to take, heedless of Martino's angry rhetoric, exemplified in his presentation of government 'interference' in the development of competition (which he claims will be beneficial to the consumer) between the telephone companies:

> "The issue should be settled on the basis of benefit to the public, not solely to serve the interests of the firms involved or of government regulatory agencies that justify their existence by denying benefits to the public, in the name of the good of that public."

When he is not worrying about whether the next Democratic President of the United States will be able to compete for strong government power over 'the most diverse society in the West' as successfully as Kennedy and Roosevelt did by monopolizing the then existent vertical communication technology, Neustadt can, however, wax enthusiastic over some of the prospects related to the technologically promoted increase in horizontal communication. The new technology has a strong chance of increasing truly democratic public participation in local politics, he considers. Direct television coverage of city council meetings without any commentary has not attracted large audiences so far, but in comparison to the numbers who actually show up at city council meetings, they are huge. Viewers get to know who the council members are and what they do, and this promotes more direct dialogue, sometimes apparently to the embarrassment of the councillors: "accustomed to anonymity (they) find themselves treated like T.V. personalities — strangers stop them in the streets to praise or revile their performances."

In that the new television, according to Neustadt, will mean longer messages tailored to smaller audiences, the quality of (local) news broadcasting may be improved for the enjoyment of those who can find time to listen to it; and free 'public access channels', which most cable systems provide, will enable local ethnic, cultural, and political groups and parties to run weekly talk shows for their activists, or organize campaigns.

> "For the price of a fundraising mailing, a group can now reach over a million people with 100 two-minute ads on a cable network. For the price of a newsletter, an organization can produce up to 10 one-hour television shows [...]. Apart from cost savings, this approach takes advantage of the emotional impact of pictures — in an America reared on T.V., video is the way to get people excited."

While vertical communication of this latter kind however — even though it is only a local phenomenon — is open to abuse, as we shall see later with regard to electronic canvassing, Neustadt foresees — as I said earlier — a glowing future for the truly horizontal communication technology of teleconferencing. While city councillors can be accosted in the street after live city council broadcasts, live broadcasts from the U.S. House of Representatives, or the Senate, are more difficult to follow up, especially if you are separated from your Congressman or Senator by the entire breadth of the United States. In 1981, the Republican Party followed the lead of General Motors and its two nearest rivals in successfully experimenting with video conferencing to get over this problem.[12] A mile away from the White House, Vice President Bush held a meeting via satellite with supporters in California.

Experience with computer conferencing in Denmark supports Neustadt's belief that systems of this kind may apparently go some way towards helping us to realise long-cherished dreams of participative democracy. Participants in computer conferences sit in front of microcomputer terminals on which they can record their own opinions in a given discussion and on which they can call up all the previous contributions to the discussion made by themselves and by the other participants since they started, or within the last few hours, or days, of the conference. Any repeated arguments or opinions are automatically registered as such, so that they may be considered in isolation or ignored.

In this way, a geographically disparate group of citizens can carry on a rational discussion over an extended period of time. So far so good: but those who habitually confuse technical aids with magic would go even further in extolling the virtues of computer conferencing. Disturbing emotional reactions are excluded, they claim, since the participants are far away from each other. Differences in social status and personality are 'ironed out', in that all the participants have unlimited time in which to present their opinions and arguments. Any personal inhibitions are overcome, because one can sit quietly at home typing out one's speech, instead of having to take the floor and win a hearing by means of superfluous rhetoric. And one has all the time one wants for having second thoughts about what one has said.

Any analysis of the snobbery, personal animosity, satirical acerbity and abundantly 'superfluous' rhetoric informing the protracted polemical exchanges in 18th C. British literary, philosophical and scientific journals, or in the 19th C. American press, for example, or even (!) in 20th C. academic periodicals, would reveal the wishful thinking behind claims like these. The spirit of Alexander Pope and Mark Twain lives on — and surely we would not, like Plato, want to exclude such colourful personalities and past masters of rhetoric from our computerized republics of the future?

Nevertheless, developments in horizontal communication would seem likely to make a potentially valuable contribution towards the creation of the sort of ideal situation of public teleological discussion in which communicative distortions are eliminated, which the Frankfurt School disciple, Jürgen Habermas, saw as the only hope for the future of a rational scientific-technical society.[13] But these horizontal communication developments have been accompanied by developments in vertical communication which — as we have seen — hardly encourage individual freedom of thought and speech. Besides electronic polling, BizNet-type lobbying, and the non-stop entertainment of an intellectually undemanding quality which I have already referred to, we would have to add the dubious effects which I.T. and telematics are likely to have on election campaigns.

More than ever before, perhaps, the party with the most money will be the party which will win the most votes, by investing the most in machines for efficient voter indoctrination. Computers will be able to 'target' messages and money, so that seductive political promises reach the most susceptible potential voters in the most persuasive way, whether in the form of different cable T.V. ads for different local populations ("we will see [...] candidates advocating bilingual education on Spanish channels, defending Social Security on channels aimed at the elderly, and playing football on sports channels" — the predictions are from Neustadt 1982) or in the form of different pre-recorded messages from the candidates, to be sent out by means of automatic dialling machines calling hundreds of carefully and strategically pre-selected people an hour, and playing back the particular 'targeted' message to them when they answer.

As always, then, in analysing the social significance of this new vertical and horizontal communication technology in relation to the concept of democracy, the questions which spring to mind are: where did the technology come from; or more precisely, are electronic polling, on the one hand, and computer conferencing, on the other, primarily the progeny of technology, or primarily the progeny of social factors? How much scope should in fact be given to technicians and technological researchers in the further development of this technology? And finally, and most importantly, which dreams, old and new, is the technology actually capable of helping us to realise?

6.2. *Today's Democratic Dilemma.*

Rousseau's opening remarks in *Le Contrat Social* about the ubiquitous bondage of free-born men, which I quoted in chapter four, still hold good today, over two centuries later. The dilemma he was referring to between freedom and constraint, between anarchy and rational authoritarianism is still very much alive. For what in effect is the fundamental element of democracy in a capitalist world? Is it the rational ordering of society by means of the power invested in the state, or is it the people's free establishment of consensus? The question has been under discussion as long as societies of this kind have existed, and it is still very much with us.

As in many other nations, the Second World War strengthened the power of the state immeasurably in the U.S.A., and, aided by Presidents F.D. Roosevelt and Truman, the Democratic Party earned a name for itself as the party which 'looks more to the people': some people, not others, as the Republicans were quick to point out! — the urban proletariat, as distinct from the farmers or the big businessmen. The latter, however, had as their representative in the 'fifties an eminent military man, General Dwight D. Eisenhower, a man who was both disinclined and unable to reverse the trend towards increased state-power in a Cold War situation. Yet, true to form, it was the Republican president who first realised the dangers for *all* American citizens of a state stronger than any ever seen before in history, with its power resting on computers and nuclear weapons. Eisenhower's Farewell Address delivered to the nation on January 17th, 1961, is not as well-known outside the United States as it should be:

> "Until the latest of our world conflicts, the United States had no armaments industry, American makers of plowshares could, with time and as required, make swords as well.
>
> But we can no longer risk emergency improvisation of national defense. We have been compelled to create a permanent armaments industry of vast proportions. Added to this, three and a half million men and women are directly engaged in the defense establishment. We annually spend on military security alone more than the net income of all United States corporations.

> Now this conjunction of an immense military establishment and a large arms industry is new in the American experience. The total influence — economic, political, even spiritual — is felt in every city, every state house, every office of the Federal Government. We recognize the imperative need for this development. Yet we must not fail to comprehend its grave implications. Our toil, resources and livelihood are all involved, so is the very structure of our society.
>
> In the councils of Government, we must guard against the acquisition of unwarranted influence, whether sought or unsought, by the military-industrial complex. The potential for the disastrous rise of misplaced power exists and will persist.
>
> We must never let the weight of this combination endanger our liberties or democratic processes. We should take nothing for granted. Only an alert and knowledgeable citizenry can compel the proper meshing of the huge industrial and military machinery of defense with our peaceful methods and goals, so that security and liberty may prosper together.
>
> Akin to, and largely responsible for the sweeping changes in our industrial-military posture has been the technological revolution during recent decades.
>
> In this revolution research has become central. It also becomes more formalized, complex and costly. A steadily increasing share is conducted for, by, or at the direction of the Federal Government.
>
> Today the solitary inventor, tinkering in his shop, has been overshadowed by task forces of scientists, in laboratories and testing fields. In the same fashion, the free university, historically the fountainhead of free ideas and scientific discovery, has experienced a revolution in the conduct of research. Partly because of the huge costs involved, a Government contract becomes virtually a substitute for intellectual curiosity.
>
> For every old blackboard there are now hundreds of new electronic computers.
>
> The prospect of domination of the nation's scholars by Federal employment, project allocations and the power of money is ever present, and is gravely to be regarded.
>
> Yet, in holding scientific research and discovery in respect, as we should, we must also be alert to the equal and opposite danger that public policy could itself become the captive of a scientific-technological elite.
>
> It is the task of statesmanship to mold, to balance, and to integrate these and other forces, new and old, within the principles of our democratic system — ever aiming toward the supreme goals of our free society [...]."
> (Eisenhower's 1961 "Farewell Address" is quoted from Heffner 1965: 313f)

It was not to be expected that Democratic presidents would pay much heed to the words of warning of a Republican, and computers started to enter the Federal Government in a big way from the early 'sixties. By 1970 there were 5,300 computers in government use, but it was not until 1972 that

Senator McGovern led the Democratic Party's successful espousal of the new 'populist' wave of the late 'sixties which has since transformed Democratic politics — a revolt *against* big government and established political organizations, in the interests of 'the little guy who can't really get a handle on the Government.' (quoted from Friebel and Händel 1974: 59)

In effect, it was to take a sober retrospective evaluation of Kennedy's 'knight in shining armour' Cold War rocket jousting, and a massive 'populist' denunciation of the disastrous weapon-testing experiment in Viet Nam which had been carried out under the auspices of both Democratic and Republican administrations, before the Democratic Party seemed able to realise the full truth behind Eisenhower's predictions. All the more surprisingly, when one recalls that Daniel Bell's seminal article, 'The End of Ideology in the West', had already appeared in 1960, the year *before* the Republican president had incited his 'fellow Americans' to do all that they could to resist the sort of anti-populist and anti-totalitarian rational managerial democracy which Bell, in his fear of a resurgence of McCarthyism, on the one hand, and of Stalinism, on the other, was later to advocate so strongly. (Revised version 1962: 393f) For, as my quotation indicated, Eisenhower was at least as afraid of the dictatorship of 'a scientific-technological elite' as he was of an over-strong and unrepresentative government.

In the 'fifties, an idealized "Jeffersonian melange of autarchic free groups" in the United States was still considered to be capable of providing significant protection for private citizens, allowing them to develop their own opinions and plans to shape governmental policy. (Laudon 1977: 19) But in the 'sixties, Daniel Bell, and other influential scholars, were to support the Democratic Party's progressive urge for a more rational government by arguing for "the centrality of theoretical knowledge as the source of innovation and of policy formulation for the society".[14] Out of his ingrained fear of demagogues, whether populist or totalitarian, Bell wanted to replace the active citizens organized into small, plural, Jeffersonian groups, 'the authentic consensus of the governed' which had been the ideal of the 'fifties, with the new heroes of a managerial democracy of functional rationality. (Laudon 1977: 20) The latter were the members of the scientific and educational estate, who, in Galbraith's opinion, alone would have the knowledge, independence, and foresight to make the society of the future both rational and humane. (Galbraith 1967) Bell, Galbraith, and others, embraced thankfully what Eisenhower had found so worrying:

> "The rise of the new elites based on skill derives from the simple fact that knowledge and planning — military planning, economic planning, social planning — have become the basic requisites for all organized action in a modern society. The members of this new technocratic elite, with their new techniques of decision-making (systems analysis, linear programming, and program budgeting), have now become essential to the formulation and analysis of decisions on which political judgments have to be made, if not to the wielding of power. It is in this broad sense that the spread of education, research, and administration has created a new constituency — the technical and professional intelligentsia." (Bell 1973: 363)

In West Germany, too, the growing strength of the state has provoked similar public debates. In the 'sixties and 'seventies, promoting General Systems Theory, the author of *Zweckbegriff und Systemrationalität*, Niklas Luhmann, proclaimed not only the end of ideology, but the end of meaning and of individual reasoning, too. He regarded with scorn the old-fashioned expectations about there being some final cause structuring human beings' societal interaction — some 'meaning' behind it all which had earlier been supposedly identifiable as some sort of cosmic order, or which had been created through social contracts.

Truth, morality and love have become the concerns of societal subsystems — of science, of juridical expertise, of family life as an isolated entity. The generation of meaning is no longer a matter of common concern. All that is left for the society to do as a whole — to the extent that it still exists as a whole, as 'a system of systems' — is to delimit its own boundaries as a composite social system, and the boundaries of its sub-systems: in fact, according to Luhmann, what constitutes any society as a society is its inappellable political system's expulsion of whatever is indeterminate and indeterminable. (Luhmann 1971: 15)

To say that Luhmann proclaims the end of individual reasoning is, of course, a question of definitions. What has actually happened is that, instead of attributing to all individual human beings the same reasoning faculty with which he himself was endowed, as Kant did, Luhmann has reduced the individual human being to "a complex error-controlled regulator, restoring its continually disturbed equilibrium through compensatory actions executed by many superimposed feedback cycles, obeying criteria of efficiency", if I may borrow Léo Apostel's earlier somewhat mocking presentation of the General Systems Theorists' case. (Apostel 1963: 7)

This may have taken us beyond Kant's voluntaristic fallacy, but by attributing rationality to the social system as a composite whole, instead of to living human beings, Luhmann has taken reason out of the hands of Kant's constitution-signing individuals and made it into a centralized abstract principle, synonymous with the value-allocative authority and efficiency of the abstracted political system, far removed from phenomenological human interaction.

The authoritarian bias of this kind of determinist model was already clearly apparent in a 1965 *Behavioral Science* article by James G. Miller, who, with the political scientist David Easton, was one of the leaders of the American school of General Systems Theorists — inspired, like Luhmann, by the work of the Austrian biologist, von Bertalanffy, whose *Problems of Life* was first published in German in 1949. According to Miller, all living systems "tend to maintain steady states (or homeostasts) of many variables keeping an orderly balance among sub-systems", and they contain "a decider, the essential critical sub-system which controls the entire system, causing its sub-systems and components to interact, without which there is no system". (Miller 1965: 193ff)

For Easton, 'the decider', in the body politic, consists of 'authorities' — legislature, president and bureaucracy, in the U.S.A. — and 'doorkeepers' — interest groups and parties — who control and process demands from the ordinary man. Insofar as the ordinary man makes demands on the authorities he is, admittedly, a part of the critical sub-system controlling the entire system — politics is not only something done by some people all the time; it is also done by a lot of people some of the time. But the role of the ordinary man within the abstracted and authoritarian political system is minimal.[15]

Back in Germany, though, as a by-product of the celebrated *Methodenstreit* between Critical Rationalists and Critical Theorists, which originated in the confrontation between Sir Karl Popper and Theodor Adorno at a conference in 1961, the Frankfurt School disciple Jürgen Habermas took up the cudgels against Luhmann's determinism. (See Habermas 1971: 141-290; on the 'Methodenstreit' see Adorno et al. 1969) He argued that no system of basic concepts comparable to that established for the investigation of moving bodies and observable events was in principle possible in the study of society. This is because societies are differently constituted as objects of possible knowledge. They form a network of intentional actions; and statements about intentional action are not reducible to statements about observable events. The investigator must gain access to his data through an understanding of meanings.

Habermas understood General Systems Theory itself as a reflection of historically specific meanings and intentions, as an attempted legitimation of the extended power of control on the part of manipulative human beings in industrially advanced societies, which, according to the laws of self-reproduction, had to ensure their survival "on the escalating scale of a continually expanded technical control over nature and a continually refined administration of human beings and their relations to each other by means of social organization". (Habermas 1963; quoted in translation from Connerton 1976: 332-346)

Habermas warned:

> "A peculiar danger arises when the process of scientification transgresses the limit of technical questions, without, however, departing from the level of a rationality confined to the technological horizon. For then no attempt at all is made to attain a rational consensus on the part of citizens concerning the practical control of their destiny [...]. When theory was still related to praxis in a genuine sense, it conceived of society as a system of action by human beings, who communicate through speech and thus must realize social intercourse within the context of conscious communication. Through this communication they must form themselves into a collective subject of the whole, that is capable of action [...]. The negative Utopia of technical control over history would be fulfilled if one were to set up a learning automaton as a central system of societal control [...]. But such a rational administration of the world is not simply identical with the solution of the practical problems posed by history. There is no reason for assuming that a continuum of rationality exists extending from the capacity of technical control over objectified processes to the practical mastery of historical processes. The root of the irrationality of history is that we 'made' it, without, however, having been able until now to make it consciously. A rationalization of history cannot therefore be furthered by an extended power of control on the part of manipulative human beings, but only by a higher stage of reflection, a consciousness of acting human beings moving forward in the direction of emancipation."

Thomas Jefferson or Daniel Bell — Jürgen Habermas or Niklas Luhmann? What, in effect, is the fundamental element of democracy in a capitalist world? Is it the rational ordering of society by means of the power invested in the state, or is it the people's free establishment of consensus? At the outset of this present section I claimed that this question, which is still very much with us[16], is a question which has been under discussion as long as societies of this kind have existed. Having endeavoured to make good the first part of my claim with reference to the post-war controversies in the United States and West Germany, it is now my business to substantiate the second, in the belief that the insights thus acquired are indispensable for the practical realisation of a qualitatively new future.

6.3. *Back to the Old Laboratory: Today's Democratic Dilemma in Yesterday's Enlightenment Philosophy.*

For illustrative purposes here, I want to focus primarily on the controversy within Enlightenment jurisprudence regarding social contracts based on particularised Nature as their point of departure, on the one hand, and social contracts based on a Nature-subsuming normative concept of Reason, on the other — positions represented by Jean-Jacques Rousseau and Immanuel Kant respectively.

The 'natural law' position was that bestial and stupid, but uncorrupted, humanity freely and spontaneously communally created and entered into a social contract, in order to ensure their own individual preservation. The terms of the contract were, however, problematic in Rousseau's opinion: "The force and liberty of each individual being the principal instruments of his own preservation, how is he to engage them in the common interest, without hurting his own, and neglecting the obligations he lies under to himself?" (This and the following quotations are from Rousseau 1977, quoted here in the translation by Beckett and Hondt 1767). According to Rousseau, the social contract had to represent a solution to this problem of finding "that form of association which shall protect and defend, with the whole force of the community, the person and property of each individual, and in which each person, by uniting himself to the rest, shall nevertheless be obedient only to himself, and remain as fully at liberty as before".

Rousseau's social contract was thus both created by, entered into, and guarded by what he called 'the general will', which was to guarantee individual liberty in the community thus created:

> "The passing from the state of nature to the civil society produces a remarkable change in man; it puts justice as a rule of conduct in the place of instinct, and gives his actions the moral quality they previously lacked. It is only then, when the voice of duty has taken the place of physical impulse, and right that of desire, that man, who has hitherto thought only of himself, finds himself compelled to act on other principles, and to consult his reason rather than study his inclinations. And although in civil society man surrenders some of the advantages that belong to the state of nature, he gains in return far greater ones; his faculties are so exercised and developed, his mind is so enlarged, his sentiments so ennobled, and his whole spirit so elevated that, *if the abuse of his new condition did not in many cases lower him to something worse than what he had left* (my emphasis), he should constantly bless the happy hour that lifted him for ever from the state of

> nature and from a narrow, stupid animal made a creature of intelligence and a man." (Rousseau 1977; quoted here in the translation from 1968: 64f)

The abuse of Man's 'new condition' which Rousseau himself was highly sensitive about, and which, in his opinion, depraved Man to a condition worse than his original state of nature, was the despotism of an unrepresentative state. The point emerges strongly from Rousseau's radical censure of any delegation of individual legislative responsibility, which party politics, lobbying, or the increased power of the state as institutionalized executive might provoke. "If the general will is to be clearly expressed", writes Rousseau, "it is imperative that there should be no sectional associations in the state, and that every citizen should make up his own mind for himself" (translation from 1968: 73). And, earlier, he argues that "Sovereignty, being nothing other than the exercise of the general will [...] cannot be represented by anyone but itself — power may be delegated, but the will cannot be". (translation from 1968: 69)

Kant provides an interesting contrast to Rousseau, in that his starting-point is different. In his *Critique of Practical Reason*, published the year before the French Revolution and a quarter of a century after the publication of *The Social Contract*, Kant refuses to compromise his ethical system, including his categorical imperative by grounding it on any basis of empirical determinism.

"All empirical motives [...] can be subsumed under the principle of *self-love* or *happiness*", he writes, but "It is the direct opposite of morality, if the principle of self-love is allowed to determine the Will. The moral law acquaints us with the idea of a nature in which pure Reason could produce the 'Highest Good'. The fact that this idea really forms the pattern of our decisions can be confirmed by ordinary self-observation. Our Reason tells us that we must subordinate our private inclinations to a general law. *This idea must reside in a non-sensuous nature where freedom reigns*" (Kant 1975; quoted in the translation by Rabel 1963: 190-194; my emphasis)

Kant, then, insists on the *a priori* existence of a God-given faculty of practical Reason within us all, a faculty which enables us *in practice* to act dutifully according to maxims which promote the goodness of ourselves and our actions, and make us detest evil actions and evil people. This insistence enables him to wave aside the objections to Rousseau's empirically-grounded theory, which, amongst other things, involved scepticism about the ability of stupid and bestial individuals to create civil societies all of a sudden!

> "The contract, which is called *contractus originarius*, or *pactum sociale* [...] need not be assumed to be a fact, indeed it is not even possible as such. To suppose that would be like insisting that before anyone would be bound to respect such a civic constitution, it be proved first of all from history that a people, whose rights and obligations we have entered into as their descendants, had *once upon a time* executed such an act and had left a reliable document or instrument, either orally or in writing, concerning this contract. Instead, this contract is a *mere idea* of reason which has undoubted practical reality; namely to oblige every legislator to give us laws in such a manner that the laws *could* have originated from the united will of the entire people and to regard every subject [...] as though he had consented to such an expression of the general will. This is the testing stone of the rightness of every publicly-known law, for if a law were such that it was impossible for an entire people to give consent to it (as for example a law that a certain class of subjects, by inheritance, should have the privilege of the *status of lords*), then such a law is unjust. On the other hand, if there is a mere *possibility* that a people might consent to a (certain) law, then it is a duty to consider that the law is just, even though at the moment the people might be in such a position or have a point of view that would result in their refusing to give their consent to it if asked." (quoted from Murphy 1970: 111)

The last sentence reveals the extent to which Kant's conception of the state legislature differs from Rousseau's, as the result of their fundamentally different starting-points. Kant's citizens not only delegate their individual responsibilities to distant legislators, but actually allow them to think for them, and pass long-term legislation for them 'behind their backs', as it were, if there is any danger that the people might let short-term considerations overrule their duty! In Kant's version of civil society it would seem that the legislators are only representative in a technical sense — the reality is qualitatively different![17]

Some thirty years after the French Revolution, Hegel, in his *Grundlinien der Philosophie des Rechts*, excluded the possibility of the hypothetical discrepancy which Kant referred to in the quotation above, between the legislators' and the people's conceptions of duty, and chided Rousseau for his suspicions about representative government. In that the representative state was the incarnation of Reason, Hegel wrote, it could never stand in the way of, nor contradict, the realisation of the empirical will of the people. Far from going against it, the state is itself the general will in reality. Rousseau's worries about the possibly unrepresentative nature of a representative state were due to the fact that, according to Hegel, he confused the civil society itself — with its association based on the sum total of mutually supportive, as distinct from mutually exclusive, private interests — with the state. For, according to Hegel, the latter is not only generally representative, but also something *more* than the mere sum of its parts in that it is the incarnation of the Reason of the total community, and as such transcends the interests of private individuals. (Hegel 1972: § 258)

So, within the space of some seventy years — almost equally bisected by such watersheds as the ratification of the Constitution of the United States, and the French Revolution — the positions had been drawn up for the constitutional debate which is still very much with us. On the one hand, we have the empirically based 'natural law' emphasis on individual human needs, and their carefully balanced free interaction — regarding with suspicion the 'rational' investiture of power in the 'representative' centralized state. And, at the other end of the scale, we encounter a system of law grounded on reason, and sympathetic towards a powerful centralized state understood to be the necessary institutionalization of reason. Any suspicions entertained by holders of *this* sort of attitude concern the civil society outside, or beneath, the central government, in which unrestrained empirical selfishness, or anarchy, may still survive.

The reader will remember, however, how I hinted, already at the end of the third section of my fourth chapter, that these — at first sight glaring — differences between the Rousseauesque and the Kantian positions are really only skin-deep. They are relative rather than absolute. For, in effect, both of these thinkers were confronted with the same problem — the conflict between individual freedom and rational subordination — and both of them dearly wanted to resolve it. In fact they shared an antinomical dilemma which seemed to point to diametrically opposite resolutions, but which in reality could only be resolved in terms of itself. We are here brought face to face with an example of one of the central tenets of the utopian philosophy of Ernst Bloch which I summarised in the third section of my second chapter: our societies abound with unresolved conflicts, and the conflict between individual freedom and rational subordination is one of the most fundamental of them. This is the essential realisation which frees the future from the tyranny of the historicists, be they optimistic or pessimistic, idealistic or materialistic.

It was the anthropologically-inclined Friedrich Engels who was one of the first of Rousseau's commentators to avoid the fallacy of attributing a 'noble savage' idealized primitivism to Rousseau. In Engels' polemical articles against Berlin professor Eugen Dühring, which he wrote in 1877-8, we can see how Marx's colleague was able to do full justice to the progression in Rousseau's thought which started in the first part of his *Discours sur ... l'Origine de l'Inégalité parmi les Hommes* (1755) with Rousseau's description of the bestial — but relatively equal and subsequently perfectible — human animal, wandering through the prehistoric forests: — speechless, unsociable, unemotional, unintelligent, undeveloping, uselessly multiplying — an eternal child in an already ancient species, unable even to recognize his own children as individuals.

Out of this hopeless state of nature, for reasons of common utility, primitive Man began to create societies, and these societies represented an immeasurable improvement in Man's spiritual condition, according to Rousseau. But the relatively harmonious tribal life gradually gave way to the miseries of slavery and despotism which Rousseau saw all around him in his own day, when the primitive tribesmen started to make tools and cultivate the soil. With cultivation came the division of the land into private property, the trees were felled and fields replaced the forests — fields which were watered with human sweat, and in which one could soon see slavery and misery taking root and ripening side by side with the crops. (Rousseau 1971: 118)

It remained for Rousseau to remedy this progression towards greater and greater inequality, by recommending the adoption of a social contract which would restore the relative equality of the tribal associations and have a similarly civilising effect on the original human animal, but which would avoid the pitfalls of the pseudo-contracts which made fools out of his own contemporaries. This was his starting point for *The Social Contract*.

The simultaneous publication of *Emile* suggests that Rousseau was taxed by the problem of how to replace the existing pseudo-contracts by his own utopian creation. His new citizens would have to be 'brainwashed in a social vacuum', as it were, to inoculate them against the vices of existing society — but they would also have to be programmed to enter into the new social contract with a whole-heartedness which — through its absolute renunciation of bestial or anarchic freedom — would ensure their own ability to enjoy to the full their own uncorruptedly moral lives.

In the meantime, in the absence of a justly observed social contract, Emile is told to live *as though* it did exist, in the hope that his example will prove beneficial and thus, presumably, facilitate an eventual 'transition':

> "You must live in the midst of your fellow-creatures, cultivating their friendship in pleasant intercourse; you must be their benefactor, their pattern; your example will do more than all our books, and the good they see you do will touch them more deeply than all our empty words." (Rousseau 1911: 438)

The above progression, which Engels, the author of *The Origin of the Family, Private Property and the State*, was one of the first to correctly perceive, makes quite clear the extent to which Rousseau was an admirer of rational civilised values rather than of some idealized primitive type of humanity. The desperately lovesick Emile is chided, for instance, in words which might have been Kant's:

> "What is meant by a virtuous man? He who can conquer his affections; for then he follows his reason, his conscience; he does his duty; he is his own master and nothing can turn him from the right way [...]. Now is the time for real freedom; learn to be your own master; control your heart, my Emile, and you will be virtuous." (Rousseau 1911: 408)

At a deeper level, it is as though Rousseau actually anticipates Kant's desire to free the human will from empirical determinism in order to render possible a moral judgement of human actions and personalities:

> "Oh, Emile, where is the man who owes nothing to the land in which he lives? Whatever that land may be, he owes to it the most precious thing possessed by man, the morality of his actions and the love of virtue. Born in the depths of a forest he would have lived in greater happiness and freedom; but being able to follow his inclinations without a struggle there would have been no merit in his goodness, he would hot have been virtuous, as he may be now in spite of his passions. The mere sight of order teaches him to know and love it. The public good, which to others is a mere pretext, is a real motive for him. He learns to fight against himself and to prevail, to sacrifice his own interests to the common weal. It is not true that he gains nothing from the laws; they give him courage to be just, even in the midst of the wicked. It is not true that they have failed to make him free; they have taught him to rule himself." (Rousseau 1911: 437)

Far from being inconsistent, then, Rousseau's works provide a true reflection of the kind of societies which were coming into being all around him. His political philosophy went beyond that of his predecessors, Hobbes and Locke, which was primarily concerned with the role of the state in the regulation of conflicts between private citizens or in the safeguarding of private property. For Rousseau was not concerned more or less abstractly and mathematically with problems of practical government, but rather with an unresolved empirical dilemma of much more fundamental consequence: *why*, in contrast to the relative equality and freedom which seemed to be their natural birthright, were his contemporaries oppressing each other and being oppressed by each other everywhere? (The point is well made in Tuschling 1978: 277ff)

In formulating the question in this way, Rousseau had *a priori* to reject any easy answers involving slickly manipulating statecraft. Getting the state — or some other authority — to solve the problem would be a contradiction in terms. In fact the mere recognition of the state as having autonomous power would be equivalent to recognizing it as an institutionalized symptom of the dilemma which Rousseau found much harder to resolve than Hegel did! The state was supposed to render it impossible for private citizens to enslave other private citizens, yet the state was not to exercise any authority of its own; the state was supposed to be the product of a free association of interested individuals, an expression of the social contract, in other words — and yet it also had to 'force' private individuals to be free, i.e. to observe the general will.

Rousseau's bid to resolve the fundamental dilemma between individual freedom and rational subordination is in fact the same as Kant's, and, in the last resort, it involves the rational compromising of individual freedom. Both Rousseau and Kant resort to a figure in which the conflict between one's freedom to do what one likes, and one's compulsion to obey the laws of one's (un)representative state, is transformed into a conflict between one's freedom to be morally virtuous and to obey (un)just laws, and one's compulsion to obey the laws of one's bestial nature, one's irrational passions. Instead of being the slave of other (powerful) men, one is in fact, according to Rousseau and Kant, the slave of a mindless empirical determinism whose spell can only be broken by the intervention of a supernatural being: Reason is the voice of God within us all, giving us the chance to be good, and hence to be 'free'. So we find Rousseau defending his *Le Contrat Social* in his *Lettres écrites de la Montagne* with these words:

> "Read it, Monsieur, this book which has been decried so much but which is so necessary; everywhere you will see the rule of law elevated above men; everywhere you will see the demand for liberty, but always under the authority of law without which no liberty could exist, and under which one is always free, however one may be governed. In saying which I am not, let us say, paying court to the powers that be: so much the worse for them; for I am representing their real interests, if only they were able to see them and pursue them. But passions blind men to their own good. Those who subordinate laws to human passions are the real destroyers of any government: those are the people who ought to be punished." (Rousseau 1823: VI, 345f)

Freedom, this key concept in Rousseau's thought, is not, then, an absolute (though threatened) quantity, which a state can protect or enforce, if necessary, with all the means at its disposal. It is, on the contrary, a term which defines the relationship between different people and between different people and the state. And the means of creating a society which is in accordance with human needs is only *apparently* the 'free human being' expressing fidelity to his own individual needs. Actually, what Rousseau focuses on is not so much the individual's realisation of his own particular human nature within the social contract, but rather on each individual's exertion of his own free will in order *communally to define the limits of his freedom*. The reader will remember the words from *Emile* which I quoted earlier in chapter four:

> "Individuals having only submitted themselves to the sovereign, and the sovereign power being only the general will, we shall see that every man in obeying the sovereign only obeys himself, and how much freer are we under the social pact than in the state of nature." (Rousseau 1911: 425)

Kant's categorical imperative focuses the same strategy. 'Act only on that maxim whereby thou canst at the same time will that it should become a universal law' is an exhortation which — as Ernst Bloch so aptly put it — reflects the 'built-in deposit' contained within the conception of the social contract — "this *quid pro quo*, which supplements the civic idealism and the imperative mood with the very 'practical reason' of the worldly tradesman". (Bloch 1977 [1949-59]: 1019f) The categorical imperative states — (categorically!) — that any specific interest which cannot be subsumed under a general law of Nature can be completely eliminated from individual behaviour.

It was Karl Marx who was the first to put his finger on the reason for the existence of this unresolved dilemma in capitalist society. In his 1843 article 'On the Jewish Question', published in the *Deutsch-Französische Jahrbücher*, he suggested that one should start by considering the 'double life' of the individual in bourgeois society, his 'heavenly' and his 'earthly' life, his life in his political community in which he asserts himself publicly as a member of that community, and his life in bourgeois society in which he functions as an anonymous private person, regarding other people as a means for the achievement of his own ends, and in which he himself is degraded to the role of a mere instrument at the mercy of hostile forces. In 1843, Marx felt that questions of education and religion — including the 'Jewish question' — as well as the question of private property, could be reduced to the fundamental conflict between the economic basis of bourgeois society and its political organisation, to the conflict between private interests and general interests, between the bourgeois economy and the state.

Not to recognize this fundamental conflict at the heart of capitalist society, which is the source of the 'double life' of each individual member of such a society, is to run the risk of falling into the trap of stressing one aspect of the conflict, only, at the expense of the other — instead of appreciating the dilemma as a single system of mutually dependent conflicting aspects, as a logically coherent and composite problem complex, in other words. It is tempting, as we have seen, for both critics and supporters of the capitalist social system *either* to criticise Man's true self in his *abstract* character of 'citoyen', of public political figure rationally protecting his private interests through morally acceptable consensus politics with reference to the role of the state, for instance, *or* to criticise Man's real nature in the shape of the morally dubious, *concretely* egoistic individual, grubbing for what he can get in the market-place. Criticism of the former role may lead to the idealisation of Man as a 'natural' individual, weakened and spoilt by his entry into society, unable to rediscover his true self unless he is freed from state despotism. And criticism of the latter role may lead to exaggerated enthusiasm for an essentially repressive state, legitimized by an idealisation of Man as a moral, rationally self-subordinating individual. The criticism falls into the trap, in other words, of reducing Man to an egoistic and anti-social role player on the economic scene, on the one hand, or to a moralizing and socially demanding hypocrite on the political scene, on the other.

The lesson to be drawn from the above analysis of the democratic dilemma in Enlightenment constitutional thinking is, then, precisely how important it is to appreciate the mutually determining duality which characterizes the society which the Enlightenment thinkers were attempting to define, and which they themselves were unable to transcend. In fact it was not until almost a century after the publication of Rousseau's *Discours sur ... l'Origine de l'Inégalité parmi les Hommes* that we find Marx writing that "the constitution of the political state and the decomposition of bourgeois society into independent individuals, whose relations to each other are legalized, while feudal and guild relations were a matter of privilege — are effected under one and the same act."[18] The 'act' — (deed or covenant) — to which Marx referred here, he was later to define as the death-warrant of feudalism and the birth certificate of capitalism — as the symbolic creation, in other words, of the economic organisation of the societies whose duality so taxed the earlier philosophers. For, in relation to this new economic organization Marx was to stress in particular the increasing prevalence of the phenomenon of individual commodity ownership. It was this phenomenon which he recognized as determining the schizophrenic role-playing of the anti-social and selfish individual, on the one hand, and the moral person observing the same rules as his counterparts, on the other. For institutionalized privately-owned commodity exchange, on the scale emerging in post-feudal times, presupposed reliable contractually regulated relationships.

So here we have the root cause of the democratic dilemma, of the 'natural' and 'rational' conceptions of constitutional jurisprudence which have evolved as conflicting but also as mutually determining ideals. And there is, as the reader will by now have realised, no easy one-dimensional solution to the dilemma available within the terms of the dilemma itself, nor any prospect of a facile or unproblematically durable compromise. Similarly, however, the reader will by now appreciate how understandable it is that efforts are continually being made to square the circle. As we have seen, the dilemma is a vitally productive source of utopian thinking in capitalist societies, and of late, as I endeavoured to illustrate in the first section of this chapter, this sort of activity has been characterized by an increasingly strong technological concern.

But, as I argued in the first section of my third chapter on the tendential content of telematics, those utopian thinkers who pin all their hopes on the new technology may all too easily fall prey to a form of technological determinism. Imagining that they are transcending the boundaries of capitalist society — in making what they themselves believe to be a new contribution to what is in effect an old debate — they may discover to their dismay that their efforts are merely circumscribed one-dimensional attempts to break out of the society's dialectical evolution, which, on the contrary, emerges strengthened from the fray. The society is legitimated by and through their radical opposition, which, in a characteristic and fascinating way, provides the ongoing social system with new life at the very moment when the opposition seeks most determinedly to transcend it. No, the lesson we can draw from our return to the laboratory of the Enlightenment thinkers is that there are no easy answers to the dilemma which still imprisons us today, as it formerly imprisoned them.

6.4. *Deadlock and Beyond.*

I concluded the first section of this chapter on the potential of I.T. and telematics technology for the future realisation of fully participative and rationally communicative democracy, by saying that the detailed presentation of the technology itself, irrespective of whether it primarily serves the purpose of horizontal, or of vertical, communication, requires answers to three questions, if its true significance is to be realised.

The first question concerned the origins of these 'instant democracy machines', and the claim I advanced in my second section was that their origins are only to an insignificant extent technological: essentially their development has been motivated by considerations of their immanent social significance. Whether we are talking about electronic polling or teleconferencing, they are both first and foremost societally determined tools. To use a genetic analogy, one might say that their social significance is dominant and their technological significance is recessive.

This being the case, the machines by themselves will naturally never be able to make any of our dreams of solving today's democratic dilemmas come true. As I argued in my third section above, these dilemmas arise because of the fundamental structures of our societies, the ways in which we have chosen to organise the production and exchange of our daily necessities. Since neither teleconferencing nor electronic polling — (nor any of the other 'instant democracy machines' reviewed in my first section) — are capable of fundamentally challenging these societal conditions, they will naturally be unable to resolve the dilemmas caused by them.

Finally, with regard to the amount of scope which should be given to I.T. and telematics technicians and technological researchers in the further development of this technology, I feel bound to say that I consider it exceedingly ill-advised to let such people continue to run the whole show, as it were. If my genetic analogy above is correct, then the existing division of labour in this field is totally lopsided. This being the case, it is a reflection of the fact that for far too long we have let ourselves be blinded by the sort of problems which technology *qua* technology offers us.

Perhaps electronic polling provides the clearest example of the point I am trying to make here. It represents an extreme case of the attitudes to democracy which take reason and rational efficiency as their constitutional norms. Yet it *professes* (apparently in good faith?) to have something to do with democratic participation. In fact what we encounter here is what one might call a classic example of the *deceptive* and *degrading* nature of technology.

Computer conferencing, on the other hand, poses more delicate problems. Here we are faced with some technology which may indeed prove to be a valuable supplement to letter-writing, or telephone conversations, as an aid to negotiations in specific contexts. But that is precisely why it stands to reason that the competence of sociologists, political scientists and philosophers should be involved in the further development of this technology.

So where do we stand today? Is the combined contribution of the improved vertical and horizontal communications technology merely to be subsumed under an ancient theme — the traditional democratic dilemma in capitalist societies between the free entrepreneur, consumer and wage-earner, on the one hand, and an institutionalised state legislature, executive and judiciary, on the other; between individual freedom and individual subordination to the rule of reason?

The question can be answered both negatively and affirmatively. Affirmatively, because, as we have seen, the traditional dilemma is still very much with us. The battle still rages between defensive and defiant individual citizens and their increasingly restrictive states. Constant attempts are made by individual citizens to defend and increase the scope of their own private freedom by defying and transgressing its legal boundaries — through tax evasion, unethical sales methods, breaches of contract, infringements of laws against pollution or of laws against unhealthy or dangerous working-conditions, robbery, embezzlement, expropriation, violent demonstrations, and other kinds of civil disobedience. While, at the same time, constant encroachments are made upon their individual freedom by a dubiously representative state, in its attempts to impose its will despotically on its citizens and reduce them — under the auspices of a well-policed democracy — to obedient worshippers of abstract Molochs.

But, while I.T. and telematics technology can easily find lucrative roles to play without overstepping the limits of the traditional democratic dilemma, their introduction has arguably led to a sharpening of the contours of the debate, with the result that it is now conducted with greater acrimony and urgency than ever before. For this reason it might be wrong merely to subsume the new technology under the terms of the old dilemma.

We could start, for example, by considering the fact that the rationalised 'democratic' despotism of the state is now in possession of tools and aids which it has previously lacked. In the first place, up until now, it has constantly run up against the barriers of bureaucracy. Its own desire for omnipotence has resulted in impotence. It has turned out to be a colossus with feet of clay because of the unfathomable complexity of its own all-too-comprehensive administration. But now at last is would seem that the combination of electronic data processing and communication can remove this previously insurmountable barrier.

Earlier, too, the rationally-founded executive machinery of the state ran up against the barrier of the inadequacy of its means of admonishing — and monitoring the behaviour of — individual citizens. Its ability to restrict individual lawlessness in the remoter recesses of society was consequently limited. It was unable to ensure the execution of its own legislative injunctions. But today it would seem that, at long last, the requisite monitoring and admonishing capabilities are technically feasible.

A third seemingly insurmountable barrier for the rationally constituted state was the centre-to-periphery legitimation problem. Increased centralized power over rapidly expanding populations came into conflict with demands for increased local and regional autonomy, and increased political participation, from more and more private citizens. But today the new technology would seem to render possible the combination of increased power at the centre with decentralisation. The experience of the multinationals has taught us that it is already possible to delegate considerable measures of responsibility to individual branches, while, at the same time, retaining effective overall control in managerial hands at a small number of administrative headquarters. Comparable delegation of responsibility would certainly be practicable under the auspices of the state, and would be desirable not least because the resultant 'decentralisation' would in reality have a supportive feedback function, consolidating the supremacy of the central government.

The rationally-founded state's *de facto* encroachments upon individual freedom would thus seem to have been immeasurably increased through the possibilities inherent in the new technology. On the other hand, though, the mere mention of the multinationals, in my last paragraph, will be sufficient to remind the reader of the way in which the new technology has already enabled industrial magnates, and others, to increase the scope of their individual freedom at the expense of any particular state. And the extent to which they will be able to continue to do, will depend very much on the extent to which all the *other* private individuals will be able to use the new technology to increase *their* individual power and autonomy, so that the state becomes more truly every man's representative against every man, ensuring the maximum scope of individual liberty and the minimum degree of state interference commensurate with the full protection of each citizen against his fellow-citizens, in their collaboration towards the joint creation of an increasingly more satisfactory mode of existence for themselves and their offspring.

In his day, for practical purposes, Rousseau considered it necessary to restrict the size of his utopia — built on an ideal of fully participative democracy — to a society the size of Corsica. (Rousseau 1977: Book II, Ch. 10) Nowadays, the combination of electronic data processing and communication provides every single citizen in a much larger society with access to information which, earlier, was restricted to a minority. Not only can every individual be provided with access to a great deal of information, but the present need for specialist qualifications, and complicated on-line searching procedures, can, given the necessary research allocations, become a thing of the past.

Earlier, the hoped-for capacity of each individual actively to participate — on an equal footing — in local and national government, came up against a barrier of relative ignorance about the society at large. Only those who were freed from the burden of other occupations and could devote their energies exclusively to tackling complicated political problems could legislate for, and govern, their fellow-citizens. Today, however, the transcendence of Nature's tyranny, through the automation of the production of our daily necessities, could conserve the spiritual, and physical, energy of each and every one of us for joint participation in decentralized governing bodies. And the technology already exists, as we have seen, to enable all of these governing bodies alike to have access to the same comprehensive information, and to reach a sufficiently similar understanding of its significance to admit of a consensus on socially desirable action, through closely coordinated discussions and joint policy-making.

The increased leisure time which increasingly comprehensive automation can provide us with, would, in fact, confront us with this highly significant choice. Are we to fritter away the extra hours, when we are not at work, in idle pastimes, or is our redefinition of the concept of work to take into account the fact that our new, and, most demanding, task could be the joint political planning, and practical government, of a more truly democratic future society?

Communication, hitherto a barrier in the way of truly representative government, need no longer be a barrier, as we have seen. Not that each and every individual would be able to reach a consensus with each and every other individual in the society, of course, but a system of local, regional, and national area networks, with point-to-point communication, would further the feasibility of broader-based discussions throughout the length and breadth of the society in question.

So the introduction of the new technology has increased, and will increase, the capabilities of private citizens, on the one hand, and the state, on the other, to fight for their potentially conflicting interests. The ancient dilemma between boundless and rationally restricted individual freedom, between individual political participation and dubiously representative government, flourishes anew under the influence of I.T. and telematics, with greater urgency and consequence than ever before. The *tendential* gap between individual citizens and their states *may be* widened; the technocratic language of the increasingly restrictive states *may* effectively prevail, and the language of individual freedom *may* suffer a decline in status. But the *latent* possibility, which is no less technically feasible, is the creation of an information and communications infrastructure for decentralized rational self-government.

One seemingly paradoxical, but highly significant, consequence of this state of affairs is that, since the technology has become so sophisticated that there are no longer any technical problems involved in the realisation of either a totalitarian, or a truly democratic, society, technology itself has rendered itself superfluous as an argument in the debate about which form of society to choose. In the course of its own development, the technology has thus — far from consolidating people's impressions of its own immanent dynamism — finally revealed its own subordinate role in the creation of our futures. Much to the dismay of the technocratic rationalists, the latest technology has returned the political discussion of its significance to the place where it belongs — to the political arena! Not that the new technology itself has become any less potentially dangerous, of course — it would be a fatal mistake to consider it *in*significant. On the contrary, the fight over this new technology can (or should be able to) concern itself more directly, from now on, precisely with the new technology's momentous, and far-reaching, social significance.

7. THE INFLUENCE OF TELEMATICS ON MODES OF PERCEPTION AND MORALITY.

In chapter 4, I argued for the necessity of a structural analysis of I.T. and telematics technology in its total context. We need to concern ourselves with the total effect of the technology on every aspect of each individual's life. We have seen how the technology is liable radically to alter fundamental social structures which have previously seemed to be fixed points in the public and private lives of each individual. Both in terms of their content, and in terms of their own interrelationship, fundamental social spheres such as the family, the state, industrial production, and political activity are likely to undergo radical transformation. The conditions of our very existence will be transformed — and, in consequence, the individual himself will be transformed.

The question of how the individual's own modes of perception and morality will be transformed by the new technology is a question of enormous scope and significance. At the same time it is, I must admit, a question about which, in the nature of things, one can hazard any number of plausible hypotheses, or informed guesses, without ever reaching much more than a reasonable degree of probability.

7.1. *The Spatial and Temporal Boundaries of Enlightenment Philosophy.*

Immanuel Kant was a nice, orderly, bourgeois philosopher, neatly categorizing rubbish as rubbish and rational thinking as rational thinking. In his critical works he strove to define the fundamental conditions for our existence and our cognitive processes, and he was well aware of the fact that a failure to comprehend these fundamental conditions would only result in an awful lot of rubbish being talked. So he addressed himself to the problem of defining how our world is constituted, dealing with Man in relation to his physical and social environment, and dealing with the concepts of space, time and morality.

But with all his talk of space and time and morality, he was himself subject to his own historically limited perceptions of space and time — he was himself a moralizer!

Kant portrayed Man in relation to his environment from his own particular point of view and on the basis of his own experience — the point of view and experience of a man of *his* social position and *his* time. At the centre of all his thinking he posited an isolated rational individual. The physical world and its dimensions of space and time are apprehended through the eyes of this artificially isolated rational individual, just as the social world is considered as a relationship between this isolated rational individual and others like himself.

The rational individual is placed fairly and squarely at the centre of the universe, but he is by no means a superman. On the contrary, he is at the mercy of external circumstances and scarcely (or only very hesitantly) dares get to grips with those circumstances. He is subject to the limitations of time and space because they are given, once and for all. He makes no attempt to transcend them — he merely defines the limits of their power.

As regards the individual's relationship to his social environment, there, too, we are confronted with a *fait accompli*, according to Kant. But in this area, at least, a definite strategy can be adopted. Not a strategy which can alter the prevailing circumstances, but a strategy which can help us to make the best of them. A contract may be entered into between the individual and the other individual members of his social environment — a contract which is so ingeniously contrived that the contracting parties are equally bound to each other: one must 'act only on that maxim whereby thou canst at the same time will that it should become a universal law' — a sound, cultivated, and at the same time eminently practical business contract, in other words.

The actions of defining limits, and drawing up a contract, are, however, fundamentally ambivalent. They tell us something about what is limited, and why the contract is necessary — about how the known world would seem to be constituted, in other words. But they also tell us about the existence of something else — something which has been excluded, about principles overriding or underlying the contract.

But the presumption of a clearly defined and self-sufficient individual subject, with clearly defined possibilities for consciously willed action, formed the ideal for ostensibly much more practical contemporary schools of thought than Kant's. English Utilitarianism, for instance, from Adam Smith to John Stuart Mill, was indeed forced to acknowledge the fact that the pre-Enlightenment legacy was scarcely a population with an overwhelming majority of rational bourgeois individuals like themselves — but Adam

Smith recommended that this small matter should be rapidly redressed through some improved public education (Smith 1976: 788), and Mill, some seventy years later, felt that it already had been — at least in urban areas, and in some capital-intensive agricultural areas in Scotland and the North of England:

> "As the idea is essentially repulsive of a society only held together by bought services, and by the relations and feelings arising out of pecuniary interests, so there is something naturally attractive in a form of society abounding in strong personal attachments and disinterested self-devotion. Of such feelings it must be admitted that the relation of protector and protected has hitherto been the richest source [...]. The arrangements of society are now such that no man or woman who either possesses or is able to earn a livelihood requires any other protection than that of the law. Of the working classes of Western Europe at least it may be pronounced certain, that the patriarchal or paternal system of government is one to which they will not again be subject. That question has been several times decided. It was decided when they were taught to read, and allowed access to newspapers and political tracts. It was decided when dissenting preachers were suffered to go among them [...]. It was decided when they were brought together in numbers, to work socially under the same roof. It was decided when railways enabled them to shift from place to place [...]. The working classes have taken their interests into their own hands, and are perpetually showing that they think the interests of their employers not identical with their own but opposite to them. Some among the higher classes flatter themselves that these tendencies may be counteracted by moral and religious education; but they have let the time go by for giving an education which can serve their purpose. The principles of the Reformation have reached as low down as reading and writing, and the poor will no longer accept morals and religion of other people's prescribing [...]". (Ford 1969: 46f)

So Mill seemed to regard the majority of the pupulace as rational, enlightened individuals, ripe to enter into the Kantian social contract with each other to their own mutual advantage.

But not everybody shared this optimistic point of view. Eight years before Mill's chapter 'On the Probable Futurity of the Labouring Classes' was published in his *Principles of Political Economy*, the calmly observing de Tocqueville had already dealt his famous death-blow to the post-Kantian 'scientific' optimism of the Utilitarians: "I believe" wrote this aristocratic survivor of the French revolution's Napoleonic aftermath, "that it is easier to establish an absolute and despotic government among a people in which the conditions of society are equal than among any other [...]". (Ford 1969: 45)

7.2. *Practical Criticism Today: Transcending the Bounds of Space and Time in our Physical Environment*

While his contemporaries were involved in discussions about the *possibilities* of realising Kant's ideals, practical criticism today concerns itself with precisely *how* we are going to set about transcending the boundaries of Enlightenment reality, the limitations of time and space which Kant took to be universal and eternal, but which, under the influence of Space Age I.T. and telematics, seem less rigidly fixed and secure than ever before. For when Kant writes that space is an *a priori* concept which forms the basis for any further observations, he is, of course, referring to a condition which no technology can alter — but also to a condition whose *oppressive* nature may be *mitigated* by telematics.

What seems to be happening under the influence of the new technology is that, while the oppressive nature of space is being contested, the individual's identity, resulting from his 'central' position in a universe of prescribed limits, is coming under threat. On the one hand, for many years now thanks to the telephone, the individual has been able to make instant verbal contact with anyone in the world, however far away they may be. Video telephones and teleconferencing are able to supplement this verbal communication with facial expression, body language and other forms of non-verbal communication. Space as a fixed principle on which to base scientific observations is untouched by these developments, of course, but it has lost its apparently unalterable phenomenological sway. But on the other hand, teleconferencing facilities permit the individual to play a central role in many different communication circles of widely varying geographical diameter virtually simultaneously, and, in turn, each individual finds himself on the periphery of many other communication circles of varying diameter. This is likely to result in a feeling of homelessness — in a lack of the multiple mutual contacts within a limited number of stable communication circles, which has hitherto contributed towards the creation of the individual's village or closed neighbourhood identity.

Nevertheless, phenomenologically speaking, one is tempted to congratulate the new technology on some considerable degree of success in limiting the oppression of the spatial dimension of our existences. The oppression of time, however, far from being contested by the new technology, would actually seem to have been aggravated by it. Time has become more and more absolute.

This is of course partly due to the fact that it is more precisely measured, and partly due to the fact that precisely measured time has become an increasingly ubiquitous reality in our daily lives. As far as the conquest of *space* is concerned, the popular and profitable science fiction myths of comics, films, novels, gambling machines and computer games have achieved a degree of no less profitable reality with the help of modern, sophisticated electronics. But no 'time machine' has yet been invented to rival in reality the free flights into past and future so characteristic of the popular dreams expressed in modern trivial literature and media fantasies. It doesn't help to be told that our conversations around the globe can be communicated digitally at the speed of light, when we ourselves are still unable to think or talk faster than we have always done to our next door neighbours! The nearest we can get in terms of time to that exhilarating *feeling* of freedom which telematics' conquest of space can give us — that feeling of being at last able to realise the centuries-old dream which Kant defined negatively for us by insisting on the precise definition of the limits to our freedom — is when we telecommunicate, or actually fly around the world, outstripping the sun, or retracing its steps, to gain or lose a few hours in relation to the parts of the world we are making contact with — or when we telecommunicate with the robots we have sent off into outer space to explore time on their own.

Speaking generally though, the conclusion must be that — in phenomenological terms — we have obtained a degree of liberation from space but are still more closely confined within the bondage of time. Time's bondage becomes all the more constrictive, too, because it has become increasingly difficult to escape from a mercilessly *linear* time perspective — a perspective involving the irreversible addition of one commutable unit to another in an infinite accumulation, which started unthinkably long before we were born and which will end, if ever, unthinkably long after we are dead. Hitherto, there has always been a tendency to escape from the inevitability and the totally anonymous insignificance of one's own mortality by seeking refuge in a cyclical time perspective, the perspective which speaks of birth, death and regeneration, of the Spring which always follows the Winter, of the morning which follows the night, of reincarnation — of doomsday or resurrection following apocalypse or crucifixion.

But with the ubiquitous introduction of the digital timepiece, the linear perspective has achieved previously unknown predominance. The traditional cyclical measurement of time can, in my opinion, be accused of the nostalgia which, as we saw in chapter 4, is characteristic of a pro-Nature attitude to social development. In preferring a traditional to a digital timepiece, the customer is going for the expensive, unperfumed, 'natural' deodorant — she is expressing a longing for a synchronisation of her own daily routine with the reassuring 'natural' rhythms of night and day and the changing seasons. The customers who prefer digital chronometers — (men rather than women, on the sciences side rather than the arts)[19] — do so presumably because the linear measurement of time is clearly an expression of a pro-Civilisation attitude to social development. Time means money, as every businessman knows, and where we have, to some extent, reduced the tyranny of time is in our ability to produce things faster and to travel faster, with greater punctuality and regularity. Digital chronometers remind us of these successes — speak to us of a world we have created by ourselves, and for ourselves, and over which we have considerable control — the world of business meetings and appointments and timetables and flight departures.

It is hardly necessary for me to point out to the reader that the digital chronometer is a perfect example of the relative unimportance of technological factors compared to the social significance of technology — a point which I illustrated in chapter 2 above in relation to the preference for communication satellites rather than a broadband network, in the European context. There are, of course, measurable technical differences in the design of a watch with fluid crystal figures rather than moving hands: digital watches require less energy and are comparatively free of mechanical wear and tear, for instance, as well as being much cheaper to produce. But if you are in the watch business, and are an adherent of built-in obsolescence to maintain your turnover, these are not necessarily good reasons for preferring to make this kind of watch rather than the more traditional kind! Nor would there seem to be any immediate ergonomic advantage for the customer: it is more time-consuming and tiring to register a row of four to six figures, several of which may be changing at the moment when one is attempting to register them — than it is to register a single pattern made by two or three hands.

No, the choice of watch would seem rather to be dictated by the customers' search for an attractive identity — either the 'old-fashioned' search for security in a supposedly harmonious natural order, or the self-congratulatory search for security in a supposedly ever-more controllable man-made urban industrial environment. As assertions of different people's identity, as proclamations of where their owners feel most security is to be found, the watches themselves take on normative significance in the ongoing attitudinal debate about what our societies have achieved, and about what it is desirable for them to achieve in the future.

In that our societies at present are not run by women or by students of the humanities rather than by scientists and businessmen, the digital timepiece with its message of linear chronometry has become omnipresent. In fact, for the majority of us, the old-fashioned clock on the wall, reasserting a reassuring daily routine, however boring, may still be preferable to the challenge and anxiety generated by digital chronometry confronting us 'too much' with the reality of our human predicament: every fraction of a second we are brought face to face with the genuinely and qualitatively new in our own personal existences and in our own total human existence on this planet, but every fraction of a second brings with it the accompanying disconcerting realisation that the past is constantly and irrevocably slipping away between our fingers.

The ability to transcend time and space is an old dream which telematics is intended to help us to realise. The feeling of global solidarity, and the practical advantages of proximity with loved ones across the miles, as well as the ability to plan ahead and to routinize and defend one's society on the basis of comprehensive knowledge of the whole world as it is today and as it has been in the past — all these are valuable, the technicians tell us, and — in their familiar and banal phraseology — they constitute the reality of tomorrow's global citizens.

But the new technology has also generated new problems in its attempts to gratify ancient desires: the 'successful' phenomenological transcendence of space has engendered a feeling of homelessness and disorientation; the 'less successful' transcendence of time has in fact proved synonymous with the recognition that time basically *cannot* be transcended, however minutely it can be measured. *We* can do things faster in relation to it — but we cannot slow it down in relation to us, and to our own mortality.

Disorientation and existential despair would seem to be the by-products of our attempts, to date, to transgress the Kantian boundaries of time and space. The original dreamers in ancient Greece and the Middle Ages are quick to remind us that they told us so: this kind of utopian thinking, they always maintained, is potentially dangerous — a challenge to God or the gods. Nowhere has the message been more clearly or more relevantly expressed, perhaps, than in Shakespeare's contemporary Christopher Marlowe's dramatisation of the *Historia vom D. Johann Fausten, dem weitbeschreyten Zauberer und Schwartzkünstler*, an anonymous fable purportedly based on the life of an early 16th C. charlatan which was published by one Johann Spies in Frankfurt in 1587. Faust, like so many other dreamers of his time, sets his hopes on alchemy, astrology and magic to satisfy the desires and longings which torture him. So completely, indeed, was Faust associated with what was new and daring in thought or invention, that, at an early date, he was identified with one of the pioneers of information technology, a printer by the name of Fust! Faust makes a pact with the devil offering him his soul in exchange for 24 hours of life with Mephistopheles as his familiar spirit:

> "Had I as many souls as there be stars,
> I'd give them all for Mephistophilis.
> By him I'll be great emperor of the world,
> And make a bridge thorough the moving air,
> To pass the ocean with a band of men;
> I'll join the hills that bind the Afric shore,
> And make that country continent to Spain,
> And both contributory to my crown [...]."
> (Marlowe 1909: 128f)

With Mephistopheles' help, Faust is quite successful in conquering space, making an aerial grand tour of the European capitals — and, in terms of time, he rivals any Hollywood silent movie, when he is able to present the Emperor Charles V with spirits in the shapes of Alexander the Great and 'his Paramour', and when he himself is permitted to make music with Homer, and love to Helen of Troy — though it is not clear in the play whether these latter are not also merely devils dressed up! It is, in fact, no part of the author's purpose to show Faustus' reward, even in this world, as imposing or dignified. His visits to the Pope and to the Emperor Charles V are characterized by what P.F. Gent, whose translation of the German story was published in London in 1592, called 'merry conceits' — but which in Marlowe's play amount to no more than adolescent buffoonery. Marlowe's message seems fundamentally to be the same as Hans Christian Andersen's in *The Goloshes of Fortune*.

But, while the theology student in the Andersen fairy-tale found peace at last in the grave, Marlowe's Faustus can scarcely expect anything but eternal torment. And, when his appointed hour draws nigh, or, as he himself expresses it in linear chronometry, when "the restless course That time doth run with calm and silent foot, Shortening my days and thread of vital life, Calls for the payment of my latest years", he panics! It is a disconcertingly modern panic, for all the talk of outmoded theology:

> "Ah, Faustus.
> Now hast thou but one bare hour to live,
> And then thou must be damn'd perpetually!
> Stand still, you ever-moving spheres of heaven,
> That time may cease, and midnight never come;
> Fair Nature's eye, rise, rise again, and make
> Perpetual day; or let this hour be but
> A year, a month, a week, a natural day,
> That Faustus may repent and save his soul!
> O lente, lente currite, noctis equi!
> The stars move still, time runs, the clock will strike,
> The devil will come, and Faustus must be damn'd [...]."
> (Marlowe 1909: 156f)

7.3. *The Social Environment: From Physical Need Satisfaction Towards Need Manipulation.*

While Kant was content to trace the boundaries of our *physical* environment as seemingly immutable limits to human activity, he pleaded for the observance of a social contract as a strategy to help us all to make the best of our *social* environment. But, in *The Culture of Narcissism*, Christopher Lasch portrays an anarchic and morally dissolute society in which personal responsibility no longer counts for very much — a modern, collective Faust-story, one might say, about the fatal consequences of giving ourselves up to social and technological temptations. According to Lasch, what is in dissolution here is precisely Kant's imperative concerning mutually responsible human action. Today, in Lasch's opinion, nobody takes responsibility for their own actions any more, nobody imposes any responsibility on anyone else. Each individual acts solely on the basis of self-love, and 'true self-love and social' are *not* synonymous, as Post-Reformation and Enlightenment philosophers had fondly hoped they would be.[20]

The reason for this is as old as urban civilisation itself. Subject to the necessity of satisfying fundamental human needs, and forced to satisfy those needs through a communal struggle against the forces of nature, small and primitive tribal and peasant societies — including many of those which are still with us in Third World countries today — were forced to accept a communal work ethic.

This, again, had consequences for child-rearing. Children had to be brought up to fulfil their adult roles within the social work force as soon as they were capable of pulling their weight. Through their upbringing and education, children were taught to identify their own needs as forming part of, and as already established by, the existing structure of communal needs. Education of this kind was an education in the acceptance of discipline: a society on the verge of starvation couldn't accept idlers.

But human needs lost their communally uniting validity as soon as urban society grew up, agricultural methods were improved, and hunger, thirst, nakedness, and homelessness became social, rather than natural, phenomena (i.e. phenomena whose existence was unnecessary, were it not for an eventual unequal social distribution of wealth). The caste system in India, for example, survives in all its rigidity in the remote villages which still today are subject to perennial famine, floods and drought. In times of plenty, the inequality of the higher castes asserts itself, but in times of dearth, harvests are shared out equally among all the villagers.[21]

In marked contrast, for example, to England, already becoming urbanised in the 14th C., where the power of the Roman Catholic Church to enforce feudal obedience was already under strain. The hero of English medieval poet William Langland's *Piers the Ploughman* can accept the prospect of working for the knight, his feudal overlord, as long as the latter protects the Church (Langland himself was a minor cleric!), and protects the ploughman from 'the thieves and wasters who ruin the world' (including animals and birds, as well as idle human beings), and administers justice incorruptibly and mercifully, does not overwork his labourers, and does not waste his time in idle revelry. But the growth of London in the 14th C. confronted the indignant Langland with a new class of absentee landlords and their hangers on, living in idle luxury at the expense of the impoverished tenants and serfs. In the second of his allegorical visions, Langland makes his hero try to turn the clock back:

> "'By God!' said Piers, 'I'll teach you all a lesson!' And with that he holloed out for Hunger; and Hunger heard him at once and started up. 'Avenge me on these wretches who eat up the world', cried Piers. Then Hunger leapt at Waster and seized him by the belly, wringing his guts till the water ran from his eyes [...]." (Langland 1966: 86)

Hunger produces the desired effect. Waster and his fellows "fled in terror to the barns, and threshed away with their flails from morning till night"; others "went to work with spades and shovels, and dug and ditched like mad to stave off Hunger".

> "Then thousands of blind and bed-ridden folk suddenly recovered, and men who used to sit begging for silver were miraculously cured! [...] And Piers was proud of his success, and he set them all to work, giving them a fair wage and as much food as he could spare."

But Langland is aware of the fact that, however ideal such a situation might appear in terms of social equality, the realities of 14th C. England were otherwise. At harvest time, the cunning labourers and beggars and tramps overfeed Hunger until he falls asleep, and then they themselves refuse to do any more work and go off to the towns in search of the best brown ale. The dreamer is left muttering vague prophesies after them that Hunger will get them in the end!

The change from communal need satisfaction to exploitative need manipulation was a fact with which Marx dealt, no less indignantly, in his *Economic and Philosophic Manuscripts of 1844*. Human needs, four hundred and fifty years after Langland's great representative English poem of the late Middle Ages, were by no means circumscribed by a limited number of minimal requirements whose satisfaction was the sole business of Victorian society!

Marx wrote:

> "Every person speculates on creating a *new* need in another so as to drive him to a fresh sacrifice, to place him in a new dependence and to seduce him into a new mode of *gratification* and therefore economic ruin. Each tries to establish over the other an *alien* power, so as thereby to find satisfaction of his own selfish need [...]. *Excess* and *intemperance* come to be (the modern economic system's) true norm [...]. The extension of products and needs falls into *contriving* and *ever-calculating* subservience to inhuman, refined, unnatural and *imaginary* appetites [...]. No eunuch flatters his despot more basely or uses more despicable means to stimulate his dulled capacity for pleasure in order to sneak a favour for himself than does the industrial eunuch — the producer — in order to sneak for himself a few pennies [...]. He puts himself at the service of the other's most depraved fancies, plays the pimp between him and his need, excites in him morbid appetites, lies in wait for each of his weaknesses — all so that he can then demand the cash for this service of love." (Marx 1959: 107f)

When Marx uses words like 'excess', 'intemperance', 'inhuman, refined, unnatural and imaginary appetites', it sounds as though he is contrasting 'artificial' with 'real' or authentic needs, and criticising the former precisely because they exceed some minimum requirements for each individual's and each family's survival. As I pointed out at the beginning of my second chapter, however, Marx was later fully aware of the difference between hunger and its satisfaction, with or without forks and knives, in civilised as distinct from primitive, societies — he was later well aware of the fact that needs are as much socially significant as they are physically dictated, even within societies which strike us as markedly primitive in comparison to ourselves — (one thinks of conspicuous expenditure on holidays and festivals in starving Indian villages, for instance).

In fact one might say that the transcendence of the necessity to satisfy the primitive needs for daily food and drink, for a minimum of clothing, and for the flimsiest of roofs over one's head, is a precondition for any utopia, which, by definition, would provide the social framework for thinking about, experimenting with, playing with, exploring, new varieties of human needs and new ways of satisfying them. As long as there is a struggle barely to exist, the need for food is a hunger phenomenon. But the extensive literature on food preparation in industrialized nations illustrates the 'refinement' of appetite which occurs when satisfying one's hunger becomes only one, relatively minor, aspect among many others in our pattern of food consumption. As Roland Barthes pointed out in his mid-1950s essay on 'Ornamental Cookery' in *Les Lettres Nouvelles*, post-war fashionable French cooking was primarily intended to *disguise* food, to 'dress it up' for the eye in socially significant clothing:

> "The weekly *Elle* [...] gives us almost every week a fine colour photograph of a prepared dish [...]. The 'substantial' category which prevails in this type of cooking is that of the smooth coating: there is an obvious endeavour to glaze surfaces, to round them off, to bury the food under the even sedement of sauces, creams, icing and jellies. This of course comes from the very finality of the coating, which belongs to a visual category, and cooking according to *Elle* is meant for the eye alone, since sight is a genteel sense [...]. Hence a cookery which is based on coatings and alibis, and is for ever trying to extenuate and even to disguise the primary nature of foodstuffs, the brutality of meat or the abruptness of seafood [...]. But above all, coatings prepare and support one of the major developments of genteel cookery: ornamentation [...]. Ornamentation proceeds in two contradictory ways, which we shall in a moment see dialectically reconciled: on the one hand, fleeing from nature thanks to a kind of frenzied baroque (sticking shrimps in a lemon, making a chicken look pink, serving grape-fruit hot), and on the other, trying to reconstitute it through an incongruous artifice (strewing meringue mushrooms and holly leaves on a traditional log-shaped Christmas cake, replacing the heads of crayfish around the sophisticated bechamel which hides their bodies). It is in fact the same pattern which one finds in the elaboration of petit-bourgeois trinkets (ashtrays in the shape of a saddle, lighters in the shape of a cigarette, terrines in the shape of a hare)". (Barthes 1973: 78f)

Positive or negative reactions to this state of affairs in industrialized nations depend on whether, as an adherent of Civilisation at all costs, one concentrates on the utopian aspects of this situation *in vacuo*, or whether, like Langland in the 14th C., one concentrates on the inequality of distribution of food and wealth, which in global perspective to-day would seem to be at least as serious a problem as any Langland encountered. So serious in fact, that, as Langland himself realised even then, any kind of solution involving a return to 'natural' or basic human needs is unthinkably naïve. In his more primitive stage of social evolution, however, it is understandable that Langland desperately *wanted* to turn the clock back — that life in the cities struck him as immeasurably decadent, as it has done (and no doubt always will) for pro-Nature primitivists since the start of urban civilisation.

Marx, however, was not a primitivist. His indignation was caused not by his society's transcendence of the daily struggle for survival, but by the way in which need manipulation was not under the control of each individual, but was instead a weapon used by others against the individual, an expression of the power struggle within an economy based on private property. The cultivation of needs in others, whose satisfaction may be lucrative to oneself, is not, of course, the same as to experiment with one's own needs. It constitutes, in fact, a breach in the observance of Kant's imperative, unless one regards the latter extremely cynically, and accepts that all's fair in love and war — in the economic warfare of every man against every man: kill or be killed, corrupt or be corrupted! Kant himself would no doubt have been horrified at such an interpretation, as his famous maxim about never treating another individual purely as one's own tool, but also as *his* own tool, makes clear. But in the 18th and 19th centuries the English Utilitarian school included zealots who would have seen nothing anomalous or dangerous in such a situation. They might, on the contrary, have pointed out the advantages of the development of the 'healthily sceptical' mentality of the critical consumer, which would presumably result from such a war of every man against every man. No, it was to take an analysis of the class structure under capitalism to convince people of the basic unfairness of the war to corrupt each other — to make them understand that the war was not between 'free and equal' individuals, but between extremely powerful producers and increasingly powerless and apathetic consumers.

In modern industrial societies, then, instead of taking basic needs as our starting-point, and nature as the object of our manipulation in an attempt to satisfy such needs, needs themselves have become objects of manipulation, and, in consequence, the content of our upbringing and education has undergone a transformation. Instead of an education in the acceptance of discipline and the identification of one's own needs with already defined and communally accepted needs, which, as I said earlier, characterized education and morality in primitive societies, the lack of rigidly defined needs in modern society has involved the collapse of moral and educational discipline and a corresponding necessity for each individual to discover for himself how he ought to behave, what he ought to become, and what goals he should set up for himself in accordance with what he himself considers to be his own needs.

The problem is not new in itself, as I have mentioned earlier, but the combination of the increased technological control over nature and the spread of literacy in industrial societies over the last two centuries has meant that what was originally a problem for urban élites has become a mass problem: a mass problem which powerful concerns have understood constitutes a very promising source of profit.

Ideals of beauty exemplify this trend rather well. In modern society, being beautiful is not synonymous with being well-fed, as has frequently been the case in primitive societies. Being beautiful in modern society — (not surprisingly, for the reader who remembers my observations, in the last section, about digitally-timed mortality!) — is synonymous with being healthy. The body is supposed to signal, in fact, that, instead of satisfying survival needs on their own terms, these survival needs are satisfied through the interplay of natural bodily requirements, on the one hand, and the demands of the medical and dietary knowledge, on the other, which one has acquired as the result of one's civilisation's successful attempts to extend its control over nature. The beautiful body, the healthy body, is not a natural, but a cultural phenomenon. And it costs money!

The collapse of traditional moral and educational discipline in the absence of any further objective need for it in industrial societies has, as I mentioned earlier, thrown the (immature) individual back upon his or her own (limited) resources. The result, disciples of Lasch would maintain, has been increasing anarchy, and a narcissistic insecurity which produces ready victims for the need-manipulators, for the sellers of an acceptable, because up-to-date and fashionable, identity. Instead of learning about basic food preparation, work in the fields, and rudimentary child-care, the children of industrialized nations are encouraged to invest in slimming diets, jogging programmes, sports equipment, and sexological literature, which promote the desire to consciously experiment with personal need satisfaction, and which illustrate the way in which the (for the victim rather costly) 'production' of the strong and healthy 'natural' individual involves a not infrequently enervating struggle (on the jogging track; at table in the company of others who are not on a diet; in bed) between body and soul.

It is in relation to this re-defined 'education' of the individual consumer — with regard to this insecure need to be dictated to, to be supplied with identity-giving idols, to be told what to think, politically, by the legendary 'strong man' — that telematics has a role to play in the society of the future. Education is no longer a question of the creation of a mature individual out of an immature one — it is about the continual *re*-creation of the individual, his re-education from one temporary identity to the next. As far as telematics is concerned, production has nothing to do with the manipulation of nature in accordance with elementary need satisfaction: production involves the manipulation of individual human beings in accordance with their own (misguided) desires. In the light of this fact, it becomes obvious that telematics is a truly *modern* technology.

8. TELEMATICS, SOCIAL CONTROL, AND THE BLIND SELF-DECEPTION OF UNREFLECTIVE TENDENTIAL CRITICISM.

8.1. *Knowledge is Power?*

The reader will no doubt recall the speech by Walter F. Bauer, President of Informatics, Inc., which I quoted in chapter four. The 500 I.T. representatives from all over the world assembled at the managerial conference in Copenhagen in 1982 were greeted by the proclamation that they, in the opinion of Mr. Bauer, were the new leaders of the world. It was as though they had stumbled upon the philosophers' stone — 'knowledge is power' intoned Bauer in Bacon's famous words, and with the confidence of the successful alchemist proceeded to sound the knell of capitalist private property. The expropriators were expropriated, only to be replaced instantly by the alchemists themselves.

In essence, as I pointed out in chapter four, Bauer merely indicated the usefulness of the new technology for the maintenance of the traditional antisocial power structure: it was no part of his intention to criticize that power structure.

It is, however, of depressing significance that Bauer's critics are inclined to share his misinterpretation of the true state of affairs. Their time is spent trying to adduce evidence to support his claim, on the grounds that it is for this reason that the new Information Society is suspect! Thomas Söderquist, for example, a radical academic teaching at Denmark's new Roskilde University Centre, has published a considerable number of articles in which he argues for the correctness, or the probable correctness, of Bauer's assumption. According to Söderquist, power in the new Information Society will be concentrated in the hands of large-scale organisations, institutions and state bureaucracies. Their function will be to plan and coordinate the new society, which they will effect with the help of knowledge — theoretical, abstract, and general knowledge, as opposed to specific, empirical and specialised knowledge. Given such knowledge, the privileged few will be able to plan the lives of the rest of the population. (Söderquist 1982)

Already in 1981, the year before Bauer's self-confident proclamation, a couple of Swedish writers had argued — in a book whose title ironically echoed Shakespeare's Miranda in the same way as Aldous Huxley did in 1932 — that those who already mastered the new technology, and had a complete understanding of how it functioned, would be able to extend their knowledge far beyond what lay within others' grasp. The authors pointed out that the optimal exploitation of the available technology in the Information Society is premissed on the supposition that one knows what information one is looking for — whereas those who lack a comprehensive understanding of the capabilities of the technology would be doomed for ever to a diet of piecemeal fragments. (Cronberg and Sangregorio 1981)

Earlier still than the Swedish study — in fact right back at the beginning of the 'seventies — Alain Tourraine produced a number of books intended to analyse the emergence of a new power structure in post-industrial societies. In what Tourraine called 'the programmed society', the emergent dominant class consisted of people who *already* controlled information, and whose theoretical qualifications enabled them to make full use of this information — *they* would be the stuff of the new élite. (See, for example, Tourraine 1979)

Whether the new Information Society is to be run by computer specialists or not is, of course, as I have earlier argued, a fundamentally open question. But Herbert I. Schiller, author of *Who Knows: Information in the Age of the Fortune 500*, is quite sure that *he* knows that I.T. is, and always will be, the obedient tool of more traditional powerful interests. With the aid of his incredibly comprehensive and irately presented body of evidence, he denounces the technology as, in the first instance, the tool of existing *economic power*: computerized communication is exclusively concentrated in the hands of a select group of highly developed industrialized nations, he points out, which — as he illustrates — facilitates the integration of peripheral regions within the commercial system of the Western World. He then goes on to denounce the new technology as an instrument of *state control*, quoting former President Carter's adviser, Dr. Frank Press, as having said that "the President's commitment to maintaining leadership includes and subsumes remote sensing as one of the many areas in space where we want to maintain our leadership". (Schiller 1981: 118)

From a statement like this it is an easy step for Schiller to take to denounce I.T. — thirdly — as being, essentially, *military technology*. For it is in fact the case that 'remote sensing' was developed as a military project, designed to gather information about military logistics all over the world, in order to safeguard the global military superiority of the United States' 'peace-keeping' force.

8.2. *I.T. as Military Technology.*

This latter aspect preoccupies many of I.T.'s critics. For example, the Battle of the Falkland Islands in the Summer of 1982 provided them with some juicy material. The war, it seems, was waged very much on the basis of advanced technical systems. On May 4th, the British destroyer H.M.S. Sheffield was sunk by the Argentinians using Exocet missiles, which were manufactured in France and brought into position and fired from French-built Super Etendard jet fighters. From the planes, the pilots could remotely control the rockets, until their own radar equipment took over the 'homing' process. Radar, laser technology, computerized command and control systems, precision attack weapons with automatic homing devices, — a deliciously compromising cornucopia of I.T. and Artificial Intelligence contributed to this coup.

The inability of the Sheffield to ward off its fate was, moreover, apparently due to a technical hitch. The rocket was sighted by helicopters, and reported to be on its way, seventeen minutes before it reached its target. Apparently the information was received, but it was mistakenly taken to refer to a British Harrier jet fighter, which experts say an Exocet missile can resemble, under the given conditions. And the Sheffield's own radar, which should have been sufficient to register the approaching danger, was either temporarily switched off, or had broken down. (Rubinstein 1982: 34ff)

To an ever increasing extent military technology *is* information technology, critics claim. I.T. plays a vital military technological role in what might be called 'a C 3 system': in military Command, Control and Communications. Within the entire cadre of American military technology, the central importance of the United States' W.W.M.C.C.S. (World-Wide Military Command and Control System) is generally acknowledged. It embraces three centres of military command: the control centre in the Pentagon, the alternative control centre at Fort Ritchie, and, as still another alternative, the National Emergency Airborne Command Center, which is located in a specially equipped E 4 transport plane. In addition, the system includes 35 computers installed in 25 different communications headquarters. All of these, and the three major command centres, are linked to the various units of the U.S. army by an extensive communications network involving thirty million miles of cable, five satellites, and a hundred earth stations. The aim is to keep the enemy under surveillance, and to command one's own forces, such that the entire military machine can constitute a single flexible and well-coordinated unit. The acquisition of information and efficient communications are thus the be-all and end-all of military technology in this respect.

On top of all this, critics can go on to point out that the computerization of the military machine has one very grave disadvantage: vulnerability — with a resultant dangerous tendency to over-react. Every single one of the components of the military technological I.T. and telematics system is vulnerable: satellites are vulnerable; earth stations are vulnerable; the overland communications network is vulnerable; the major command centres can be put out of action; even the emergency airborne command centre is vulnerable, in that it has to take on fuel and supplies at regular intervals, and may have difficulty in finding an airstrip which is intact.

It is an indisputable fact that military technological communications systems have exhibited two main trends in their recent development: the systems have become increasingly centralized, which is, of course, a necessary precondition for effective coordination; and they have come to rely more and more on advanced technology — technology which is, undeniably, vulnerable. Critics have compared these information systems to chains — their effective operation dependent on an ever increasing number of links, each of which is becoming more and more vulnerable from day to day. Since the operational efficiency of the entire military machine is dependent on these increasingly vulnerable chains, the incentive to strike first has become all the more compelling — to put the enemy out of action before one's own vital installations are destroyed. (Lerner 1982: 53ff)

So the opposition has at least two trumps in their hands — they can say that I.T. and telematics have rendered military systems increasingly dangerous to themselves and to humanity; and they can point to military technological systems as examples of the fact that, to an increasing extent, military technology has become synonymous with information technology, with the additional consequence that the latter is often the product of military research and development. But the irresistible, and to my mind fatal, temptation into which they so often fall is to conclude from such arguments that I.T. is an improbable tool for democratic government, and that it is more likely to be of assistance to existing power groups who wish to maintain and tighten their hold over the populations they seek to exploit.

8.3. *The 'Natural' Opposition.*

Although the military-industrial complex is a formidable opponent, the critics of the new technology have one enormous and reassuring advantage: they represent 'natural' unspoilt humanity.

More or less plausibly synchronized with the history of capitalism, the Marxist primitivists among them often serve up the familiar story about how our authentic human needs, originally flourishing in a rich and fertile past, have become corrupted, degenerate, reduced to one-dimensionality in our lamentable present. Our contemporary mass media are the hidden trumps in the hands of the depravers, and telematics has merely completed our downfall. Deprived of his own 'true human nature', modern Man has instead been given the role of mindless operator, and victim, of coin-operated gambling machines and computer games. And indeed, critics of military technology, and of contemporary political leaders, not infrequently appear to have a secret pact with pre-Capitalist 'authentic' humanity — which, when the occasion arises, will triumphantly be reinstated!

The fallacy behind pro-Nature primitivism involves, of course, the elevation of 'authentic' human needs to static, universal phenomena, with the accompanying tendency to historicize, in the search for a plausible explanation of just how and when technology suddenly turned sour on us. In fact, technology and human needs are interrelated, dynamically evolving, categories: (human) nature will always be a historically specific and socially conditioned abstraction, having little to do with any tangible reality. Thus our modern concept of (human) nature is, in effect, a product of our capitalist societies, but those who fight for this abstraction are often blind to the way in which the forces they criticize have actually generated the ideal they uphold — a fact which I illustrated at the beginning of my fourth chapter by juxtaposing the relative optimism and pessimism of N.F.S. Grundtvig and Hans Christian Andersen in the first phase of the Industrial Revolution. The costs and the benefits of the scarcely consciously registered common denominator, the new social system, were antinomically evaluated, as the reader will remember. And even if they talk at cross-purposes, critics of technology and technological optimists share that same antinomical point of departure, which explains why critics of power so often speak in the language of power — why they have a tendency to wallow in lurid descriptions of the crimes perpetrated by those in power! Calculations of new political leaders' probable infringements of civic liberties are full of gory details; run-downs of military installations and the technology of war are sometimes voluptuously scary.

The resistance of the oppressed, expressed as it so often is in the language of oppression, is the reverse of the medal — it is 'all part of the game'.

8.4. *Power Old and New: Confiscation v. Self-Castigation.*

Precisely this is my point: criticism of telematics as an instrument of repression participates in a game which is the invention of those who want to repress. The criticism is expressed within the logic of repression, and thus itself becomes a component part of this repression.

My contention is, in other words, that the struggle between those who have power, and those who do not, is only superficially a fight 'for' or 'against' existing society. Actually, we are dealing with two opposing power groups' struggle *within* existing society. This is partly due to the fact that they both speak the same superficial and fundamentally anachronistic language. And partly because they are both *necessarily* comprised by the logical pattern of a debate which, together, they constitute.

Accordingly, neither side spends any time on trying to find out precisely what new kind of power telematics really represents. For telematics is not repressive in the way in which its critics normally accuse it of being, or at least not quite so unambiguously repressive. Its critics tend to *simplify* telematics in order to make it fit into their standard critique of those in power. But this is both erroneous, and an unnecessary lapse in argumentative quality, because, as the result of this oversimplification, critics of the technology deprive themselves of the possibility of ever turning the technology to their own use. They deprive themselves of the possibility of influencing its design and development.

Characteristic of such criticism is its lack of imagination: confronted by something new in the shape of telematics, it can do no better than reduce it to something old — to an instrument of personal power, a tool of bureaucratic power, a war machine — to a traditional manifestation of power.

Power in the traditional sense was exercised through confiscation: those in power maintained it through their ability to confiscate the property of their subjects, and, in the last instance, their lives. The death penalty is the fundamental symbol of this kind of power.

But there is another way in which power manifests itself, which involves the oppressed's internalization of behavioural norms and values, reinforcing obedience to the *status quo*. Winston Smith's fate, after he has been in the Ministry of Love in *1984*, is appalling not because he has been deprived of his clothes and all his possessions (he didn't start out with very much!), nor because he is deprived of his youthful vigour, and virtually his life, through the ill-treatment he receives (his health wasn't all that good in the first place!) — nor even because he is deprived of Julia, the golden girl of his sensual and politically emancipative dreams. What is appalling about his fate is that he is successfully brainwashed into not wanting her any more, into not criticising what his intelligence tells him is arrant nonsense, into sanctioning himself, whenever he detects a desire in himself to go against the prevailing orthodoxy. The haunting message of the novel concerns the ability of the ongoing power structure to kill potential resistance in people without killing the people themselves, without necessarily confiscating either their property or their lives. When a metaphysically postulated Big Brother can make those people love him whom his disciples maltreat as badly as they do Winston, then we are confronted with a quasi-religious power which turns each individual into his own judge, and his own executioner if he oversteps the bounds which he has been taught to respect.

One thing is fiction, though, with the Grand Guignol effects of the Ministry of Love in *1984* — quite another is reality in industrial societies as we know them today. Yet even with the comparatively primitive telematics technology which is already widely available to us, we daily subject ourselves, of our own free will, to doses of a discreet, and, as it were, subliminal form of socialisation, which preserves and promotes the existing power structures of our societies. Every day we absorb — with fascination — examples of how to live: which house or luxury flat to buy, what to buy for its furnishing and decoration and improvement, what clothes and food and drink to buy — but, most important of all, examples, to, of how we ourselves and our families should *look* and *behave,* both inside and outside the home, in order to receive the social acceptance of our similarly 'attractively normal' friends, colleagues and business associates. With varying degrees of 'luxury', of course (though with *less* variable expenditure involved!), this unforgiving, relentless, and critically self-castigating pursuit of a glamourized normality arguably pertains at every level of society, from the executive with his well-ironed shirts, opinions, and behaviour, to the unemployed rocker with his uniformly noisy and provocative clothing, motorbike, attitudes, and activities.

Power of this kind need scarcely have recourse to external sanctions. The individual punishes himself — with a bad conscience, if in minor matters he fails to live up to the norms he daily programmes himself with, with days off work, depressions, a nervous breakdown — even, in the worst instance, with self-confiscation, i.e. suicide. Each individual (or the immediate social groups to which he belongs) is his own judge and executioner. Each individual tends not to spare himself, tends, rather, to be a hanging judge. More people commit suicide each year in Denmark than are killed in traffic accidents ....

Several hundred years have elapsed since power thrived in the traditional sense in Western Europe. Kings, dukes, feudal overlords ruled by virtue of their monopoly of the exercise of power. Their power consisted in the fact that they held the lives of their subjects in their hands. But, in post-feudal times, death began to lose its absolute power as knowledge increased about means of preserving and prolonging life. Improvements in agriculture, medicine and the economy, and in the societies' ability to develop and reproduce themselves, gave some relief from the ever-present threat of death characteristic of feudal times, but also contributed to the growing body of knowledge about how such societies might be transformed and self-regulated. The formulation of theories of political economy was one of the ways in which this tendency manifested itself scientifically, from Quesnay's tables of laws concerning the economic circulation in capitalist society, to Adam Smith's 'invisible hand'. Once a society 'automatically' ensures its own maintenance and improvement through the momentum of its own economy, the feudal overlord becomes superfluous.

The change from the consolidation of power through threats of deprivation in this life and damnation in the next, to the consolidation of power through self-administered brainwashing and do-it-yourself punishment, is not of course a transformation which takes place from day to day. It requires decades, perhaps even centuries. And even though the new form of power involving the self-programming of social norms has assumed a central position in today's industrialized societies, it still does so against a persistent background of traditional manifestations of power. In the old days, capital punishment was the natural order of the day; today it has been abolished virtually everywhere, but its spectre still haunts us from the wings. Today, punishment is meted out with rehabilitation as its ultimate purpose — but thoughts of revenge, of the maintenance of public order through terror, still exist, though they are perhaps considered to be pretty 'uncultivated' anomalies.

Essentially, however, we are witnessing trends in industrial societies towards the development of bloodless mechanisms for the maintenance of existing social orders, the development of humane, democratic — fully automatic — self-programmed living. This is why technology mediating socialisation of this kind both seems to be, and — in a very fundamental sense — actually is, the most modern technology we have. It is progressive, attractive, fashionable. Indeed, it is surely no exaggeration to claim that telematics is, in fact, the most advanced instrument of self-regulatory power which has ever become available to us — with its capacity, as a highly technically developed and omnipresent socializing tool, to make each individual the willing victim of his own internalized prejudices. Free of the trappings and symbols of physical oppressors, the invisibly governed members of today's welfare states govern themselves mentally at least as harshly as they were ever governed in feudal times.

If the above assumptions about the historical transformation of modes of power are correct, then the inevitable conclusion must be that many of the contemporary attacks on more traditional manifestations of power serve only to reinforce acceptance of the new kind of power.[22] If you like, you might say that criticism of capital punishment is criticism of a medieval manifestation of power. Of course criticism of this kind is important, because it consolidates and extols an historical advance. But, at the same time, it allows the new method of social control to get off scot-free. The criticism of medieval barbarity is an indirect expression of satisfaction with the new!

Even the Peace Movement sometimes seems to me to be guilty of this kind of quixotic attack on anachronisms, which can involve a dangerous blindness towards more insidious threats. I believe, for instance, that it is an anachronism to regard war as an extension of diplomacy — a comparatively new state of affairs, which, of course, it is essential to do everything in our power to prolong. But the qualitatively new element in the situation would be an understanding of war not as an extension of diplomacy but as a contrast to it — not as a present reality, as part of the business of everyday life, but as a remote abstraction, as a contrast to the business of everyday life. To talk seriously about destroying the entire population of the earth ten times over, or a hundred times over, or a thousand times over, would be tantamount to participating in serious political negotiations between the inmates of a lunatic assylum. Such figures are totally incomprehensible and constitute, therefore, a contrast of extreme abstraction to the real business of day-by-day diplomacy. But, for all its abstraction, the threat of total destruction is, however, ever present at the back of people's minds, and as such it contributes to the insecurity and the fear of unorthodoxy which promotes the desperately conservative acceptance of the *status quo* at all costs. As such, the abstract threat of total destruction reinforces the new form of social control.

Critics of telematics technology, which we have earlier defined as the culmination of the new form of *self*-regulatory power to date, often miss the point for the same reasons. What they tend to try to expose is, as we have seen, the existence of a small, self-appointed Machiavellian élite *behind* the new technology, or they try to prove that the technology is 'really and truly' *military* technology. The retrograde nature of their obsessive concentration on the — allegedly covert — past content of telematics technology is aptly symbolized by their appropriation of the anachronistic 400-year-old Baconian epigram, where some of Orwell's Ministry of Truth slogans might be more critically to the point: 'War is Peace', for example, or 'Ignorance is Strength'. No, criticism of this kind is too easy, and it costs you nothing. It is easy, because it is in complete accord with the spirit of our day and age. It costs you nothing, because it presents no threat to the new form of power, to the new kind of social conditioning, but, on the contrary, indirectly, and usually unconsciously, expresses a form of satisfaction with it. Critics of the new technology of manipulation who sensationally 'expose' allegedly conspiratorial groups of 'manipulators', or who 'expose' its connection with (anachronistic) military technology, are themselves guilty, in my eyes, of anachronism and self-deceit. They criticize some faint survivals of the past under the impression that they have 'seen through' telematics — which is how they are anachronistic, and how they deceive themselves. For, if the truth be known, their criticism is the best ally of the new, sophisticated form of social control. In 'exposing' the new technology, they affirm its efficiency. In *1984* neither Goldstein nor Big Brother are presumably still alive — or may ever have existed at all — but in continually denouncing the one and singing the praises of the other, the inhabitants of 'Airstrip 1' manifest their inability to think beyond these fictions — their duck-speaking inability to think anything other than what everybody else thinks.

9. MEDIATING THE QUALITATIVELY NEW: SOME SEMINAL EXAMPLES OF ONGOING SOCIAL EXPERIMENTS IN SWEDEN AND FRANCE.

9.1. *Proving the Pudding: All Good Theories are Practically Useful!*

Always there is the tendency to interpret the significance of telematics one-dimensionally. Some consider it categorically an instrument of oppression. Others, no less categorically, an instrument of liberation. Others again insist on its neutrality: technology is virginal, they say, its significance will always depend on whose hands it falls into.

Let me first remind the reader of the fallacy involved in this latter misconception. Any form of (communications) technology will possess social significance, which will influence the technology's own design and development. A part of this social significance will always consist of the implicit or explicit societal purpose which informs the design and production of the technology. The characteristics thus imparted to the technology will adhere to it, and will influence its subsequent possible usage.

The socially significant content of a multi-media cable network, for example, is eminently apparent in its structure. One has only to note who has access to the databases connected to it; which groups of users are nodally situated within the network; to what extent (and how) is access to the network's production facilities restricted. Or we could take videotex systems as an example: which particular social group of users' characteristic preoccupations are reflected in the choice of the alphanumeric search terms? What kind of socialisation is mediated through the 'menu' pages, with their particular lay-out and manner of listing the options or facilities available? What kind of manipulatory power is manifested in the major information suppliers' use of not particularly informative, but ostensibly entertaining graphics, with their blinking lights and childish appeal?

An even more obvious — and yet, in a curious way, much less obvious — example would be the old-fashioned communications media's stereotypic design, which has acquired a seemingly 'natural' inevitability in the course of time. The telephone, for example, is used for communication from one place of work to another or from one family to another, whilst radio and television establish links from private or public centralized authorities to private homes. In a manner which, by now, should not come as a surprise to us, the technological logic coincides precisely with the structure of the societies within which the technology was developed. The Indian who once remarked that telephony was unsuitable for use in village India because the sound of the bell was not loud enough to attract the attention of the entire village, and, worst of all, only one person at a time could listen in to it, or speak into it — that man had discovered the limitations of the technology, the way in which it imposes its social significance upon all its potential users.

'Technical specifications' are, similarly, actually specifications of the social significance of a given technology. This is very simply illustrated by the fact that a telephone which mediates communication from a single individual to a large audience by means of a cable is called a radio or T.V. 'microphone', while a radio which mediates communication by means of radio waves between two individuals only, is known as a (radio) telephone. Technology is, in other words, defined in terms of its social significance, despite the frequent assertions to the contrary which are put forward to commend (profitably produced) technology to potential customers on its own (often exaggeratedly abstruse) terms.

Technology, then, contains social significance and this significance informs the technology and adheres to it, even though one might subsequently want to use the technology for purposes other than those for which it was originally designed. The resultant temptation (which, however, is no less fallacious) is to conclude from this fact that technology is either essentially 'good' or essentially 'evil'. But this kind of one-dimensional conception of technology, while very properly taking into account the tendential content of the technology which has a crucial influence on its design and development, leaves *out* of account the fact that the technology also has latent social significance, for example with regard to utopian ideals of human freedom, mutual respect, and communion.

The ambivalent nature of technology derives, of course, from the abundance of contradictions prevalent in the society which produces it — an abundance of contradictions whose existence is testified by any criticism of the technology. For what else would provoke such criticism, were it not for an absence of consensus about means and ends within the society whose technology is being criticised? Any attempt — in the interests of defending controversial technology — to deny that such criticism reflects a lack of social consensus, deserves to be dismissed as an unusually obdurate form of philosophical idealism. While any attempt to deny the fact that this lack of social consensus about ends and means is deposited in the technology would, at best, amount to a form of materialism which has temporarily forgotten its historical epithet!

As I have already demonstrated in the structure of the opening chapters of this book, an analysis of I.T. systems has to *start* with the — fundamentally theoretical — distinction between technology *qua* technology and technology *qua* socially significant phenomenon. For technology does, of course, possess both a physio-logical and a socio-logical content, if I may be permitted to use the terms in their original senses. Subsequently, however, one can begin to reassemble the artificially separated component parts, analysing the ways in which the technical and the societal contents mutually affect each other. Subsequently one can analyse, in other words, the ways in which the technology's societal content has influenced its technical design and capabilities, on the one hand, and the ways in which the technical content of the technology has influenced its social significance, on the other — for example by obstructing, or accelerating, the realisation of its own latent utopian potential.

The reader will, no doubt, recognise that my remarks about satellite-, as opposed to cable-T.V., at the end of chapter two, provide an illustration of the first kind of analysis, together with the remarks I made at the end of my fifth chapter about the managerial control function of much of today's office automation technology. My remarks in chapter seven about digital or old-fashioned watch design would provide a further illustration, together with the example I gave above of the limitations of telephony in village India.

In illustration of the other kind of analysis — the analysis of how the technical content of the technology influences its social significance — I would remind the reader of my remarks concerning the dangers of electronic polling, in chapter six, as well as my remarks in chapter seven concerning the feelings of insecurity and homelessness which have resulted from the sophistication of the technology which has enabled us phenomenologically to transcend the boundaries of space. My remarks in the last chapter, concerning diplomacy and the abstract threat of destruction by the most efficient war technology ever developed, would provide a further example, and — on the positive side — I would remind the reader of my concluding remarks in chapter six about how the level of technical sophistication in both horizontal, and vertical, communication technology is now so far advanced that technocratic rationalists are confronted with an ambivalence which forces them to consider the political alternatives on their own terms, rather than in the pseudo-scientific terms which they themselves would prefer to use!

In this and the following chapter, however, it is not my intention to elaborate any further the theoretical framework for the political assessment of I.T. and telematics technology which it has been the book's primary purpose to expound and recommend. On the contrary, in the following pages I want to exemplify the *usefulness* of the theoretical framework (and of the concept of social significance in particular) for the purposes of applied research with regard to policy-making.

9.2. *The Necessity for Enthusiasm.*

Reconciling the latent potential of telematics with its more overt tendential content is difficult, if not impossible, but in the last two chapters of the book I shall be recommending what seems to me to be the only viable approach to the problem of putting telematics technology to the service of a more truly democratic society, to the service of a qualitatively different future. It is an approach involving publicly-influenced, interdisciplinary, long-term experimentation with the technology in appropriately selected and studied social contexts.

I started this section by saying that reconciling the latent potential of telematics with its more overt tendential content is difficult, if not impossible! But in my opinion it would be mistaken to accuse Daniel Bell, Alvin Toffler, Yoneji Masuda — and all the others whose day-dreams have been articulated in their writings — of peddling untruths. Marxist ideology critics may disagree, but for me it's not a question of reducing ideology to economics; phenomenological perceptions to some objective material reality; 'superstructures' to 'bases'. It's not a question, in other words, of crushing people's hopes with the dry-as-dust scepticism of 'scientific socialism'. What we are trying to analyse is an enormously complex social organism, shot through with contradictions, which it would be a decidedly reprehensible instance of reductionism to circumscribe within some dominating evolutionary tendency. And further, within the context provided by this complex social organism, we are trying to understand, and get to grips with, the comprehensive complexity of technical systems which clearly do display a predominantly commercial bias, but which nevertheless also contain within them latent potential which no such commercial bias, however blatant, can belie.

It's an old mistake, which socialist theorists should have got beyond, to turn their backs on whatever may or may not be possible, in order to devote their attention exclusively to whatever social transformations are actually and verifiably taking place under their noses.[23] It was a fatal blunder for the German socialists in the 1930s, for instance, since it played right into the hands of the Nazis — as Ernst Bloch reminds us. The socialists correctly saw what was coming, but they provided no inspiring alternatives.

Characterizing the unenthusiastic and uninspired economic analyses of the Marxist pedants of those days, which so inexcusably gave Hitler and Goebbels the monopoly of the German people's hopes and dreams, Bloch wrote:

> "They remind me of the results of chemical analyses in trade descriptions to be found on bottles of mineral water. Such an analysis is doubtless entirely correct, but it is no advertisement, and it is hardly complete, for it says nothing about what the water tastes like when you drink it."

Realism, let me hasten to add, is of course necessary; but dreams and hopes are not to be left out of account, precisely because they are, in themselves, elements of reality. Which is why it is wrong to dismiss contemporary scenarios and utopias as mere manipulation. They articulate the collective dreams of our existing societies, they are themselves products of our societies, and it is precisely in their relationship to our existing societies that their importance lies.

For me the inevitable conclusion is that, as a research worker, it is essential that one should approach new technology of the kind we are dealing with here, with a fundamentally enthusiastic and open-minded attitude. Not, of course, with the kind of naïve enthusiasm which may amount to a gratuitous legitimation of the unhindered realisation — in commercial terms — of the anti-social tendential content of the technology. But still with a moderately, and realistically, enthusiastic attitude — rather than with an all-too-sober attitude, which might dismiss the technology out of hand as being merely a manifestation of some late capitalist economic trend, or as being a mere tool in the hands of some evil institutionalized power. As we have seen, it could be a serious mistake to abandon dreams and hopes to those who represent the reactionary bias of the new information technology. No, it is up to us to wrest from these man-made tools their hidden potential for the development of our own fuller and richer humanity.

To give an idea of what some 'enthusiastic' social experiments with telematics could look like in practice, I have chosen to present one Swedish and several French projects in this chapter, before going on to elaborate the theory behind such experiments in my final chapter, and offering some practical guidelines for similar experiments in the future. The ongoing experiments which I have selected illustrate very clearly *both* how necessary such 'enthusiastic' initiatives are, *and* how vulnerable they are to delusions, of their own, and others', making. The critical strategy which strives to demonstrate how our societies *could be*, always runs the risk of losing sight of the fact that, in actual fact, they have not yet got that far! All too easily, we are confronted with efforts to realise and defend purely abstract utopias, the narrowly-conceived products of drawing-boards rather than the more realistic and complex products of controlled social evolution.

9.3. *Social Experiments with Telematics in France, Sweden and — ?*

Experiments with information and communications technology outside Europe are generally better known than the European social experiments, which is one reason for concentrating on the latter here in this chapter devoted to the presentation of some concrete examples of the experimental approach which I want to advocate.

There are, however, other reasons; at least when it comes to leaving out of account such well-known projects as the Hi-Ovis experiment in Japan, or the Qube-experiment in Columbus, Ohio. The former is generally agreed to have been disproportionately technically oriented, with the various button-pushing participants in the diminutive urban district chosen for the experiment merely dragged in to lend the whole thing an air of authenticity. And the electronic banking, shopping, and polling, in the Qube-experiment, also involved rather too much button-pushing, and not enough imaginative social thinking, as I pointed out in the first section of chapter 6 above.

I am, however, well aware of the fact that there are some far more promising projects under way in Canada, for example, and in Holland and Germany, to stay on this side of the Atlantic — but lack of space, rather than any other considerations, forces me to leave these latter social experiments aside.

9.3.1. *Grannskap 90: A Swedish Experiment with Remote Terminal Office Work.*

As we have seen, modern communications technology permits us to send text and pictures virtually instantaneously between geographically distant places by means of digital transmission networks. This fact opens up entirely new perspectives with regard to decentralized places of work, and with regard to new kinds of work itself. Remote terminal office work, for example, becomes a possibility. Already virtually half of Sweden's total labour force is involved in various different kinds of information processing — at least according to some estimates. And a substantial proportion of these 'information workers' are already equipped with telephones and keyboards and V.D.U.s. (The Swedish information given here was aquired on a field study trip to Nykvarn in early 1983).

That remote terminal office work is technically feasible is an indisputable fact. The disputes arise with regard to the various different estimates of the social consequences of remote terminal work. Some fear that it will lead to the increased isolation and reduced influence of the information worker, sitting all alone behind his domestic terminal. Deprived of professional and social intercourse with his colleagues, burdened by such domestic duties as child-minding and housework while he is trying to get on with the job, and constantly monitored by his employer, his 'emancipation' from the office will be merely synonymous with a new refined form of slavery. On the other hand, there are those who regard remote terminal office work in a more positive light: no more transport problems; flexible working hours; familiar and personally created surroundings which one otherwise spends virtually all one's waking hours working somewhere else to pay for.

In order to experiment in practice with I.T.'s and telematics' latent potential for countering the general social tendency — and the new technology's own generally recognized tendency — to isolate the individual worker, the Nordic Institute for Social Planning (Nordplan) initiated a project with what they call a 'Grannskapscentral'. The word 'grannskap' means 'neighbourhood' in Swedish, and the 'grannskapscentral' is a moderately-sized communal office situated in a particular neighbourhood. Equipped with voice, text, and data communications equipment, the office enables workers from the same neighbourhood to work together, doing different kinds of jobs for different employers elsewhere in the country. Some of the workers at the 'grannskapscentral' work there every day; others divide their weekly working time between the neighbourhood office and their own former offices elsewhere.

A number of difficulties had to be overcome before the project could get started: lack of interest on the part of the local authorities; union anxiety that projects of this kind would undermine existing shop-floor solidarity; and managerial scepticism with regard to the possibility of a reduction in productivity resulting from the extra (not insubstantial) capital outlay. Nevertheless, all these difficulties were finally overcome; amongst other things, by means of sponsorship agreements with various firms, who agreed to supply equipment free of charge. And in November 1982 the 5,000 inhabitants of the little community of Nykvarn, located some 25 miles outside Stockholm, were able to witness the inauguration of Sweden's first 'grannskapscentral'.

There were 10 workers at the 'grannskapscentral' in Nykvarn when I visited it in early 1983. It was, of course, far too early to draw any hard and fast conclusions from the project, but already some significant advantages and disadvantages had made themselves felt. Unanimous satisfaction was expressed about the reduction in commuting time, and about the fact that the new office was in the immediate vicinity of the workers' homes. Satisfaction was expressed, too, about the fact that the neighbourhood office has dispelled the isolation normally endemic to remote terminal work, in a manner which was generally considered to be socially acceptable. But dissatisfaction was expressed about the fact that one now had to go to work in two different places: one's former office, where one's participation in one's professional fellowship suffered from the relative infrequency of one's visits, and the neighbourhood office, where the fellowship was mainly centred on leisure time activities.

Hilkka Paavonen is the daily supervisor of the project, in which she herself participates, spending part of her time at the neighbourhood office working for a distant employer like all the others, and part of her time keeping a log-book monitoring developments on the project on a day-to-day basis. She is now firmly convinced that entirely different — and significantly more detailed — things may be learnt from a practical social experiment of this kind than may ever emerge from any theoretical speculations about the potential social effects of the introduction of the new information and communications technology. According to Hilkka Paavonen, it is a remarkable experience to observe the way in which work *qua* social activity undergoes a gradual transformation: originally characterized by an instrumental/functional orientation, it daily comes more and more to resemble a communal leisure-time activity. Since the 10 new 'colleagues' are doing different kinds of work for different employers, their place of work becomes a place where, as neighbours, they discuss such things as their children's schooling, their own living conditions, and many other aspects of the lives they lead in their 'after hours'.

And indeed, in my opinion, top priority must be given to monitoring this kind of development on a project of this kind. The transformation of work as a phenomenological entity must be monitored, and its positive or negative consequences, in the lives of the participants in the experiment, must be carefully and continuously evaluated. If work really does undergo something approaching the radical transformation which Hilkka Paavonen claims to have observed, then the results of experiments like this with remote terminal office work in neighbourhood offices may have enormous consequences for social organization in capitalist societies in the future.

On its own terms, the Swedish 'grannskapscentral' project has both experimental and demonstrative functions. At the local level, useful lessons may be learnt from it as an experiment with regard to remote terminal office work as a community-based activity. And at the same time it serves to demonstrate the fallacy of the assumption that remote terminal office work necessarily implies the isolation of the information worker behind a domestic terminal.

Seen from the outside, however, the Swedish project scarcely fulfils any of the criteria which I will list in the sections to come as being crucial to my definition of a truly valid social experiment. Its scope is far too limited for that - which, added to the fact that none of the present workers at the neighbourhood office are engaged in typical routine office-work, renders any general conclusions highly dubious, even if they are not publicly made known until a sufficiently long period of time has elapsed to confirm their reliability.

Enthusiasm, as I mentioned in my introduction to this chapter, is necessary, but may lead to delusions. To avoid them, it must be countered with a healthy degree of realism. Despite Hilkka Paavonen's very conscientious, but unfairly burdensome, labours, the continuous evaluation of the project may justly be criticized for not being sufficiently comprehensive. And in a truly valid social experiment, the participants themselves would have much more say in the design and development of every aspect — technical as well as social — of their 'grannskapscentral'. The Swedish project at Nykvarn is, in my opinion, to be regarded as more of an inspiration for a social experiment than as an actual social experiment itself.

9.3.2. *The Framework for Social Experiments in France.*

Of all the nations in the world, France is probably the one to have carried out most experiments with I.T. and telematics systems to date. This is largely due to a supportive political framework favouring such experiments on two grounds, for they contribute to the realisation of France's industrial policy and communications policy alike.

In December 1976, five years before the creation of Britain's ministry of technology, then President Giscard d'Estaing gave the top-ranking official at the French Ministry of Finance, Simon Nora, a few months in which to prepare a preliminary report "to stimulate thinking on how the computerization of society should be carried out". (Nora and Minc 1978: 3) Nora's report was to help the President to define the task of a commission whose duty was to make guideline proposals to the government — a commission which a closed session of the Council of Ministers in April 1975 had already agreed to set up. The reason for their decision was doubtless the same as the one expressed in the President's letter to Nora:

> "The applications of the computer have developed to such an extent that the economic and social organization of our society and our way of life may well be transformed as a result. Our society should therefore be in a position both to foster this development and to control it so that it can be made to serve the cause of democracy and human growth". (Nora and Minc 1978: 3)

Together with a younger inspector of finance, Alain Minc, and a team of expert consultants, Nora spent over a year preparing what was to become a controversial best-seller on its publication in January 1978: *L'Informatisation de la société*.

From their position at the Ministry of Finance, Nora and Minc were, of course, perfectly aware of the economic implications of a government computerization policy. But, for them, the larger political issues — the question of the concentration or decentralization of power in the French society of the future — were paramount: "The social effects of telematics", they wrote, "are undoubtedly more important than its economic effects, because they throw the traditional games of power into disorder". (Nora and Minc 1978: 49)

Given telematics' ambiguous potential — its tendential content favouring the centralization of power, and its latent potential as an instrument of decentralization — Nora and Minc felt that it was imperative for the state to side with the decentralizers, following a policy of deliberate intervention:

> "As of today, one must centralize only what has to be centralized, fragment anything that can be fragmented, and deal with essentials right away, reserving only exceptional matters for action at a higher level. [...] The government cannot limit itself to promoting equally all the modes of organizing data-pro-

> cessing techniques. The pressure in the direction of structured, centralized networks is so strong that it is necessary to counteract it. Some people claim then that the government engages in a discriminatory policy by favoring the promotion of decentralized, small-scale computerization. Yet it is the only way of maintaining some degree of autonomy and responsibility for the weakest actors on the social stage". (Nora and Minc 1978: 6)

Nora and Minc's impressive piece of pioneering work bore fruit which, in technological terms, might be considered at least as ambitiously visionary as the report itself. I refer, of course, to the construction of an experimental fibreoptic cable network in Biarritz, which Giscard d'Estaing gave his blessing to a year and a half after the publication of the report.

Nor has the subsequent swing to the left in French politics spelt the end of France's computerization under the paternal government auspices recommended by Nora and Minc. On the contrary, Mitterand's presidency has witnessed the implementation of many of their recommendations. In the first place, Mitterand has created the ministry of communications which Nora and Minc considered a *sine qua non* for a coordinated government development policy. The first minister of communications in France was George Fillioud, and, together with two other ministers with a keen interest in experiments with telematics, Louis Mexandeau from France's P.T.T., and Jean-Pierre Chévènement from the ministry for industry and research, he has initiated a number of projects which are in keeping with the humanist principles upheld by Nora and Minc. Indeed, in the beginning of 1982 Jean-Pierre Chévènement invited two researchers, Armand Mattelart and Yves Stourdzé, to prepare a report on the subject of technology, communications, and cultural diffusion. (Mattelart and Stourdzé 1982) The report was completed in August the same year, and is of particular interest in the present context because its authors made a point of stressing the importance of 'social experiments with telematics'. Mattelart and Stourdzé defined the necessary procedures for such experiments as follows:

1. The scope and exact locations of the experiments should be the outcome of *negotiations between the local authorities involved and the central government*.

2. The experiments themselves must be technically *'open-ended'*: an example they give is the highly successful electronic mail system which was not originally intended to be part of the major interactive videotex project in three Parisian suburbs which was started in July 1981, but which was evolved as the result of an initiative on the part of the local citizens participating in this

project.

3. The experiments should focus on *communal* network usage. Throughout the present century the development of electronic media has reflected a preoccupation with the needs of private individuals. It is therefore of vital importance that the network's interactive potential be developed so that the electronic media may serve communal interaction needs.

4. *The experiments should take place over a reasonably long period of time* (a year or more), for the pace of the development of new technology usage is slower than the normal pace of technical development *per se*.

5. *Traditional location criteria for such experiments should be reconsidered.* Geographical factors have traditionally been decisive for the scope and location of the experiments, but — precisely because they are fundamentally 'social' experiments — it might perhaps be better to let other social criteria define the experiments' boundaries: occupational, ethnic, or other interest groups, might for instance provide stimulating experimental contexts.

6. Care must constantly be taken to strike a balance between the necessary coordination of these experiments and their no less *essential autonomy*. Standardized solutions are to be avoided at all costs, but this should not exclude the possibility of different local populations and groups learning things which are of mutual interest and benefit from each other's different experiences. (Matelart and Stourdzé 1982: 19) Here again, incidentally, one is reminded of the seminal influence of Nora and Minc's report: "No global scenario", they had written, "can be imposed from a single center without suffocating society or paralyzing the government. Therefore, it is necessary to conciliate a maximum of freedom and a minimum of coordination, to facilitate change rather than impose it." (Nora and Minc 1978: 101)

Not, perhaps, as idealistic as Mattelart or Stourdzé, but by no means unsympathetic towards their conclusions, Louis Mexandeau, formerly France's P.T.T. minister before the postal and telecommunications service became annexed to the industry ministry in the March 1983 reshuffle, considered that social experiments with telematics should at least satisfy the following three requirements. In the first place they should redress the deficiencies of traditional market surveys for the technology; it is difficult, if not impossible, accurately to predict the demand for electronic services which the public have not previously had access to, or any practical acquaintanceship with. Secondly, they should provide common ground for a dialogue between technicians and social scientists, who have traditionally been insufficiently knowledgeable about each others' fields, and whose collaboration is essential, in Mexandeau's opinion, for the successful development of viable information and communications systems. And, thirdly, social experiments of this kind should take place in clearly defined social, cultural or geographical contexts, permitting easier supervision, control and analysis, and reducing investment risks. (Mexandeau 1982: 11)

In effect, France has followed a clear and relatively unambiguous I.T. and telematics policy since the publication of Nora and Minc's *L'Informatisation de la Société* in January 1978. Yet the various social experiments with the new technology in France have so far exhibited considerable diversity. The fact that some of the experiments were initiated under the Gaullist Giscard d'Estaing's presidency, and others under the socialist Mitterrand's, may not be entirely insignificant after all.

9.3.3. *French Pilot Projects: Technology in Quest of Social Needs.*

As the result of the enlightened political climate which I have described above, the development of interactive videotex has been tackled in quite another way in France, where the latent potential of the technology for the creation of a decentralized and truly democratic information society has not been sacrificed on the altars of the Molochs of Economics or Technology, as has been the case in Britain and Denmark respectively. Instead, a number of different pilot projects have been based on the same initial assumption that videotex was not yet ready to be turned over to the free market, and attempts have been made in the various projects to adapt videotex, as a virginal piece of information and communications technology, to a variety of different social needs. The largest and most costly of these pilot projects is perhaps the '3V' videotex project in the three Parisian districts of Vélizy, Versailles and Val-de-Bièvre, which was started in July 1981 and which has the participation of 2,500 users. Each of these users has been equipped with a V.D.U. and an alphanumeric keyboard, and all the terminals are linked to a central database by means of the telephone network. (The information given about the projects in Paris, Grenoble and Nantes was acquired 'first hand' in the spring of 1983).

Télétel, as this videotex project is called in France, is primarily designed to provide an electronic information service. All the users have access to some 180 information providers who provide traditional information services — time-tables, pages from reference books, etc. — as well as a number of other technically more demanding interactive services — banking, ticket reservations, more advanced forms of on-line searching, etc. A number of services have also been added with continually updated information. However, two other experiments have been carried out under the auspices of Télétel which are perhaps even more of interest. The first of these is the electronic mailing system, which was referred to in my previous section. The 2,500 users in the three districts involved in the Télétel project can send electronic mail to each other which they have typed out in their terminals. Instant or delayed written electronic communication from person to person, or from one person to a group of others, has become a possibility, in other words, within the terms of the Télétel project. Following the same principles as an answer-phone system, the electronic communication is automatically deposited in an electronic 'mailbox'. At its recipient's leisure, it can be retrieved and displayed on his V.D.U. 'Circular letters', too, can simultaneously be sent out to a large number of pre-selected recipients — notices of meetings in a bridge or chess club, for instance.

Apparently, this experiment has been highly successful. Almost all the project's participants have subscribed to this electronic mailing system. Societies and private persons alike have made use of it; an electronic 'personal column' has come into being; and study groups have been created among closed groups of users, in which a number of people study together and communicate with each other by means of instant or delayed electronic correspondence.

The second innovation within the framwork of the Télétel project is a C.A.L. (computer aided learning) experiment called 'Didaotel'. This experiment involves as many as 20,000 pages of information, corresponding to some 300 study hours, and interactive question-and-answer facilities form an integral part of the learning service.

All in all, and most importantly, this ambitious '3V' videotex project has served the purpose of casting light on the wide variety of uses to which videotex may be put. Not only can it supply a vast range of useful and topical information, but it can also facilitate written communication between private persons and between officials and rank-and-file members of clubs and organisations. Perhaps uninformed criticism might dwell on the fact that Télétel has proved to be unexpectedly costly. But, as the reader will no doubt have realised by now, the long-term results of social experiments of this kind — whether measured in terms of marketing and product development or in terms of benefits to the consumers — are, to put it mildly, cheap at the price.

A more serious criticism might be that a still disproportionate amount of time has been spent on the technical rather than the social aspects of the experiment.

There are, however, several other videotex pilot projects in France which deserve to be mentioned here — projects in which videotex is used as a means by which local public authorities can provide citizens with necessary and useful information. One of these is in Grenoble. The system is called CLAIRE, and it was initiated in December 1981 after a couple of years' preparation. The system involves a central database (which is located in Paris, incidentally!) and 35 terminals which have been installed in various public places in and around Grenoble — in post offices, shopping centres, municipal offices, public libraries, etc. The database has 15,000 pages of information, partly of an official nature concerning municipal affairs — opening-times, legal advice, social service information, public meetings, etc. — and partly concerning local clubs and associations. 2,000 of the latter have been assigned a couple of pages each in the database on which to present their aims, officials' addresses, most important activities, regular meeting-times, forthcoming events, etc.

As I mentioned above, this project in Grenoble was only initiated after two years of intensive preparation during which sociologists studied the information needs of the local population and, by means of surveys, established which people and institutions had earlier been approached to satisfy those needs. At the present time the project is fully under way, and it is subject to regular assessment by a team of research workers from Grenoble University. Not insignificantly, cable-TV networks have existed in Grenoble for a long time, due to its mountainous location, and in time it is hoped that it will be possible to link the information system to one of these cable networks in the city. The idea is to develop a multi-media cable system, with the city authorities as cable owners, and with the city's own population providing and availing themselves of their own services. The plan is, in other words, to combine national, international, and local T.V. reception with CLAIRE, the existing interactive videotex information system.

Far away from the Alps — on the other side of the country, in fact — a similar municipal information service has been developed in Nantes. TELEM-NANTES it's called, and, like the videotex system in Grenoble, its aim is to provide rapid, comprehensive, and easily available information to the local citizenry. In addition, it is hoped that the population will acquire a useful degree of familiarity with modern information technology, and the system will act as a good advertisement for the city generally. As in Grenoble, TELEM-NANTES is in the hands of the local public authorities. It is run by the municipality — though any societies, cultural institutions, etc. are free to provide it with information — and the 30 public terminals have been set up in post offices, public libraries, and similar places.

In contrast to the '3V' pilot project mentioned earlier, the videotex information systems in Grenoble and Nantes are relatively inexpensive. Something in the region of $170,000 were invested in the Nantes project, including a generous investment by the French P.T.T., and the annual running costs for men and materials barely exceed a similar moderate figure. So such systems are scarcely a burden on the budget of any larger city — Grenoble, for example, has 300,000 inhabitants — and they will presumably become even less expensive in the future, when mass-produced terminals hit the market in a big way, and database capacity is extended so that a single database can be shared by several cities, with attendant economies of scale. But the financial side is, of course, always only of relative importance, as we shall see. The great virtue of these two projects is that they are run by the cities themselves as public enterprises, aiming to discover through social experiments in practice what sort of a future videotex may have as a local information system.

The projects clearly suffer, however, from the fact that they are not — as yet — as technically advanced as the more costly Télétel '3V' system. Two-way communication is not yet possible within the systems, and, according to local officials, members of the public are unable to use them without assistance from the staff at the institutions where the terminals have been installed. A further weakness, too, is the very time-consuming procedures involved in updating or supplementing the databases. Instead of using a modern database management system to imonitor usage levels and permit automatic updating by the information providers themselves, the local authorities in Grenoble and Nantes only permit the information providers to make alterations to the database via public officials, after filling out innumerable forms!

The local information systems in Grenoble and Nantes are thus quite clearly 'first generation' systems. But, in contrast to so many other videotex projects, the social experiments with the new technology in France have, as a clearly defined long-term goal, the satisfaction of current and future local communications needs, and most people have no doubt at all that in Grenoble and Nantes we have only seen the initial stages of a much more comprehensive development of locally-based, and user-friendly, information and two-way communication systems.

9.3.4. *Marseille: 1,000 Microcomputers in the 'Belle de Mai' District.*

In contrast to the three videotex-projects mentioned in the previous section, what is characteristic of the 'Belle de Mai' project in Marseille is its attempt to transcend the limits of the centralized information provision: in the Marseille experiment the idea is that the participants themselves will supply, administer, and use their own databanks.

In his capacity as Mayor of Marseille, France's Home Secretary Gaston Deferre signed a deal in 1982 under which the so-called World Centre for Computing and Human Resources — (which I shall be dealing with more fully later on in the present chapter) — was to carry out an experiment in Marseille, with the aim of studying the reactions of the inhabitants of a limited area of the city to the possibilities and challenges of the new computerized information technology. At the present time of writing, the 17,000 inhabitants of the relatively poor 'Belle de Mai' district — many of whom are immigrants, incidentally — are witnessing the installation of 1,000 microcomputers under the supervision of 15 research workers (physicists, psychologists, sociologists, educational researchers, etc.), who are to be responsible for planning, coordinating and evaluating the project, as well as for instructing the local population in how to operate the equipment. (Information about this and the following project was acquired on a study visit to Marseille in the spring of 1983).

The first phase of the experiment is exclusively educational: 500 pupils at the local Edouard Vaillant state school have already had the chance to learn to use computers using M.I.T. researcher Seymour Papert's LOGO-system. The — as yet unfinished — second phase involves equipping clubs and societies in the area with microcomputers, and developing systems linking them together through the telephone network. According to the supervisors of the project, the idea is to adapt the technology to the requirements of the various participants, whether private individuals or associations. In previous experiments with telematics, users have merely gained access to databanks already in existence; in the 'Belle de Mai' project, the idea is that the individuals and organizations concerned are to be enabled to build up their own communal databank.

One of the most positive aspects of this experiment is, then, the attempted transcendence of the rigid distinction between information suppliers and users. And another positive aspect is the decentralisation of the information storage. But it is an open question whether the participants in the experiment who have no special training will be willing to learn a system like LOGO, in order to operate the equipment which is being placed at their disposal. And it is an even more open question whether one actually can leave it up to the local population concerned to carry out a social experiment to the extent intended here. At Marseille, the idea is that the local population of the 'Belle de Mai' district will carry out their own social experiment, will compile their own databases. But the problem would seem to be that, in the initial phase of the experiment, the participants are to be given what by any previous standards would be considered to be a very low level of supportive service.

9.3.5. *The Fibreoptic Cable Network in Biarritz.*

This, the first Nora-Minc inspired project in France, was started in September 1979 under Giscard d'Estaing's Gaullist presidency. In marked contrast to the Marseille experiment, with its considerable dependence on its users' own initiative, and deliberate subordination of the technical aspects, the Biarritz social experiment has had a rather more typical technical bias. From the first, the aim was to give experts insight into the operation of a typical small town fibreoptic cable network — its construction, utilization and maintenance — under realistic conditions. The public demand for — and exploitation of — two-way audio-visual services was to be monitored; and France's industrial production of fibreoptic cable was to be helped to develop, with Biarritz becoming an international showroom for the industry. In keeping with the pilot project's avowed primary purpose (i.e. the furtherance of France's industrial policy), Biarritz became the chosen location not only because of its reasonably small size, but also because of the reputation the town already enjoyed as an internationally famous seaside resort.

Installing the star-switched fibreoptic cable network — cabling the many different households — has been more technically demanding than was originally expected, and the cabling was not completed until late 1983. Facilities to be provided through the network include rediffused radio and television programmes, local interactive information and entertainment services, and a video telephone service. There are to be 15 separate T.V. channels and 12 channels for stereophonic radio reception. But the video telephone service will undoubtedly be the most demanding in terms of cable capacity: as well as dialogue, live black-and-white images are simultaneously to be transmitted from private home to private home; between private homes and public offices and local shops; and between 'professionals', i.e. internally between local offices and local businesses. Additional cable capacity will be utilized for an interactive videotex service (of the kind already operating in the French '3V' experiment, for instance) as well as for a local video programme bank or videothèque, where orders may be received from private homes for entertaining, cultural, or educational programmes which may subsequently be rediffused down the cable network.

The fibreoptic cable network in Biarritz is to become operational in early 1984. Technically, as I have indicated above, it is highly advanced. Socially, however, it has encountered growing scepticism from French telematics researchers. As a social experiment it is already virtually obsolete, even before it has had the chance to get off the ground.

9.3.6. *The World Centre for Computing and Human Resources.*

According to Jean-Jacques Servan-Schreiber, author of *Le Défi Mondial*, computers have always been the tools of cultural imperialism. To date they have never accepted any language other than English, Japanese or French, perhaps, in exceptional cases, but, for example, never on any account Ouolof — the native language of the majority of the population of the former French colony of Senegal! This fact, Servan-Schreiber maintained, has contributed to the growing inequality between the highly industrialized nations of the world and the Third World countries. But the discrepancy between the Northern and Southern nations is in reality to no one's advantage, and Servan-Schreiber has therefore recommended a technical and economic Third World development programme of previously unknown dimensions — a new global Marshall Plan, as it were.

Such, at any rate, was the ideological background for his 1981 application to the new socialist president, François Mitterand, for funds to help him to found his idealistic French computing centre. And Mitterand clearly saw certain possibilities in the idea, for he gave Servan-Schreiber a government grant of some 20 million dollars over two years to help get the project on its feet. The President's decision was made in September 1981. The official opening of the Centre took place on November 20th the same year. And in March 1982 the Centre was fully operational.[24]

Situated in the Avenue Matignon, two minutes' walk from the Champs Elysée, the imposingly named 'Centre Mondial Informatique et Ressources Humaines' now houses a research staff of 25, 10 of whom are from the U.S.A., including several from M.I.T. There can be no doubt about the global pretensions of the Centre: its concern with the growing gap between the rich and the poor nations of the world; and its more specific concern with the relationship between automation and unemployment. But it has nevertheless become increasingly clear that the Centre's high-level R. and D. is above all expected to stimulate the *French* microelectronics industry, and to help prepare the way for the successful computerisation of the Centre's *own* society! Seymour Papert, whose LOGO system of learning has been used by the Centre in the 'Belle de Mai' project in Marseille, as I mentioned earlier in this chapter, has already left the Centre in protest against this growing tendency to pander to its host country's industrial policy.

Not that the Centre's overriding scientific aims are in any way problematic. Its declared intentions involve uniting social science and computer technology, and developing them sufficiently fast to beat the growing negative effects of automation. A basic tacit assumption at the Centre is that the development of computer technology exhibits two conflicting tendencies. The first involves increasing factory and office automation and rational managerial control. The second tendency, repressed by the first, involves the possible development of personal computers which will directly correspond with the needs and qualifications of ordinary people. The aim of the research work at the Centre is to place this second tendency on an equal footing with the first, by concentrating, for the time being, on this 'repressed' tendency — by developing, in other words, technology which anybody and everybody can use as spontaneously as they speak, write, or draw.

The essential duality of the problems raised by the new technology is clearly expressed in the Centre's manifesto, where it is stated that the Centre's research area is not computer science in any traditional sense, nor any of its derivatives such as office automation, numerical control, or hardware and software for existing large-scale systems. On the contrary, its aim is to unite social science and computer technology in what is somewhat vaguely termed a joint 'science de l'artificiel'. Similarly, full employment, in the traditional sense, is in the Centre's ideology less important than the full employment of each individual's personal resources, engaging both halves of the brain.

The same idea informs the organisation and design of the Centre, too. Far from being an ivory tower, it is situated right in the heart of Paris, with direct access from the street 24 hours a day, seven days a week. The ground floor is equipped for teaching, and is filled with a constant stream of visitors — schoolchildren on computer courses, or just curious passers-by who drop in to have a look around, to try out the machines, or to make enquiries.

Both ambitious and comprehensive, the Centre's R. and D. programme requires not inconsiderable resources, however. During the course of the first two years the 20 million dollar grant will be used, amongst other things, to pay for an increase in the number of highly-qualified research workers. By the end of 1983 there should be a hundred of them, working under optimal conditions in three main fields — doing theoretical research; social experiments in France; and pilot projects in the Third World. As far as the first two fields are concerned, comprehensive social experiments with telematics have been planned for the Aix-Marseille region, and current theoretical projects include 'computerization, cultural development and education'; 'man-machine interface problems'; 'the relationship between programming and natural languages'; 'decentralized access for computer users'; and 'user-friendly microcomputer design'.

The first of these theoretical projects was under the leadership of the American Seymour Papert until, as I mentioned earlier, he broke his two-year contract in protest against the French government's not entirely disinterested curiosity about his work. Concerned with the use of computers in the classroom, Papert's project was based on the initial assumption that traditional schooling is repressive. "I think schools generally do an effective and terribly damaging job of teaching children to be infantile, dependent, intellectually dishonest, passive and disrespectful to their own developmental capacities", he wrote in a *Times Educational Supplement* article published in May 1982. And he continued:

> "The anti-social nature of school undoubtedly has roots in the class structure of society and in the nature of the Freudian unconscious. As long as important bodies of knowledge (such as school mathematics and the written language) are not rooted in the desires and the life experience of children, schools will have to teach them artificially and by force". (Papert 1982)

Papert believes that computers in the classroom, far from reinforcing the repressive tendencies of schooling generally, can act as a force to revolutionize the children's learning environment. Using the sort of software which he has developed, C.A.L. systems permit children to learn mathematics on a do-it-yourself basis in a manner similar to the way in which they acquire their own native language.

An avowed idealist, Papert feels that if the latent potential of classroom computer technology is developed along similar lines everywhere, then "school, defined as a place where the three R's are imposed by force (or by the kind of subterfuge called 'motivation' which is just as bad) will no longer be necessary. Society will be able to face the task of inventing environments in which children can develop as social, loving, honest human beings without distorting this goal by the crudely technical one of stuffing the multiplication tables into their heads". (Papert 1982: 41)

At the Centre Mondial Informatique et Ressources Humaines, it is, however, the Third World pilot projects which have aroused the greatest interest so far. At the moment there are two of them. The first of them aims to develop the software which will permit the Ouolof-speaking population of the former French colony of Senegal to make use of microcomputers. At the present time, some of the scientists at the centre are doing the theoretical work on the software, while others are helping children from Senegal to learn how to operate computers. Later on, the aim is to develop portable computers responsive to voice control in local languages, which will cost less than 500 francs—i.e. less than an old-fashioned black-and-white T.V. set.

The second of these projects involves the development of microcomputers for Third World medical personnel. Stocked with data about the diagnosis and treatment of various illnesses, these computers are to present their information largely by means of graphics, so even illiterate personnel will be able to make use of it.

In order to realise all its projects, the World Centre for Computing and Human Resources has had to draw on many different contacts in the electronics industry from all over the world. Nippon Electric from Japan has contributed some speech recognition equipment, for example, while other high-capacity computing equipment has been obtained from the American firm of Digital. And microcomputers from Apple (another American firm), from the British firm of Sinclair, and from Thompson-CSF of France, are undergoing modification and refinement as part of the Centre's R. and D. programme.

I have already hinted that the host country's interest in the centre might be more compromising than helpful, however, and, in the face of Papert's withdrawal, one is tempted to ask whether there is any reason why the Centre should not be moved to any other host country, in view of its declared international aims and its collaboration with the electronics industries of many different countries around the world. According to Nicholas Negroponte, another M.I.T. research worker at the Centre, there are, however, at least two good reasons for keeping it in France (as reported in Bonnet 1982).

The first is that it would be folly to ignore the relative sophistication which has already been attained in many areas by the French telecommunications and microelectronics industry: a fact which makes the nation a stimulating milieu for I.T. and telematics research. And the second reason is the political one that France alone, of all the countries of the world (including Japan), has decided to take up the challenge offered by the world economic recession and develop its society in accordance with a vision of a *qualitatively* different future. Social and political factors in France have thus combined to make available large sums of money for social experiments, which avowedly aim to combine support for France's microelectronics and cable industries with the socially responsible development of I.T. and telematics technology.

There can be no doubt at all about the fact that, as Negroponte maintains, the French government is determined to help the nation's electronics industry as much as it possibly can. The former minister for industry and research, Jean-Pierre Chévènement, considered such support to be one of the highest priorities for President Mitterrand, and at the time of writing there are rumours in government circles of a proposed total investment of some 17 billion dollars in the electronics industry for the period 1982-86. Private and public sector activities are to be coordinated within an overall framework, permitting long-range planning which will make it possible to combine research, education, industrial production, and the cultivation of private and public demands for the industry's new products.

So the only hope at Servan-Schreiber's World Centre for Computing and Human Resources — and it is a fervent hope — is that this national economic tendency will complement, rather than sabotage, the socially progressive development of I.T. and telematics technology. And in actual fact it is this balancing act which constitutes the essential experiment of the World Centre itself, at the present time. If the Centre does succeed in holding these two normally conflicting tendencies in an acceptable balance, we shall be able to conclude that the entire project amounts to an admirable practical realisation of the concept of 'social experiments with telematics'. But Papert's defection scarcely augurs well for the future of the Centre, and most observers would agree that there are a great many daunting practical difficulties ahead. Enthusiasm, in other words, has been (and will again be) put to a very stiff test on this ambitious project.

10. THE ONLY CONCEIVABLE WAY FORWARD — SOCIAL EXPERIMENTS WITH TELEMATICS: THEORY, SUMMARY, PRACTICAL GUIDELINES, CONCLUSION.

10.1. *Some Fundamental Points in the Definition of the Theoretical Concept of Social Experiments with Telematics.*

In briefly defining the scientific approach which it has been the purpose of this book to recommend — the 'social experiments with telematics approach' — one would have to start by insisting on the fact that these experiments take ongoing social conditions as their point of departure rather than any particular technical system. The distinction must be made, in other words, between *technical* or *technological* experiments whose primary purpose is to test out some new device or technical system, and in which human participation is merely a necessary precondition, and *social* experiments, whose primary purpose is to test the function and significance of technical systems in and for specific social settings. The basis and the point of departure for the latter kind of experiments is the structure of social needs, or — to use a better explanatory concept — the 'societal demand'. For it is in this way that social experiments are also to be distinguished from traditional methods of market analysis. Not the needs of the market, but the needs of the society as a whole are the object of this kind of analysis, and this, in turn, means that social experiments can remedy the deficiencies of traditional methods of market analysis, due to the fact that so many of the markets for new I.T. and telematics systems do not already exist, and so many of their potential customers are not identifiable in advance.

The second point one would have to insist on is that social experiments with telematics are dynamic development projects in which the technology is not regarded as already 'perfected', but as 'perfectible' — i.e. it has to be continually modified or supplemented — in a Hegelian dialectic, as it were — throughout the duration of the experiment. This means that social experiments with telematics emphasize the importance of an open-ended and progressive R. and D. policy for the new technology.

Taken together, these first two points concerning social experiments with telematics conflict with more traditional and generally held beliefs about technology. Traditionally, technology has been thought of as being primarily based on the natural sciences, on the traditional study of objective and eternally valid laws of nature. As such, it has enjoyed a sacrosanct final authority, providing an expectant and grateful mankind with immutable 'finished' products. More recently, this 'objective', 'value-free', natural scientific rationality, which has legitimated so many different products of technology, has been challenged as a cover, frequently promoting the interests of various sections of society at the expense of others; promoting economic interests, for example, or totalitarian state interests.[25]

Social experiments with telematics, however, allow technology to be developed neither purely in order to satisfy economic interests, nor purely in order to satisfy the interests of (unrepresentative) governments requiring more efficient means of state control. By means of the social experiments which I am advocating, the societies themselves will be able to develop the new technology to suit their own varieties of needs, instead of becoming enmeshed in a web of technical systems legitimated from above in terms of some abstract reasons of state.

This is not to say that I would consider it possible or desirable to produce complex I.T. systems in amateur street-corner community workshops! Telematics systems are the joint products of a combination (albeit a frequently unacknowledged combination) of social and natural science, and it would of course be absurd to deny the extremely sophisticated technical content of the technology. But what I have been arguing against throughout this book is the fallacy of neglecting, or marginalizing, the attendant social, political and cultural content which is ultimately of far greater importance. All too often, this latter content is 'smuggled in', as it were, when technical systems are introduced into our societies, in that, regrettably, the natural sciences frequently — and unawares — serve ends which more properly belong within the domain of the social sciences. I refer, of course, to the fact that much technology, which at first sight seems merely to be involved in the 'innocent' and truly admirable manipulation of physical nature, frequently turns out subsequently to be at least as much involved in the — somewhat less innocent and admirable — covert manipulation of human beings.

But let me repeat: it is, of course, out of the question seriously to entertain any hopes of amateur, community-produced, 'do-it-yourself' I.T. and telematics technology. On the other hand, though, existing clearly-defined social communities can — and in my opinion should — function as workshops, in themselves, for developing the social aspects of these information and communication systems. Of course this means that there will be no small amount of conflicts and ambiguities inherent in the 'social experiment with telematics' situation: the virtue of the approach is merely to ensure that the technology at least has some chance to develop in accordance with the real developing needs of all its enormous amount of potential users; that our societies at least have some chance to influence the further design and development of the technology which is placed at their disposal, however narrow the particular social interests it may originally represent.

As far as technology is concerned, a further consequence of my recommended approach is that a particular type of technology is necessary for the success of the social experiment. It must be an essentially flexible sort of technology, in that its technical content must not unambiguously and irrevocably prescribe its social significance. Atomic energy, for instance, is an example of technology of this latter inflexible kind: its social significance can never avoid the necessity of the well-controlled, centralized, hierarchical society. Telematics, on the other hand, would seem to be essentially flexible: any given I.T. system which consists of a network and a number of linked services is by no means already a finished product, but rather constitutes the starting point for a process of further development.

A further point one would have to insist on, in defining the concept of 'social experiments with telematics', is the fact that the concept has normative significance. This means, in other words, that any proposed pilot project has to satisfy certain stringent criteria if it is to be regarded as a true social experiment. Far from being loosely applicable to any sort of telematics project, the concept, if it is formulated sufficiently precisely, can thus serve as a yardstick by which to judge and evaluate such projects. Used normatively in this way, 'social experiments with telematics' provide, incidentally, no guarantee that the latent potential of the technology on trial actually can be realised in the kind of societies we know today. On the other hand, it is worth noting that such experiments do not automatically exclude this possibility in advance, but rather — with a persistent optimism — they ensure that at least some attempt is made to discover whether the latent potential of the technology perhaps can be realised under existing social conditions after all.

Finally, one would have to insist on the fact that the concept of 'social experiments with telematics' rests on the assumption that human needs are not static entities, but are in effect continuously evolving. As I have tried to argue in my earlier chapters in this book, specific human needs cannot constitute eternally valid norms for judging or evaluating the social significance of technology. New human needs are continuously being created, and existing patterns of needs are constantly being modified, as the result of the ongoing interaction between man and man, and man and nature — controlled, or not yet controlled. Stripped of its normative or critically reactionary pretensions, the assertion of an eternally valid 'human nature' boils down to a single, irrevocable choice, which civilisation as we know it today has already made a very long time ago: the choice between bestial need satisfaction and civilisation itself.

The essentially relative nature of human needs is yet another argument supporting the choice of existing, clearly socio-culturally defined, local communities as the optimum forum for the development of telematics technology: communities which are in effect already phenomenologically defined precisely by existing collective needs for such things as fellowship and intercommunication and communal political and cultural activities.

In addition to insisting on the above fundamental points, it might also be advisable to emphasize that the concept of 'social experiments with telematics' is not a concept formulated in order to *compete* with any other existing concepts, such as the concept of 'technology assessment'. This latter concept can neither be threatened nor vindicated by the launching of the concept of social experiments with telematics, which makes no pretensions to conceptual imperialism. In relation to technology assessment in any traditional, literal sense, social experiments with telematics are something quite different: they are, as I mentioned earlier, open-ended, progressive, and future-oriented, and instead of starting with the technology itself, they start with ongoing social conditions and needs.

Technology assessment is, of course, a blanket term covering a multitude of widely and essentially different evaluative projects and activities; which fact in itself provides some justification for the formulation of a new and more precise concept. But, in mentioning the concept of technology assessment here, I am simply referring to the traditional American definition of it as provided by the Office of Technology Assessment in Washington, D.C. According to this definition, technology assessment involves a variety of policy studies which systematically analyse the effects on society which occur when some technological innovation is launched, or is launched onto a wider market, or is modified in some significant way. Assessment of this kind focuses on the unintentional or indirect consequences of technology, or on consequences which only appear at some later date. One of its aims can also be to enable decision-makers to exercise effective social control over the technology concerned. (Coates 1982)

If we can accept a fairly narrow definition like this of the concept of technology assessment, then we can point to at least three significant contrasts between technology assessment, on the one hand, and social experiments with telematics on the other. In the first place, as I have just mentioned, the logical point of departure for technology assessment is technology itself, while social experiments logically start out from an analysis of a whole society, or at least of a representative segment of a society. Instead of with a technological system, social experiments with telematics start, in other words, with a system of communal human needs.

Secondly, the aim of technology assessment is to describe, and/or predict, the consequences of the introduction of the technology which is under analysis. The purpose of a social experiment with telematics, on the other hand, is to pinpoint and describe societal needs for information processing and communication — whether in the commercial, political, or private spheres of the society or community under analysis — with a view to ensuring the appropriate design and development of I.T. and telematics systems capable of satisfying such needs.

Thirdly, technology assessment frequently has a potentially regulative function — i.e. it frequently prepares the ground for legislation regarding new technology — while social experiments with telematics tend to come into the picture at an earlier stage, since they are more concerned with the promotion of technological development itself. The technical systems actually used in social experiments with telematics are by no means regarded as finished products in any way, which are to be regulated *post factum*, as it were: they are regarded rather as embryonic systems which are to be developed in mutual accord and correspondence with continuously developing societal needs.

10.2. *Why and How Social Experiments with Telematics Can and Must Be Carried Out.*

In this section I want to try to answer three very basic questions on a rather more pragmatic level. Why should one carry out social experiments with telematics? How must one carry out social experiments with telematics?

And why and how is it possible to carry out social experiments with telematics?

The answer to the first question involves sociopolitical considerations; the answer to the second involves considerations of commercial and industrial policy; and the answer to the third involves a consideration of the specific nature of telematics technology itself.

In sociopolitical terms, the reasons why one ought to carry out social experiments with telematics are, of course, based on the desirability of designing information and communication systems which contribute to the spiritual and material welfare of each and every citizen within any given society. As we have seen, such systems can have enormous influence on each individual's working life, political life, and private life respectively. This means that it is a matter of vital necessity that the potential societal advantages and risks, associated with the various different ways of integrating these technical systems into the societies concerned, be tested under careful and socially responsible supervision, and under conditions which are dictated by the actual needs of the potential users of the systems.

With regard to industrial policy and commercial considerations, it seems to me that one must necessarily carry out social experiments with telematics in capitalist societies with private (and public) commercial interests in mind. It is, in other words, my own opinion that any sober and realistic assessment of the situation in these countries must point to the pursuit of industrial and commercial policy goals as a necessary precondition for the launching and successful completion of social experiments with telematics. On the other hand, I don't ultimately foresee any insurmountable difficulty in bringing social experiments with telematics into line with commercial policy considerations. In the long run, it can only be in the overall interests of industry, of the business world generally, and indeed of any capitalist nation's entire economy for that matter, to participate in such experiments, since they provide a desirable context — if not the only conceivable context — within which to develop the carefully monitored, and realistically guaranteed, full marketable potential of I.T. and telematics technology.

However, in that they seek to combine both socio-political and industrial policy considerations, in the manner I have indicated above, social experiments with telematics do undeniably take place in a socially complex and conflict-ridden arena, in which a multitude of different interests are represented. And that a delicate balance may after all be found between these potentially conflicting interests can only be due to the fact that the interested parties in social experiments with telematics are ultimately mutually dependent: on the one hand, the equipment used in the experiment is so costly and comprehensive that 'do-it-yourself' social experiments with the technology without the active support of the industry would be impossible; while, on the other hand, to develop such comprehensive equipment in the vacuum of an industrial laboratory without the active support of representatives of the enormous future market for the technology would be a no less impossibly costly mistake for industry to make.

In answer to my third question, about how and why it is relatively easy to carry out social experiments with telematics technology in particular, I shall be repeating my earlier arguments about the open-ended social significance of information and communications systems. It is — in other words — possible to carry out social experiments inasmuch as telematics technology is essentially flexible and capable of being used for a variety of different purposes. Its open-ended latent potential can be realised under a wide variety of different modes of social organisation.

10.2.1. *The Sociopolitical Aspects.*

The three managing directors, two directors, and chief executive who made up the Prime Minister's Information Technology Advisory Panel, and whose initial recommendations to the government were largely responsible for Britain's — in my opinion — fatally misconceived cabling policy, were at least aware of the paradoxical nature of their recommendations. On p.48 of their report we find them writing that although cable will offer great opportunities for new forms of entrepreneurial activity and substantial direct and indirect industrial benefits, "[...] the initial financing of cable systems will depend upon none of these things, but upon estimates of the revenue from additional popular programming channels". (Aldrich et al. 1982: 48)

It is indeed true that the long-term goal of the British cabling policy is to provide the population with a variety of new services — which, apart from electronic banking and electronic shopping, might, with some stretch of the imagination, just possibly include better access to information, which, in turn, might provide the basis for more — electronically mediated — participative democracy, in the best sense in which the latter possibility might be conceived of. But the immediate goal to be attained, in order to get cable system subscribers to finance the network, is the provision of more canned T.V. entertainment — a short-term goal, in other words, which would seem to be curiously incompatible with any longer-term ideal of serious democratic enlightenment. Where the British cable systems report invites criticism is in pointing out this paradox, but in not giving any indication of how it might be resolved — (and in generally selling out the sociopolitical aspects to considerations of industrial policy). The report, in other words, provides evidence of an awareness of the fact that the prescribed cable systems policy will have profound sociopolitical consequences, without this awareness prompting its authors to give any serious thought at all to an evaluation of the consequences they refer to. In this way, the potential beneficiaries of the new telematics systems become no more than a means to an end: an end which has everything to do with industrial policy, and nothing to do with the users as ends in themselves, i.e. as potential beneficiaries of the latent advantages which the new technology could in itself — and quite correctly — be the means to provide them with. (Hearst 1982)Thus the clear tendential content of telematics technology is allowed to predominate at the expense of its latent potential, and the unpredictably and qualitatively new Information Society is aborted at birth.

Insofar as the I.T.A.P.'s recommendations became government policy, I would want to point out that — besides the obvious sociopolitical unacceptability of this betrayal of confidence and enforced prostitution of the general public — such an attitude contains another (and no less acceptable) paradox. As a general rule, sophisticated technological innovations are not launched onto the market until they have undergone thorough testing and are pronounced technically sound. If, in spite of these precautions, technical hitches should arise, industry is prepared to take the blame and compensate customers where necessary. But it is quite another matter as far as politicians are concerned. Parallel with the introduction of tried and tested new technology, sociopolitical innovations of far-reaching consequences are heedlessly and wantonly introduced without any form of prior testing at all, and when the hoped-for collaboration between men and machines in the new sociopolitical situation predictably develops flaws, and finally falls apart, the politicians themselves are the last to take the blame for their own irresponsibility!

Of course I wouldn't dream of suggesting that technical and social systems are one and the same thing, or that social systems can ever be tested as definitively as technical systems. But I *would* want to make a very strong claim for the proposition that the widespread belief obtaining at the present time, the belief that populations generally should welcome almost any technological innovation with respectful gratitude, is as misconceived as the emperor's expectations about the reception which would be accorded his new set of clothes, in the famous fairy-tale by Hans Christian Andersen.

From a sociopolitical point of view there can be no doubt at all of the necessity and desirability of supplementing 'technology assessment' with a sociologically-founded open-ended experimental approach; with R. and D. — in other words — which focuses on the society which is to evolve hand in hand with the developing technology at its disposal. This sort of R. and D. requires realistic and representative social conditions and competent sociological planning, execution and evaluation. It has become all the more urgently necessary as the influence of I.T. and telematics technology on the functioning of existing social systems has increased exponentially.

As I have sought to explain and illustrate in this book, telematics technology is open-ended as far as its social, political and cultural implications are concerned. Various different kinds of societal content are contained within its varied design and development. In making choices about the design and development of the I.T. and telematics systems of the future, one is thus choosing between potentially different media political and sociopolitical futures. And even where these choices have been made unawares (i.e. where the development of I.T. and telematics systems has been narrowly considered only in terms of industrial policy), sociopolitical choices have in actual fact been made. Hence the obvious necessity for clarifying the issues, for analysing the implications of alternative strategies for designing and developing the technology; hence the necessity for social experiments with telematics.

10.2.2. *Commercial and Industrial Aspects.*

There are three main reasons for recommending that the commercial and industrial aspects of I.T. and telematics systems should involve the public sector, i.e. that the development of these systems should take place within the framework of a publicly controlled and supervised social experiment. In the first place (if one disregards 'internal' office automation networks) information and communications systems are public, in the sense that they constitute a communal infrastructure: a fact which immediately suggests the advisability of developing such systems under the auspices of local and state authorities.

In the second place, the development costs of I.T. and telematics systems involve investments of no small magnitude, which makes state participation in R. and D., and a supportive national technological development policy, clearly desirable. And, finally, the fact that I.T. and telematics systems are essentially conglomerations of different I.T. and telematics equipment — the fact, for instance, that the development of a nationwide integrated broadband network is inextricably bound up with the development of the services which such a network can provide — again calls for a supervisory body which is independent of any short-term and narrowly-conceived commercial interests, and which can guarantee public influence on the development of such systems down to the last detail.

I am, of course, aware that the degree of public influence which I would consider desirable in social experiments with telematics is hardly likely to recommend these social experiments to industry, at least in the first instance. Nevertheless, I would remind the reader that the British attempt to build up a commercially viable national broadband network *without* sufficient public control, in my opinion has left the future of British industry clutching little more than a bunch of loose and incompatible coaxial cable ends in its otherwise empty hands. And the launching of Prestel, without having first learnt valuable marketing lessons through cooperation with public authorities in publicly influenced social experiments, was anything but a minor disaster for British Telecom in commercial and industrial terms. In other words, it would seem after all to be the case that — just as the uncontrolled development of information and communications systems is sociopolitically irresponsible — so, too, the development of these systems without publicly influenced social experiments is unlikely to prove very attractive in commercial and industrial terms.

10.2.3. *The Technological Aspects.*

The reasons why one *ought to* carry out social experiments with telematics are, as we have seen, sociopolitical. But the reason why it is *possible*, and in fact relatively easy, to assess the consequences of, and to further develop, I.T. and telematics technology on an interdisciplinary basis within the framework of a social experiment, is that, as I have earlier claimed, this technology has a high degree of social significance, and the outcome of the conflict between its overt tendential content and latent potential has not already been predetermined in some one-sided fashion, at the expense of its less commercial aspects.

I based this claim on the fact that I.T. and telematics technology have to be assessed in interactive systemic terms. A fibreoptic cable network is the example *par excellence*, of course, since it is quite literally based on a combination of a number of different kinds of technology: laser physics and electronics in connection with optical transmission and switching; glass fibre engineering; digital packeting and conversion technology; phototelegraphy;

etc. And its purpose is to link a wide variety of other technical systems which are based on various other kinds of technology — on computer science, algebra and mathematics, above all, but also on radio-telephony and geo-stationary satellite technology for instance, on silicon chip and transistor and microfilm engineering, on holography, and on video disc technology, on printing, and graphics, and indexing, and cathode ray physics, and alphageometrics: the list is endless! But the technological diversity and complexity of the network itself, and of all these linked technical systems, is more than matched by the diversity and complexity of the social systems within which the technology is intended to play a major role: from local and national political decision-making to international banking; from industrial and office and agricultural management to meteorological services and robotics; from media political and cultural policy to every aspect of education — for children and adults alike. And the point I have been trying to insist on is that — while a single technical system in isolation, such as the pulsed transmission of light-waves from a laser to a photodiode through some light-conducting material, is fundamentally influenced by purely physical factors, and therefore requires a high degree of natural scientific knowledge for its development, a complex multiple technical system of the kind we meet in telematics, whose aim is to transmit, store and process socially significant symbols, is fundamentally influenced by the social system within which it is supposed to function, and of which it is itself an integral part.

As I mentioned at the very beginning of chapter 1, the word 'telematics' was itself a French compound, which they found it necessary to invent in order to do justice to the fact that an integrated system of telecommunications and information processing amounts to something more than just the sum of its parts. For, as I have tried to illustrate throughout this book, what we are dealing with here is an integrated technological system of which socially significant symbols are transmitted, stored, and processed, and within which it is impossible to draw any hard and fast line delimiting the territories of the natural sciences and the social sciences respectively. This means that the appropriate and adequate assessment and further development of telematics technology can only take place in environments which reflect the integral complexity of telematics itself: in representative social environments, in other words.

And the integral complexity of telematics systems also means that the full social significance of the technology is very sustantially open-ended. Telematics systems beckon us alluringly towards the future, promising us the realisation of age-old utopian dreams — to the simultaneous delight of the enthusiasts and irritation of the sceptics among us. But, in that they contain not one but many potential futures within them, they themselves cannot take us by the hand and lead us down any one particular path towards a qualitatively new future. Traditional 'retrospective' technology assessment is thus wholly inappropriate to the problem with which this particular kind of technology confronts us: the problem of our own scientific assessment and development of desirable futures for ourselves. In fact, logical positivism in any traditional sense cannot help us. Instead, we need a scientific praxis which can help us to release the full latent potential of telematics technology in all its open-ended complexity. Given the flexibility of the technology, the social experiment with telematics becomes the obvious choice; indeed, the only feasible solution.

10.3. *Social Experiments with Telematics as Strategic Praxis in Relation to Utopian Theory.*

> "Es gibt für mich keine eindeutige Wahrheit. De Möglichkeit (die Annahme) der Wahrheit entsteht aus Zweifeln und Widersprüchen". Peter Weiss, *Aus dem Notizbüchern 1960-71.*

In the last chapter I gave some examples from France and Sweden of what social experiments with telematics could look like in practice. In the present chapter I went on to define the concept theoretically, stressing its normative function. In the preceding section, I have concentrated less on 'what' and more on the 'why' and 'how' of social experiments with telematics, but before going on to elaborate more practical guidelines for social experiments with telematics later in the chapter, I want, in this section, to focus again on the 'why' and 'how' of social experiments with telematics, but this time on a less pragmatic but more philosophical level. I want, in fact, to define and defend the concept of social experiments with telematics in terms of utopian theory and practice.

In a recent attempt to analyse utopian thinking in the works of contemporary social critics — such as Haug, Sohn-Rethel and Goux — another Danish admirer of Ernst Bloch, Ole Thyssen, found it helpful to distinguish between what he calls 'classical' utopias and 'integrated' utopias. (Thyssen 1976) The former, which Thyssen found exemplified in the writings of Plato or Fourier for instance, were purely abstract constructs: daydreams, as it were, of idealised alternative societies in which existing social contradictions from 'real life' found their resolution within the framework of a closed mythological universe.

In the history of ideas, as Thyssen points out, utopian thinking is generally considered to have reached a turning-point when it was confronted by Karl Marx's historical materialist criticism. Some historians even maintain that it ceased to exist altogether. Others, including Bloch, claim that it continued to exist, but only after it had undergone a radical transformation. Thyssen refers to the works of Ernst Bloch himself, and to those of Marcuse, as illustrating the correctness of the latter conclusion.

What Thyssen calls an 'integrated' utopia is a utopia which does not escape from contemporary reality into an illusory world of artificially resolved conflicts, but which in itself actually constitutes an integral part of the ongoing process of social development. Instead of distancing itself from a concrete description of a given society, it informs such a description, and is in fact a determining principle behind such a description. In Bloch's phrase, the classical utopia has 'come to itself' as it were, has abandoned its delusions of absolute power, and has accepted its historical function. No longer content to 'go it alone', Thyssen's integrated utopia enters into an alliance with concrete social criticism as a ubiquitous — but often invisible — normative principle.

As I argued in my second chapter, technology is not just the study of things technical; in effect it is the study of how to gain control of things in order to achieve given ends — of how to gain control over nature in fact, in order to satisfy human needs. It is, in other words, a threefold study of how to increase the power of Man, how to satisfy human needs, and how to achieve given ends — (or at least attempt to achieve given ends!) — with the aid of human ingenuity. And technology is also the study of transformations: of the transformation of physical nature which technical systems — designed with the aid of human ingenuity to satisfy human ends — go to work on; of the transformation of the society which is incarnated within and influenced by the technical systems; of the transformation of the human needs which the technical systems were originally intended to satisfy.

Technology, the 'study of technical systems', is thus, in my definition, the study of the whims of nature, the ingenuity of Man, and the leashed or unleashed forces for the transformation of nature, Man, and society which are immanent within the technical systems themselves. Significantly, too, technology is the *integral* study of all these phenomena as mutually dependent and interactive elements — elements which are all simultaneously present within the single entity, the technical system itself.

This study of future-oriented technical systems can appropriately be expressed in terms of Ernst Bloch's concept of the heuristic model. As Bloch puts it in his sublimely optimistic post-Hegelian terminology: "Every heuristic model is methodologically a 'thesis', and every thesis involving concrete anticipation refers to a concrete experimental model which participates in the creation of the world itself and its creatures" (Bloch 1977 [1965]: 88). For our purposes, the heuristic model is what is to be realised in the social experiment with telematics.

Mediating the qualitatively new means thinking in terms of 'becoming' rather than in terms of 'being'; and when we think in terms of 'becoming', the concept of overt or latent tendencies contained within the present can be extremely helpful. For the process of becoming should never be confused with some sort of trite reading of the history of civilisation as a simple journey from bad to good. It must always be understood as an accumulation and intensification of conflicts and contradictions within an ongoing social system at any time, whose potential resolution necessarily points beyond them into the future. The process of becoming thus always involves experimentation, and the whole history of civilisation constitutes in itself an ongoing social experiment.

To put it in Bloch's words again, this process of becoming is described in terms of

> "the inherent momentum of conflicts and contradictions in the process of the progressive realisation of the progressively realising self in the world. By turns, the fundamental question 'What?' merges everywhere into the question 'To what end?' — a question which the heavily pregnant world is on its way to providing us with an answer to in terms of itself *qua* ongoing experiment [...]. The questioning becomes integrated within a hypothesis, which still does not amount to a definitive answer, but which gives the questioning a particular aim and direction. And thus the possibility develops to test the hypothesis against some evidence, in that the 'How?' of intervening, experimenting, and ratifying, gives rise to the creation of anticipative models [...]. Thus conceived, in a manner which radically differs from that of logical positivism, these types of experiments and models are part of the work in progress — the work continuously in progress — in the 'laboratorium possibilis salutis': they are part of material reality's laborious onward trail." (Bloch 1977 [1975]: 241f)

Telematics, as we have seen, commends itself to us in utopian terms. But if telematics is understood by itself only to be the incarnation of a single future, the utopia which it offers us can only amount to an abstract one. Instead of Ole Thyssen's 'integrated utopia', what we are then offered is not a real, qualitatively different future, but an impossible dream, a wishful, pathetic idealisation of the present. Only when the realisation is made that telematics is the incarnation not just of one but of many possible futures; and only when some of these futures are recognised as the latent potential of the technology, born of the concrete societal contradictions with which we are burdened at the present time, while others are recognised as the more predictable and 'legitimate' futures which are in line with more general societal tendencies at the present time; and only when this latter, more predictable, tendential content of telematics technology, and its former, less predictable, latent potential, are *analysed together* — only then can we start to talk about an 'integrated utopia', only then do the promised utopias have a chance of becoming concrete realities.

Focussing on the latent potential of the technology in isolation can never be more than abstract enthusiasm. Focussing on the all-too-predictable tendential content of the technology — and turning one's back on its latent potential — can never be more than a barren form of realism.

In themselves, the developing social systems with their aspirations — which are incarnated, as it were, in telematics technology — are not unambiguous. On the one hand there are the aspirations for greater individual freedom, and for more decentralised political participation, while on the other hand there are the aspirations for greater productivity and for a higher degree of efficient centralized coordination of the various social activities undertaken by individual citizens. The fact that such fundamental social ambiguity is incarnated in new technology means that statements about its social significance ought not be made in absolute terms but in relative terms, terms which relate the potential of the technology to desired ends, and which assess it 'strategically', as it were, in terms of its relative ability or inability to realise those ends.

To state categorically, for example, that atomic energy was invented in order to benefit mankind is not a very helpful thing to say to the survivors of Hiroshima and Nagasaki — or to others — who are worried about the dangers of radioactive waste; or about the potential release of radioactivity from atomic power stations into the atmosphere as the result of faults in their construction or operation, or as the result of damage by terrorists or hostile powers in time of war; or even about the rather remote possibility that the spread of atomic power stations will increase the temptation for more (implausibly ingenious?) terrorists to make home-made atomic bombs. On the other hand, though, the no less categorical statement that atomic energy is completely senseless, is a lie which it is all too easy to refute — and which is thus no more helpful, in assessing the desirability of this particular example of (relatively) new technology.

What is called for here is a *strategic* assessment of the social significance of atomic energy. We would have to address ourselves to the fact that — in contrast to wind or solar energy, for instance — atomic energy is more in harmony with aspirations for greater productivity and more centralized social organization. Industry and commerce, large institutions and conurbations, could be easily and (relatively!) reliably supplied with electricity produced by means of atomic energy, while wind and solar energy could come into their own in a more decentralized rural scenario, which makes the latter technology more in line with aspirations for greater individual freedom, perhaps.

It would, at any rate, seem foolish to deny the fact that what we have called the dominant tendential content of atomic — and wind and solar — energy respectively is to provide electricity for large-scale institutional consumption, in the former case, and to provide electricity for small-scale individual consumption in the latter case. But it would be no less foolish to deny that atomic energy contains the latent potential, as we have called it, for supplying electricity to relatively isolated small-scale communities, while wind and solar energy could no doubt be developed to supply industry with sufficient energy to keep efficient, low energy robots operating night and day …

In a nation like Denmark which has no hydro-electric power, no coal, and very little offshore oil and gas of its own, but no atomic power stations as yet, despite the substantial uranium deposits in Greenland — and which, for geographical reasons, has a social structure which is perhaps not as centralized as is typically the case in highly industrialized nations, the solution would seem to be a combination of atomic energy and wind and solar energy, in that the tendential content of the different forms of technology might act as a check upon each other. But a further analysis of the social significance of atomic energy suggests that a balance of this kind would be difficult to maintain. For the contrast between wind and solar energy and atomic energy is not just a contrast between the amount of energy generated per installation: it is also a contrast between the modes of social organization required to defend the installations against sabotage or abuse; and the relative consequences of sabotage or abuse which render desirable varying degrees of social control, and which place individual citizens under varying degrees of 'centralized' threat over which they themselves have no control.

Atomic energy, in other words, is tendentially analogous to the vast centralized databases in Wicklein's *The Electronic Nightmare*, while wind and solar energy is perhaps more reminiscent of the decentralized databases which are to be built up, under the auspices of the Centre Mondial Informatique et Ressources Humaines, in their social experiment in the Belle de Mai district of Marseille which I gave an account of in my last chapter. But the very fact that these diametrically opposed kinds of energy-supplying technology are analogous to two different developments of *one and the same* kind of telematics technology will, doubtless, remind the reader of a point I made in my second section above. What makes telematics technology eminently suitable for social experiments is precisely that, in contrast to atomic energy, it is so open-ended: the dice are not so heavily weighted in favour of its tendential content at the expense of its latent potential, as it were. For, in the last instance, this is where the criticism of atomic energy must set in. It is not a question of whether the *technology* is 50% safe, 90% safe, or 150% safe: the real problem is that this form of energy supply steers us so inflexibly, so inexorably, towards one particular kind of future society.

It is quite otherwise with telematics technology — the advantage of which lies not so much in its relative safety nor in its technical ingenuity; Wicklein, for example, would actually claim that it is far less safe than atomic energy, while any atomic physicist would deny that telematics technology exhibits any more technical ingenuity than the latest atomic power station! No, paradoxically, in terms of considerations of safety, in contrast to atomic energy the advantage of telematics technology lies precisely in its *unpredictability*.

For, as I have argued in chapters 5-8 above, the very patently open-ended latent potential of telematics technology in effect sharpens the tone of ongoing debates about what sort of society we already have, and what sort of society we would utimately prefer. It aggravates fundamental conflicts between the enforced egoism of the population in the market place and the resultant enforced cooperation of the population in the political and legal spheres, and it highlights the dilemma between the illusory freedom of the 'natural' — and the unnecessary slavery of the 'civilised' — individual within our pitifully undemocratic so-called democracies.

As far as the working life of each individual was concerned, we saw how the prospect of domestic work stations ambiguously satisfied the aspirations both of those who desire to rationalise work processes and increase productivity, and of those who want to make working conditions more human and bridge the gulf between work and free time. Ambiguously, at any rate, in capitalist societies, in that, while transport and office expenses are saved and productivity can be increased under much more effective managerial control, and while the workers themselves can vary their own working hours within their own personalized surroundings, and escape the stress of commuting, the conditions for shopfloor solidarity and collective bargaining will be seriously endangered. The consequences — for those still in work — may be a longer, more professionally and socially isolated, and more frustrating, working day, after all, with even less time for the children, for one's marriage, or for other social activities. While — for those no longer in work — the 'right to idleness' may seem a cold comfort as long as work is synonymous with money and power.

As far as the political life of each individual was concerned, the open-ended potential of telematics for improving both vertical and horizontal communication pointed again towards conflicting possible futures. On the one hand it pointed towards a society run rationally and efficiently according to the vertical dictates of an implausibly representative professional élite of politicians and experts, whose virtually unshakeable predominance over the rest of the population would be based on a vertical 'one man one button' rigged electoral response to all their initiatives. While, on the other hand, it pointed towards a society run according to a more plausibly conceived — (a less abstract and more truly Rousseauesque) — 'general will': the actual will of everybody, including minority groups whose differences of opinion might be willingly compromised on one particular occasion, if they were guaranteed a full hearing and the possible acceptance of their will on other occasions. Here, the latent potential of telematics technology for horizontal intercommunication, and interaction, could permit full decentralized access to information and full and equal participation in public policy-making.

And as far as the recreational life of each individual was concerned, we saw how the ambiguous potential of advanced CATV systems has already manifested itself. On the one hand we have our latter-day Faust on his sofa, plagued by his own helpless passivity and homelessness; as Mephistopheles' T.V. cameras transcend time and space to bring him the whole world and a string of sexy actresses to boot, but where he slowly and inexorably loses his soul in compensatory identification with Christopher Lasch's celluloid idols. And, on the other hand, we have what could be a much wider variety of programmes for the individual viewer to select; programmes which he can watch as many times as he likes, having juxtaposed the books on his shelves with videotapes. And if he gets bored with the physical inactivity of watching a thought-provoking programme or reading a perhaps no less mentally stimulating book, he may join his friends in the neighbourhood and help them to produce their own local T.V. programme, or he may use his video telephone to spend the next few hours in the company of — and to enjoy stimulating conversation with — some kindred spirits living at some distance from his home.

Finally, prompted by Orwell's doomsday vision, we saw in chapter 8 the ambiguity of the latent potential of telematics technology for self-imposed social control. If the mythical universe of television entertainment, within which we daily immerse ourselves, has replaced the medieval mythical world of the gospels and the Old Testament and the regular moral exhortations of the clergy, to the extent that we — more or less unconsciously — judge each other and ourselves in accordance with the dramatized morality which we hourly and daily subconsciously absorb from television, then the question arises as to whether this T.V. entertainment is to become a controlled, democratic tool encouraging independent thought, or whether it is to become an uncontrolled and pseudo-democratic expression of the power of uncontrolled commercial forces within our societies. Are we to condemn ourselves to death — (slowly or fast, either through pills and alcohol, or through suicide) — for not being able to achieve the fictive normality of a Texas oil dynasty? Or are we sensibly and firmly to reproach ourselves and others for selfishness and greed?

In contrast to more traditional technology which involves the manipulation of raw or refined materials from our natural environment, telematics technology manipulates our own human nature, our psyche, since its purpose is to store, process and transmit symbols — the stuff of our minds, rather than external matter. Does this mean that what we are dealing with here is an improvement in human communication in the direction of socially beneficial telepathic communion, or does it mean that we are about to experience a form of mental pollution which is so total that we will no longer be able to realise and criticise what is happening to us?

As I wrote in the preceding section, telematics systems beckon us alluringly towards the future, promising us the realisation of age-old utopian dreams — to the simultaneous delight of the enthusiast and irritation of the sceptics among us. To a greater extent than many other kinds of technology, telematics commends itself to us in terms of 'becoming' rather than of 'being', in terms of its immanent latent potential.

At the same time, this particular technology renders problematic the traditional distinction between technical and social science: a distinction which has to be replaced by collaboration. In that this technology is the study of tools which manipulate symbols rather than external matter, it disregards the distinction between ourselves and our natural environment: the tool manipulates the inner nature of its user.

Finally, this particular kind of technology distinguishes itself from many other kinds of technology through its intrinsically systemic character. It has to be thought of in terms of a coordinate system of different varieties of technology, an integration of different technical systems.

Telematics technology beckons us alluringly towards the future. But, in that it contains not one but many potential futures within it, it cannot by itself take us by the hand — as I put it in the previous section — and lead us down any one particular path towards a qualitatively new future. Theoretically, as we have seen, the only adequate scientific approach to the problems and challenges surrounding this new technology — the only approach which will provide us with the necessary freedom of choice to realise its promise of the qualitatively new — is the heuristic model, in Ernst Bloch's definition. And in terms of strategic praxis, the social experiment is the practical realisation of this heuristic model — the only scientific praxis which can release the full latent potential of telematics technology.

At the outset of my last chapter, I pleaded for the desirability of supplementing realism with enthusiasm in our attempts to reconcile the latent potential of telematics with its more overt tendential content. In social experiments with telematics both realism and enthusiasm are necessary. A *realistic* assessment of the technology in context is required, to guarantee the realisation of its tendential benefits for the industrial policy of the society concerned. Social experiments with I.T. and telematics systems involving microcomputers and fibreoptic data transmission obviously have considerable interest for the microelectronics and cable industries, both with regard to the development of the home market and with regard to improved export qualifications. And, beyond this, there are the potential secondary and tertiary spin-off effects to bear in mind. For not only will the construction of an integrated broadband cable network create opportunities for the provision of innumerable information and communication services: it will also rationalize the informational infrastructure of the entire nation's industry.

An *enthusiastic* assessment of the technology in context is required, if the many different potential futures which it contains are to be related to existing 'alternative' social movements. Created and strengthened by societal conflicts and contradictions — some of which the new technology itself has thrown into urgent relief — these movements for popular mobilization, participation, and decentralization exist alongside the mainstream tendencies in today's industrial societies towards centralized hierarchical rigidity, and popular passivity and impotence. How long these alternative social movements will exist is a dubious but still open question. It renders all the more urgent the adoption of social experiments with telematics. For, as strategic praxis, such experiments can and must ensure that both the latent and the overt tendential content of the new technology is held in balance — they can and must ensure that its latent content profitably supplements and complements its mainstream tendential content — so as not to throw away this unrivalled opportunity in human history for mediating that which is truly and qualitatively new.

10.4. *Practical Advantages of Social Experiments with Telematics.*

The Inadequacy of Traditional Market Research.

Traditional techniques of market research are useless with regard to the launching of new I.T. and telematics technology. Among scores of examples, one might mention the representative survey of French householders lacking telephones, which was undertaken by the *Revue française d'opinion publique* in 1965. 76% of those answering the questionnaire maintained that they didn't need a telephone. Now there are five times as many telephone subscribers in France as there were in 1965! (figures from Mexandeau 1982)

Indeed, as far as communications technology is concerned, it is frequently the case that normal expectations about the potential social demand for, and utilization of, such technology fall far short of reality. Thus, in view of the inadequacy of traditional market research, there is a real need for carefully monitored pilot projects under representative social conditions, precisely in order to investigate the potential demand for, and utilization of, communications technology. The discovery and development of the societal demand for new technology is one of the main purposes of social experiments with telematics.

Who Should Have Most Say in the Design of I.T. and Telematics Equipment: Artists, Salesmen, or Potential Users?

Strange though it may seem to us now, the concept of 'industrial design' is a relatively new phenomenon in Danish industrial and commercial history. Originally, a couple of decades ago, the word 'design' was synonymous with the word 'finish', or even with the word 'fashioning'. In the electronics industry, however, the word has become synonymous with 'packaging': the packaging of electronic components behind chrome or veneer in various articles of household equipment, for example.

In terms of user-friendliness, practicality, and ergonomics, the concept of design has become more and more relevant with regard to I.T. and telematics systems and devices. It is not just a question of whether the equipment looks, sounds, and feels, good. It has to function within specific social contexts — in public libraries, primary schools, tourist bureaux, boardrooms, private homes, in the reception halls of luxury hotels and in airport lounges. This kind of design can no longer be exclusively the concern of interior decorators: in social experiments with telematics, sociologists, social psychologists, and the potential users of the technology themselves, can have an equal hand in its design. The development of good, socially acceptable and functional design for the new technology is another of the main purposes of social experiments with telematics.

The Desirability of the Democratic Planning of Societal Infrastructures.

Doubts are frequently expressed about whether it is reasonable that the consumer should have little or no influence on commercial products until they have been launched onto the market; about whether it is reasonable, in other words, that industrial and commercial interests alone should decide the extent and variety of the consumer's choice.

Other aspects of this problem have to be taken into account, too, as far as communications systems are concerned. For here it is not just a question of individual products which — at least in theory — consumers are at liberty to accept or reject: here the consumer is confronted with complete technical systems. Systems which, moreover, are further differentiated from other consumer products by their possession of two very essential characteristics. In the first place, these systems constitute an infrastructure for the society, or community, in question, which it is hardly reasonable to expect that the individual citizen will be in a position to accept or reject at any later stage. And secondly, in that this societal or communal infrastructure is publicly shared, it would seem all the more reasonable that the public itself should have a say in its design and further development.

Social experiments with telematics facilitate democratic decision-making about new I.T. and telematics infrastructures, in that a representative number of potential users have an equal say with a large number of experts in the evaluation and modification of the technology, and scientifically monitored and assessed social experiments in representative communities can provide a useful, stimulating, and reliable basis for other communities' prior assessments and decisions with regard to the new technology.

The Desirability of the Empirical Testing of New Communications Systems.

Traditional technology asssessment suffers from two fundamental drawbacks. Either an assessment is made *after* the technology has already come onto the market, in which case the results seem merely to legitimate already made — (and irrevocable) — decisions about the nature of the technology. Or, if the technical systems are tested *before* they come onto the market, the results of such tests are hardly any less questionable since they are either made abroad in other cultural environments, for instance, or else they are made under simulated conditions which bear too little resemblance to the reality for which they are destined.

The problems are even greater as far as I.T. and telematics systems are concerned. Theoretical assessments of these systems are unusually difficult to make in advance, and previous experience with similar systems in other cultures is also of dubious validity at anything other than a fairly high level of generality. For the successful total development of I.T. and telematics systems is precisely a matter of their responsiveness to very specific social and cultural conditions. Hence the necessity for testing such systems in representative areas of the actual societies in which they are to function, with careful and thorough monitoring of the consequences of their introduction, and detailed registration of their utilization levels and patterns.

The Full Future Development of I.T. and Telematics Technology is Impossible to Predict.

The first cars ever to be made resembled a traditional horse-drawn carriage without the horse. And the habit of measuring the capacity of internal combustion engines in terms of horse power is still with us. Habitual thinking about technology dies hard, and the qualitatively new is, by definition, unthinkable in advance.

As far as I.T. and telematics technology are concerned, our imaginations are patently inadequate to the task of conceiving all the qualitatively new ways of interacting and communicating which exist, as latent potential, within technology of this kind. But one thing we do know for sure: this technology is going to surprise us — *if* we give it half a chance! Which is another reason why social experiments with telematics are desirable. Experiments, that is, which enable users of the technology to explore its potential creatively — communally as well as individually — so that both its design and its mode of functioning may be developed and improved. Beyond all recognition, as it were.

Private Bureaucracy and Public Enterprise.

Normally, the intervention of public authorities, whether local or national, in the affairs of private industry is considered likely to be more of a hindrance than a help. But, as far as the development of I.T. and telematics technology is concerned, the reverse would seem to be true. Here, it is the public authorities who fall over themselves to get everything they possibly can out of the technology, while the manufacturers of the technology themselves tend to retard developments; up to their necks in technicalities, the latter have great difficulty in seeing beyond their noses — or at least in raising their eyes from their microscopes or from their mounds of technical paperwork! The successful recent development of Danish hearing-aids, now a highly esteemed export item, is a case in point: without our advanced public welfare legislation, the ingenuity of our electronics engineers might never have been so successfully exploited.

The full development of I.T. and telematics technology, in continuous response to the burgeoning societal needs which the technology itself helps to fertilize, requires full cooperation between social scientists and engineers from both the private and the public sectors. And it requires full cooperation between private cable and micro-electronics businesses and public authorities, who will ensure that the full benefits of the technology become available to the communities they represent and serve. Social experiments with telematics can provide the necessary framework for this kind of collaboration.

10.5. *Summary of the Concept of 'Social Experiments with Telematics' and Some Concrete Guidelines.*

Presuppositions.

The first proposition underlying the concept of 'social experiments with telematics' is a *moral* one: the assumption is that social experiments with telematics *ought to* take a given society and its specific societal needs as their starting point. The needs of the populations of today's highly industrialised societies, for example, are not so much fundamental human needs, as societally conditioned and structured needs, bound up with specific societal roles. And, when I say that these social experiments with telematics technology ought to take specific societal needs as their starting point, I am in fact merely bringing the concept into line with the shared explicit ideals of all democracies.

For social experiments with telematics ought not to satisfy *only* the commercial pursuit of profit, nor *only* the profit-seeking needs of potential customers as they are reflected in the existing market demand for I.T. and telematics technology. Nor, on the other hand, should they seek to satisfy *only* the needs of public authorities (on whatever level) — needs for 'vertical' legitimation and control. On the contrary, the experiments should take *both* these sets of needs into account and, in addition, strive to satisfy the specific needs of each and every individual citizen in his three basic roles. For each individual citizen has needs which are specific to his working life — (his need, for example, to be fully socially responsible and creative); needs which are specific to his political life — (his need to be fully informed about the options facing himself and his society at any time, and his need to discuss his views with others and have genuine influence over his own and his society's future); and needs which are specific to his private life — (the spiritual as well as the physical needs of himself, his family and his community).

The second assumption underlying the concept of social experiments with telematics is an *empirical* one, and thus, unlike the first, is open to discussion. This is the assumption that I.T. and telematics systems are not finished products but systems which are under continuous development. For it may be demonstrated empirically that, in office systems, in L.A.N.s, in other communications networks, the components are constantly being removed, modified, replaced by something better. And the structure of the networks themselves is under constant transformation, in response to increasing demands for the integration of more and more hitherto independent L.A.N.s or local CATV systems or national and international packet switching networks, etc.

The third assumption underlying the concept of social experiments with telematics is also an empirical one. It is that societal needs — the needs of all the potential users of I.T. and telematics systems, in other words — are not absolute, static, and immutable, but undergo continuous dynamic development and transformation as elements of socially, and historically, specific demand structures; demand structures which are generated out of the dialectical interaction between developing individuals, developing societies, developing technology, and developing — (synthetic) — and static nature.

The final assumption is also an empirical one. This is the assumption that I.T. and telematics systems reflect an increasingly closer integration of technology and human behaviour. A television set, for instance, is at one and the same time an informational tool, a recreational tool, a behaviour-modifying tool, and a money-making tool. Of course it is important not to forget that, when all's said and done, a T.V. set *is* still a tool, just as a garden spade is still a garden spade, even though it may be used for shovelling coal, making money, or committing murder. The difference between a T.V. set and a garden spade is not a qualitative one in *that* sense. But what we are talking about is a *quantitative* difference, a difference based on the far greater degree of teleological complexity, and the far closer dialectical relationship between man and machine, which informs the design of a T.V. set — (or of any other example of I.T. or telematics hardware or software, for that matter) — and which constitutes its social significance.

Definitions.

The concept of 'social experiments with telematics' rests on the above assumptions and must thus be defined, and realised in practice, in accordance with them. In keeping with the first assumption, the word 'social', for instance, points to the fact that *individual and communal societal needs are given top priority in these experiments*. And since the discovery, and satisfaction, of these societal needs for telematics technology is the basic aim of experiments of this kind, they have to take place in social space which is structured by representative ongoing patterns of communal needs, communal interaction and communal traditions.

It is impossible to give a more precise statistical or geographical definition of the optimum context for these experiments, just as it is impossible to give any very precise recommendations with regard to their optimum duration, since the specific technology and societal needs which are in focus in each different experiment may vary considerably. The framework might vary from three classrooms in a school, for instance, if the focus is on CAL and junior citizens' educational needs, to cities the size of Biarritz, or Grenoble, if the focus is on the needs generated by an integrated broadband cable network. Less ambitious integrated cable network experiments might, however, very profitably take place in typical provincial small towns. Towns which, in terms of cultural geography, have functioned for a number of years as reasonably independent and self-contained communities, with their own clearly defined traditions and culture.

If we go on to try to define the use of the word 'experiment' in the concept of social experiments with telematics, we would have to insist on the fact that what is referred to here is a heuristic communal experience of 'learning by doing'. *The emphasis in these experiments is on future-oriented development*, whether it is the I.T. and telematics systems and services themselves we are referring to, or whether it is the local community's individual — or communal — needs and functional activities.

The future orientation of this kind of experimental activity means that the more people involved who have an anticipatory capability (like artists, for instance), the better the results are likely to be. At all events, the experimental framework must be as open as possible, and all the participants — artists, technicians, social scientists, businessmen, civil servants, politicians, and as many as possible of the users of the technology — must be given ample opportunity during the experiments to compare experiences, and to help each other to further develop the potential of the technology to keep pace with the joint further development of their own needs.

Finally, and in keeping with the last underlying assumption mentioned above, the definition of 'social experiments with telematics' as a linguistic collocation would involve us in a specification of *the essentially interdisciplinary nature of these experiments*. Experiments of this kind provide opportunities for much-needed practical collaboration between two traditionally separate branches of knowledge — sociological expertise and technological expertise.

The Supportive Framework.

For the practical realisation of the concept of social experiments with telematics — as I have defined it above in accordance with its fundamental presuppositions — it would seem necessary to form a supportive research team whose function would be to select and chart the proposed experimental community, and to assist in the planning, coordination and evaluation of the experiment itself. Such a team would, of course, reflect the interdisciplinary approach which is fundamental to social experiments with telematics as we have seen. But experience has shown that the entire team of academics — whether they represent the social sciences or the natural and technical sciences — must be entirely independent (and, in particular, economically independent) of any of the interested parties in the social experiment; whether the latter are businessmen supplying equipment or services, local authorities supplying services or premises, or users, willingly spending time, energy, and perhaps even their own money on the project.

"Social experiments with telematics take place in a socially complex and conflict-ridden arena", I wrote in my second section above, and in the same section I tried to argue that it is in everyone's interest that an independent supervisory body should prevent short-term and narrowly-conceived commercial interests from sabotaging the development of the full potential of the technology. The comparative failure of the recent trans-national videotex pilot project in Denmark, for instance, has made it abundantly clear that the reluctance of public authorities to finance social experiments of this kind to the extent necessary for their successful completion can have a disastrously abortive effect. The research team cannot, and must not, be under constant pressure from public authorities to save money: insignificant savings in the short run could have fatal consequences for the eventual success of the investment. And, finally, I would remind the reader of my warning, at the beginning of the last chapter, against the dangers of possible over-enthusiasm on the part of the users participating in the experiment. Their views cannot, and must not, influence the sober and critical assessments of the research team; abstract utopias must not be allowed to sabotage the possible realisation of integrated utopias.

"Reconciling the latent potential of telematics with its more overt tendential content is difficult, if not impossible", I wrote pessimistically at the beginning of my last chapter. The sort of difficulties with which, as we saw in that chapter, the social experiments with telematics in Sweden and France are so bravely struggling must make it abundantly clear to the reader how desirable, and necessary, it is to have an independent referee in social experiments with telematics.

The function of the independent supportive research team is, as I mentioned earlier, to select and chart the proposed experimental community, and to assist in the planning, coordination, and evaluation of the experiment itself. Since social experiments with telematics, as I have defined them, must take individual and communal societal needs as their starting point, and since the whole aim of these experiments is to develop these needs — and the technology to satisfy them — it is obvious that the research team has to make a thorough survey of the experimental community it has selected *before* the actual experiment can get under way. The social, political, and cultural conditions obtaining in the chosen community must be analysed in advance partly in order to furnish the foundation for the actual planning of the experiment, and partly in order to provide a basis for subsequent comparisons which can register the changes in the community which the introduction of the new technology brings about.

Charting existing individual and communal societal needs is more easily said than done, especially if the phrase leads one to imagine that the needs are in any way static or purely individual. Before the technology arrives, as well as during and after the social experiment, both individual and communal needs within the community in question will, of course, be dynamically developing and changing. What the research team has to do, in other words, is to 'find out what's going on' in the community it has selected. The colloquial phrase does, in fact, give a more precise indication of what is happening, and of what has to be done. Before the social experiment can get under way, the supportive researchers must discover 'what is going on' — individually and generally — in the family life of the community, in its political life, in its various clubs and associations, etc., etc.

The results of this initial investigation are of the utmost importance for the detailed planning of the experiment. For, at the planning stage, the role of the supportive team is to help the local population to choose technology which is truly relevant to their established social, political and cultural requirements. Moreover, it must be the concern of the supportive research team at the planning stage to ensure in advance that the social, political and cultural effects of the introduction of the new technology will lend themselves to analysis and reasonably objective evaluation.

Above all, however, it is essential that the supportive team should encourage the members of the community concerned to participate as fully as possible both in the planning and in the continuous evaluation of the social experiment. The whole point of social experiments is to free each and every individual citizen from the tyranny of other men's 'good ideas' — whether these other men are technicians, businessmen or public authorities. It would be fatal if the participants in the experiments were to avoid the tyranny of the latter élites only to find that they have become the victims of a new academic élite — of the self-styled 'supportive' researchers themselves, in other words. In the opinion of the French Information Society promoters, Simon Nora and Alain Minc, the end justified the means when they appealed to the Gaullist president to 'engineer' the introduction of a decentralized and more democratic society, in words redolent of Machiavellian statecraft. But social experiments with telematics are intended precisely to avoid the dangers of this Machiavellian paradox.

The emphasis on the fullest possible participation of the members of the chosen community in the continuous evaluation of the social experiment is necessary, too, if the technology is to be improved continuously throughout the experiment, in sensitive response to qualitatively new and unforeseen needs. For the supportive research team, this means that not only do quantitative measurements, questionnaires, and their analysis, have to be constantly updated, but also that continuous series of qualitative interviews have to be arranged, as well as series of meetings designed to elicit group or communal evaluations of the ongoing experiment.

In order to evaluate the overall social, political and cultural effects of the introduction of the new technology, it must also be the task of the supportive research team to *coordinate* the various subsidiary projects undertaken in the chosen community, partly in order to permit a cross-fertilization of ideas between the various subsidiary projects, and partly because the total effect on the community of the various projects involved in the experiment will be more than just the sum of its parts. For the *interplay* of the various projects will also have significance, both in the lives of the individual members of the community and in the life of the community in general.

Potential Benefits.

The fundamental aim of social experiments with telematics is a democratic one: it is to improve the quality of the lives of each and every member of the society concerned. In representative communities, all the potentially interested parties, and all those who may be affected by I.T. and telematics technology, can become involved in the planning, execution and evaluation of social experiments with the new technology, so as to influence its development in directions which will be of advantage to each and every one of their fellow citizens. Whether their project is successful is something which only the participants themselves, and later their fellow citizens too, of course, can judge.

For participants in the microelectronics or telecommunications business, or for potential suppliers of related services, social experiments with telematics have obvious advantages over more traditional market research, in that they can give a unique picture of potential demand and utilization patterns in relation to specific technical systems and devices *before* the latter are launched onto the open market.

For politicians, and for all who are concerned with the longer term results of the introduction of I.T. and telematics technology, social experiments with telematics offer a unique opportunity to assess the available societal options and thereby avoid expensive 'mistakes'.

In that the experiments take place in representative communities within an impartial and highly-qualified interdisciplinary research framework, and in that the experiments have as their aim the development of new, more user-friendly, and more widely relevant I.T. and telematics systems, social experiments with telematics thus represent a compromise between the R. and D. interests of the industries involved, and the democratic desire of each and every citizen in the given society to have a genuine chance to influence media and communications policy.

10.6. *Conclusion: Advanced Technology in the Service of Mankind.*

Every age has its utopias, its visions of a better society: a society which simultaneously, fascinatingly, both reflects, and differs from, any societies already existing.

Towards the end of the long road from the medieval poet Langland's 'fair field full of folk' to electronic polling in Columbus, Ohio, we encounter one of the utopian visions of our own time — the dream of an Information Society. It reflects existing industrial societies to the extent that it is cluttered with advanced technology. But at the same time, as a utopia, it constitutes a protest against existing industrial societies, in that it envisages patterns of human fellowship which are today under the threat of extinction.

The dream of an Information Society has also found more concrete expression in the metaphor of the 'global village'. What is conceived of here, in utopian terms, is the ability of I.T. and telematics technology to open doors and windows onto a world full of possibilities, of information and experience, which have hitherto only been available in the metropolis; while at the same time enabling citizens of tomorrow to remain within communities which retain all the advantages of traditional provincial town life with its easy manageability and familiar neighbourhood fellowship.

It is a dream of the transcendence of the rigid distinction between work and free time, which is so characteristic of modern industrial society. Remote terminal links can bring work back into our homes, just as new communications systems can open our homes towards the wider society around us.

And it is a dream of the revival of a healthy grassroots political and cultural climate, so that there need no longer be any question of letting others determine our lives for us, and our culture need no longer be synonymous with mass-produced entertainment. Instead, politics and culture will become synonymous with communication and participation, with 'do-it-yourself' policy-making, and 'do-it-yourself' entertainment.

I.T. and telematics technology create these visions for us because of their essential ambiguity. On the one hand, the dreams have a ballast of technical realism: 'technically' it is already possible to realise them. While on the other hand, I.T. and telematics technology seem in themselves to constitute the worst conceivable threats to the realisation of any dream of a better future.

For I.T. and telematics technology could just as easily turn out to be socially repressive: depriving large sections of the populations of tomorrow's societies of the ability to determine their own futures by withholding information from them, and allowing powerful minorities to retain the monopoly of all information in their own hands. I.T. and telematics technology could just as easily create frustrating and lonely home offices, permitting omnipresent managerial control within the illusory privacy of one's own four walls. And I.T. and telematics technology could just as easily complete the social isolation of tomorrow's citizens by offering them stupefying mass-produced entertainment all day long, with home-shopping and home-banking 'saving them the trouble' of having to get up from their armchairs and distance themselves from the hypnotic fascination of their flickering screens for as much as a single moment.

The utopia of the Information Society rests, then, upon an ambiguous foundation, riddled with conflicts and mutually contradictory tendencies. Our task at the present time must be to build something qualitatively new out of the tensions generated by these ongoing conflicts. For there are extremely powerful reactionary forces behind such tendencies as mass-produced pulp entertainment, or union-defying, minutely controlled, 'home office' piece-work, etc.

Against such forces, means have to be found to break the monopoly of commercially-employed so-called 'experts' over the design and development of the potentially liberating technology. The means I have been recommending in the last two chapters of this book involve the creation of publicly influenced R. and D. frameworks for the development and testing of I.T. and telematics systems; social experiments with telematics, in other words, in which experts advise, but do not decide everything over the heads of the actual experimenters, over the heads of the local populations themselves.

Ready-made technical solutions are unacceptable. Communal workshops must be set up for the realisation and assessment of democratically inspired visions of improved human fellowship — visions in which I.T. and telematics technology can play a vital role. And a necessary precondition for the establishment of such communal workshops is knowledge: knowledge about the technology itself, and knowledge about the fact that the technology has become so advanced, of late, that the tyranny of the arguments based on the claim that only technicians could operate it, or on the claim that the technical limitations of the technology compelled us to accept it on *its* own terms, rather than on *ours*, has been broken at last. Never again must we allow ourselves to be blinded by science with regard to this technology. From now on it must become ours — ours to do with as we think fit. It must enter the service of all mankind.

If, on the basis of this kind of attitude, we succeed in establishing a sufficient quantity of 'communal workshops', of social experiments with telematics as I have defined them in this book, then there may just be a chance that I.T. and telematics technology may help to bring to birth a qualitatively different and better future for us all, rather than merely tightening the hold upon us of the existing forces of repression.

FOOTNOTES

1. The definition given here is in line with the one used by international research workers — at IDATE, for example, the French research establishment at Montpellier, or at GAMMA in Montreal. But it should be noted that 'Informatique' or, in Britain, 'Information Technology' (I.T.), are sometimes used synonymously with 'telematics'.

2. The first of these facts is attested by a welter of economic studies; the latter development is (for example) well-documented in T. Forester (ed.) (1981).

3. Translated here by P. Edmonds, this quotation is from N.F.S. Grundtvig (1877: 444 [1838]). This work is a lecture on the history of the preceding fifty years, which Grundtvig held in 1838. Denmark celebrated the bicentenary of Grundtvig's birth in 1983, and an anthology of his writings was published in 1984 in an English translation by E. Broadbridge, N.L. Jensen et al., *A Grundtvig Anthology: Selections from the Writings of N.F.S. Grundtvig (1783-1872)*, Cambridge, U.K. (James Clarke and Co.) 1984.

4. I use the term 'Marxism' here with reference to the social science method which was invented and developed by such disciples of Marx as Engels, Kautsky and Lenin. Marx himself once declared that he was not a Marxist. While conceding that his disciples could find a substantial amount of ammunition for their method in Marx's works, I am inclined to agree with him!

5. The point is well made in a doctoral dissertation by the Danish historian of ideas, Hans Jørgen Schanz; see H.J. Schanz (1981: 34ff). (The dissertation contains a summary in German).

6. Marc Uri Porat initiated his work on the so-called 'Information Economy' with nine volumes of detailed studies, entitled *The Information Economy*, (1977). The figures quoted here are from Robert D. Hamrin (1982). Curiously enough, they are not identical with Porat's own figures in his nine volume work, as the reader can verify by glancing on to my p. 54. The trends are the same, though!

7. M.I.T.I. (trans. M. Boman), *Rapport fra informations industri komiteen, rådet for industriel opbygning* Copenhagen (Sept. 1981) p.12-26. Translator's note: I have not been able to get hold of the English edition and must therefore assume full responsibility for the precise phraseology of the quotations given below in Qvortrup's text — P.E.

8. The quotation here is from Daniel Bell, 'The Social Framework of the Information Society', in Michael L. Dertouzos and Joel Moses (eds.) (1980: 193f) (cf. ibid. p.168) but Bell was advancing similar ideas right back at the end of the '60s.

9. The reference, of course, is to Georg Lukács' analysis of bourgeois antinomical thinking in 'Die Antinomien des bürgerlichen Denkens', *Geschichte und Klassenbewusstsein* (1968) [1923].

10. See, for instance, the plea for a 'planned transition' to a knowledge-based economy, and the listed prerequisites for the transformation of educational institutions, which are offered by C. Dede, J. Bowman and F. Kierstead in 'Communication Technologies and Education: the Coming Transformation', in Howard F. Didsbury, Jr. (ed.) (1982: 174-182).

11. It is to Charles E. Wilson, Secretary of Defense in the Eisenhower administration and one-time president of General Motors, that we owe the phrase "What is good for the United States is good for General Motors, and vice-versa". See D. Bell (1962: 399).

12. "The Big Three auto makers will (and currently do) use interactive technologies for business planning and decision making. It's cheaper than flying around the country to various meetings". (K.C. Laudon 1977: 17).

13. For an excellent summary of his utopian thinking with regard to consensus politics, as it is expressed in his 'Vorbereitende Bemerkungen zu einer Theorie der kommunikativen Kompetenz' and 'Wahrheitstheorien', see T.A. McCarthy, 'A Theory of Communicative Competence', in *Philosophy of the Social Sciences* (1973: 135-156).

14. This quotation is actually from his later work — D. Bell, op. cit. (1973: 14) — but his 'post-industrial society' concept had already appeared in an article in 1964.

15. For a loyal but critical brief introduction to Easton's political thinking in the 'sixties, see W.J.M. Mackenzie (1967: 102-110).

16. Pardonably, perhaps, some serious modern thinkers are guilty of trying to deny the continued existence of this ancient conflict, between the state and the society at large, over which is to have the right to represent the individual citizen. After 200 years of philosophical wrangling, one still meets optimistic claims about the possibility of establishing a compromise between boundless, and rationally restricted, individual freedom. An exposition of this particular fallacy which — no matter for surprise, due to its 'easy solutions' — received a high degree of attention in Denmark recently was the work of two politicians and a well-known literary figure: see N.I. Meyer, K.H. Petersen and V. Sørensen (1978).

17. Kant's 'Über den Gemeinspruch: Das mag in der Theorie richtig sein, taugt aber nicht für die Praxis' was first published only four years after the outbreak of the French Revolution — see *Berlinische Monatsschrift* XXII (September 1793) p.201-84. Section II of the essay — containing the passage I have quoted — is entitled 'On the Relationship of Theory to Practice in Political Right', and is subtitled '(Against Hobbes)': in H. Reiss and H.B. Nisbet, *Kant's Political Writings*, Cambridge U.K. (C.U.P.) 1970, p.73-87.

These two facts may help to explain Kant's very absolute position here: — "[...] Even if the power of the state or its agent, the head of the state has violated the original contract by authorising the government to act tyrannically, and has thereby, in the eyes of the subject, forfeited the right to legislate, the subject is still not entitled to offer counter-resistance", writes Kant! Actually he subsequently modifies his position by emphasizing the importance of 'the freedom of the pen' to criticize legislators, and the moral obligation of the latter to abide by his proposed rational rule of thumb that "Whatever a people cannot impose upon itself cannot be imposed upon it by the legislator either". Kant finds Hobbes' proposition that the head of the state has no contractual obligations towards his people 'quite terrifying' — but he is himself in complete agreement with Hobbes that the people have no right to overthrow him by force!

18. K. Marx and A. Ruge, eds. (1967: 206) — translation by P. Edmonds. Marx's article 'On the Jewish Question' is available in English translation in several different editions of his earlier works, as well as in David McLellan's comprehensive and balanced selection from the complete works: see D. McLellan (ed.) (1977: 39).

19. Findings based on a recent unpublished survey in Denmark, involving a limited sample of secondary school students. They would, of course, not necessarily be valid in other industrialized nations where (young) women might be more 'liberated', and humanities students less 'old-fashioned'!

20. The reference is, of course, to Alexander Pope's versified popularization of the ideas contained in Lord Shaftesbury's *Characteristics of Men, Manners, Opinions and Times*, London (1711), which came to Pope via his friend Lord Bolingbroke, and which the poet immortalized in his *Essay on Man*, London (1733-34). The famous quotation is from the concluding lines of Epistle IV.

21. A good economic appraisal of the resilient Indian socio-economic reward system — known as the 'jajmani' system — is to be found in a report based on village studies in South India: Scarlett Epstein's 'Productive Efficiency and Customary Systems of Rewards in Rural South India'; see R. Firth (ed.) (1967).

22. The theories propounded here about traditional and modern modes of power are based on Michel Foucault's analyses, see M. Foucault (1975) and M. Foucault (1976).

23. A typical example of this fallacy would be Herbert I. Schiller's — otherwise brilliant — study which I mentioned in the opening section of chapter 8 above (H.I. Schiller, op. cit.).

24. Information about the Centre was acquired 'first hand' in 1983. J.J. Servan-Schreiber and Nicholas Negroponte have produced a 'manifesto' which is to be continually updated — *Centre Mondial Informatique et Ressources Humaines: Mission and Programs*. A useful introductory article dealing with both the ambitions and the problematic aspects of the Centre is to be found in *Le Nouvel Observateur* (June 5th, 1982): G. Bonnot, 'Informatique: Comment la France invente le nouveau cerveau du monde'.

25. Cf. H. Marcuse (1972: 119f): "In the social reality, despite all change, the domination of man by man is still the historical continuum that links pre-technological and technological Reason. However, the society which projects and undertakes the technological transformation of nature alters the base of domination by gradually replacing personal dependence (of the slave on the master, the serf on the lord of the manor, the lord on the donor of the fief, etc.) with dependence on the 'objective order of things' (on economic laws, the market, etc.). To be sure, the 'objective order of things' is itself the result of domination, but it is nevertheless true that domination now generates a higher rationality — that of a society which sustains its hierarchic structure while exploiting ever more efficiently the natural and mental resources, and distributing the benefits of this exploitation on an ever-larger scale. The limits of this rationality, and its sinister force, appear in the progressive enslavement of man by a productive apparatus which perpetuates the struggle for existence and extends it to a total international struggle which ruins the lives of those who build and use this apparatus.
[...] Society reproduced itself in a growing technical ensemble of things and relations which included the technical utilization of men — in other words, the struggle for existence and the exploitation of man and nature became ever more scientific and rational. The double meaning of 'rationalization' is relevant in this context. Scientific management and scientific division of labour vastly increased the productivity of the economic, political and cultural enterprise. Result: the higher standard of living. At the same time and on the same ground, this rational enterprise produced a pattern of mind and behaviour which justified and absolved even the most destructive and oppressive features of the enterprise. [...] Certainly it is quite natural, and does not seem to call for an explanation in depth, that the tangible benefits of the system are considered worth defending — especially in view of the repelling force of present day communism which appears to be the historical alternative. But it is natural only to a mode of thought and behaviour which is unwilling and perhaps even incapable of comprehending what is happening and why it is happening, a mode of thought and behaviour which is immune against any other than the established rationality. To the degree to which they correspond to the given reality, thought and

behaviour express a false consciousness, responding to and contributing to the presentation of a false order of facts. And this false consciousness has become embodied in the prevailing technical apparatus which in turn reproduces it."

REFERENCES

Abraham, J.H.
1973 *The origins and growth of sociology*. London: Penguin.

Adorno, Th.W. et al.
1969 *Der Positivismusstreit in der deutschen Soziologie*. Neuwied/Berlin: Luchterhand.

Aldrich, M.J. et al.
1982 *Report on cable systems: A report by the information technology advisory panel*. London: Her Majesty's Stationary Office.

Andersen, Hans Christian
1958 "The goloshes of fortune". In Svend Andersen (ed.), *Hans Christian Andersen: Fairy Tales*. Odense: Flensteds Forlag. [1838]

Anonymous
1770 *An essay on trade and commerce*. London.

Apostel, L.
1963 "Can metaphysics be a science?" *Studia Philosophica Gandensia* 1.

Barthes, Roland
1973 *Mythologies*. St. Albans: Paladin.

Bauer, Walter F.
1982 "Computer services in the information society". Unpublished transcript of speech made at a world conference for computer business representatives, Copenhagen 1982.

Bell, Daniel
1962 *The end of ideology in the West: On the exhaustion of political ideas in the fifties*. New York: The Free Press.

1973 *The coming of post-industrial society: A venture in social forecasting*. New York: Basic Books.

1980 "The social framework of the information society". In Michael L. Dertouzos and Joel Moses, *The computer age: A twenty-year view*. Cambridge, Massachusetts: MIT Press.

1980 "Introduction". In Simon Nora and Alain Minc, *The computerization of society: A report to the president of France*. Cambridge, Massachusetts: MIT Press.

Benedetti, Franco de
1979 "The impact of electronic technology in the office". Paper presented at the conference

on 'Tomorrow in World Electronics', London March 21 and 22, 1979. Quoted in Vincent Mosco and Andrew Herman, *Radical theory and electronic media*. New York, stencil, 1980.

Bierstedt, R.
1959 *The making of society: An outline of sociology*. New York: Random House.

Bloch, Ernst
1977 *Subjekt-Objekt: Erläuterungen zu Hegel*. Gesamtausgabe vol. 8. Frankfurt a. M.: Suhrkamp Verlag. [1949]

1977 *Das Prinzip Hoffnung*. Frankfurt a. M.: Suhrkamp Verlag. [1949-1959]

1977 *Tübinger Einleitung in die Philosophie*. Gesamtausgabe vol. 13. Frankfurt a. M.: Suhrkamp Verlag. [1965]

1977 *Experimentum Mundi: Frage, Kategorien des Herausbringens, Praxis*. Gesamtausgabe vol. 15. Frankfurt a. M.: Suhrkamp Verlag. [1975]

1982 "Anticiperet realitet — hvad er utopisk tænkning, og hvad kan den?" In J.E. Andersen et al. (eds.), *Ernst Bloch — en introduktion*. Aarhus: Modtryk.

Bonnet, G.
1982 "Informatique: Comment la France invente le nouveau cerveau du monde". *Le Nouvel Observateur*, June 5th.

Coates, J.F.
1982 *A technology assesment workbook*. Washington, D.C.: Office of Technology Assessment.

Connerton, P. (ed.)
1976 *Critical sociology: Selected readings*. London: Penguin Books.

Cronberg, T. and I.-L. Sangregorio
1981 *Du sköna nya vardag: Om datateknik och boende*. Stockholm: Prisma.

The Danish Government
1983 *Redegørelse nr. R 19 om udviklingslinjer for telekommunikationsnettet af ministeren for offentlige arbejder givet 10. maj 1983*. Folketinget (The Danish Parliament).

Dede, Christopher, Jim Bowman and Fred Kierstead
1982 "Communications technologies and education: The coming transformation". In Howard F. Didsbury (ed.), *Communications and the future: Prospects, promises, and problems*. Bethesda, Maryland: World Future Society.

Druet, Pierre-Philipe, Georges Thill and Peter Kemp
1980 *Henimod et teknologisk demokrati*. Copenhagen: Lindhardt og Ringhof.

The Economist
1982 "Tomorrow's leaders: A survey of Japanese technology". *The Economist*, June 19.

EEC Commission
1979 *Det europæiske samfund og de nye informationsteknologier* (The European Community and the new information technologies). Bruxelles: KOM(79).

Firth, R.
1967 *Themes in economic anthropology*. London: Tavistock Publications Ltd.

Ford, B.
1969 *From Dickens to Hardy: Volume 6 of the Pelican Guide to English literature*. London: Penguin.

Forester, Tom (ed.)
1981 *The microelectronics revolution*. Oxford: Basil Blackwell.

Foucault, Michel
1975 *Surveiller et punir*. Paris: E.G.

1976 *Histoire de la sexualité, 1: La volonté de savoir*. Paris: E.G.

Freemann, Chris
1981 "Unemployment and government". In Tom Forester (ed.), *The microelectronics revolution*. Oxford: Basil Blackwell.

Friebel, I. and H. Händel
1974 *Britain-USA now: A survey in key words*. London: Longman.

Galbraith, J.K.
1967 *The new industrial state*. Boston: Houghton Mifflin.

Grundtvig, N.F.S.
1877 *Mands Minde 1788-1838*. Copenhagen. [1838]

Habermas, Jürgen
1963 *Theorie und Praxis: Sozialphilosophische Studien*. Neuwied/Berlin: Luchterhand.

1971 "Theorie der Gesellschaft oder Sozialtechnology? Eine Auseinandersetzung mit Niklas Luhmann". In Jürgen Habermas and Niklas Luhmann, *Theorie der Gesellschaft oder Sozialtechnologie - Was leistet die Systemforschung?* Frankfurt a. M.: Suhrkamp Verlag.

Halal, W.E.
1982 "Information technology and the flowering of enterprise". In Howard F. Didsbury, Jr. (ed.), *Communications and the future: Prospects, promises, and problems*. Bethesda, Maryland: World Future Society.

Hald, A.P.
1982 "Towards the information-rich society". In Edward Cornish (ed.), *Communications tomorrow: The coming of the information society*. Bethesda, Maryland: World Future Society.

Hamrin, Robert D.
1982 "The information economy: Exploiting an infinite resource". In Edward Cornish (ed.), *Communications tomorrow: The coming of the information society*. Bethesda, Maryland: World Future Society.

Hearst, S.
1982 "Der Kampf um das Kabel in Grossbritannien". *Media Perspektiven* 7.

Heffner, R.D.
1965 *A documentary history of the United States: An expanded edition*. New York: Mentor.

Hegel, Georg Wilhelm Friedrich
1972 *Grundlinien der Philosophie des Rechts*. Frankfurt a. M.: Verlag Ullstein. [1821]

International Data Corporation
1983 *The impact of I.T.* London: Management Publications Ltd.

Jensen, N.L. et al. (eds.)
1984 *A Grundtvig anthology: Selections from the writings of N.F.S. Grundtvig (1783-1872)*. Cambridge, UK: James Clarke & Co.

Jyllandsposten
1983 Article in *Morgenavisen Jyllandsposten* (Danish national daily).

Kant, Immanuel
1973 *Kritik der praktischen Vernunft*. Stuttgart: Reclam. [1788]

1975 "Beantwortung der Frage: Was ist Aufklärung?" In *Was ist Aufklärung?* Göttingen. [1784]

Lafargue, P.
1883 *Le droit à la paresse: Réfutation du 'droit au travail' de 1848*. Prison de Sainte-Pélagie (la Fédération du Centre)

1970 *Textes choisis*. Paris: Editions sociales.

Langland, William
1966 *Piers the ploughman*. Harmondsworth: Penguin.

Lasch, C.
1978 *The culture of narcissism*. New York: W.W. Norton & Company.

Laudon, K.C.
1977 *Communications technology and democratic participation*. New York: Praeger Publishers.

Lerner, E.J.
1982 "Strategic C 3: A goal unreached". *I.E.E.E. Spectrum*, Oct. 1982

Luhmann, Niklas
1971 "Moderne Systemtheorien als Form gesamtgesellschaftlicher Analyse". In Habermas, Jürgen and Niklas Luhmann, *Theorie der Gesellschaft oder Sozialtechnologie — Was leistet die Systemforschung?* Frankfurt a. M.: Suhrkamp Verlag. [1968]

Lukács, Georg
1968 *Geschichte und Klassenbewusstsein*. Georg Lukács Werke Bd. 2. Neuwied/Berlin: Luchterhand. [1923]

Lundvall, Bengt-Åke
1983 "Fremtiden vil bringe kvinder i strid modvind". In the Danish national daily *Information*. (Copenhagen), Feb. 14th.

Mackenzie, W.J.M.
1967 *Politics and social science*. London: Penguin.

Mandel, Ernest
1972 *Der Spätkapitalismus. Versuch einer marxistischen Erklärung*. Frankfurt a. M.: Suhrkamp Verlag.

Marcuse, Herbert
1972 *One-dimensional man*. London: Sphere Books Ltd.

Marien, Michael
1982 "Non-communication and the future". In Howard F. Didsbury, Jr. (ed.), *Communications and the future: Prospects, promises, and problems*. Bethesda, Maryland: World Future Society.

Marlowe, Christopher
1909 "The tragical history of doctor Faustus". In *The Plays of Christopher Marlowe*. London: J.M. Dent. [1604]

Martin, James
1981 *Telematic society: A challenge for tomorrow*. New York: Prentice-Hall.

Martino, J.P.
1982 "Telecommunications in the year 2000". In Edward Cornish (ed.), *Communications tomorrow: The coming of the information society*. Bethesda, Maryland: World Future Society.

Marx, Karl
1959 *Economic and philosophic manuscripts of 1844*. Moscow: Progress Publishers.

Marx, Karl and A. Ruge (eds.)
1967 *Deutsch-französische Jahrbücher*. Darmstadt: Wissenschaftliche Buchgesellschaft.

Masuda, Yoneji
1981 *The information society as post-industrial society*. Bethesda, Maryland: World Future Society.

Matelart, A. & Y. Stourdzé
1982 *Mission technologie, diffusion de la culture et communication: Note de synthèse*. Paris: Ministère de la Recherche.

McCarthy, T.A.
1973 "A theory of communicative competence". *Philosophy of the Social Sciences* 3.

McLellan, David (ed.)
1977 *Karl Marx: Selected writings*. Oxford: Oxford University Press.

Mexandeau, L.
1982 "Comment révéler les besoins?" *Le Monde*, October 17th.

Meyer, Niels I., K. Helveg Petersen and Villy Sørensen
1978 *Oprør fra midten*. Copenhagen: Gyldendal.

Miller, J.G.
1965 "Living systems: Structure and process". *Behavioral Science* 10.

M.I.T.I.
1981 *Rapport fra informations industri komiteen, rådet for industriel opbygning*. (Translated by M. Boman.) Copenhagen.

Molitor, Graham T.T.
1982 "The information society: The path to post-industrial growth". In Edward Cornish (ed.), *Communications tomorrow: The coming of the information society*. Bethesda, Maryland: World Future Society.

Murata, Masatoshi
1982 "Information network system and its impact on society". In *L'experimentation sociale en télématique: Actes des 4e journées internationales*. Montpellier: IDATE.

Murphy, J.G.
1970 *Kant: The philosophy of right*. London: Macmillan.

Neustadt, R.M.
1982 "Politics and the new media". In Howard F. Didsbury Jr., (ed.), *Communications and the future: Prospects, promises, and problems*. Bethesda, Maryland: World Future Society.

Nora, Simon & Alain Minc
1978 *L'Informatisation de la société: Rapport à M. le Président de la République*. Paris: La Documentation française. (English translation: MIT Press 1980.)

Nørretranders, Tor
1982 Articles in the Danish national daily *Information*, July 3rd 1982.

O.E.C.D.
1981a *Information activities, electronics and telecommunications technologies: Impact on employment, growth and trade*. Paris: I.C.C.P.

1981b *Microelectronics, productivity and employment*. Paris: I.C.C.P.

O'Neill, Paul
1982 "Dr. Charles Kao sees a bright future for the fiber industry". *International Fiber Optics and Communications* 3:4.28-34.

Papert, Seymour
1980 *Mindstorms: Children, computers, and powerful ideas*. USA: Basic Books.

1982 "Tomorrow's classrooms?" *Times Educational Supplement*, May 3rd.

Persson, P.O. et al.
1980 *80-talet på en bricka: Datateknik, utveckling och miljö 1980-1990*. Stockholm: Riksdataförbundet.

Porat, Marc Uri
1977 *The information economy*. Washington, D.C.: Office of Telecommunications.

Rabel, G.
1963 *Kant*. Oxford: Oxford University Press.

Reiss, H. and H.B. Nisbet
1970 *Kant's political writings*. Cambridge: Cambridge University Press.

R.I.T.E.
1982 *A vision of telecommunications policy in the '80s*. Tokyo, Research Institute of Telecommunications and Economics.

Robertson, J.G.
1962 *A history of German literature*. Edinburgh: W. Blackwood & Sons.

Rousseau, Jean-Jacques
1823 *Oeuvres complètes*. Paris: P. Dupont.

1911 *Emile*. (Translation by Barbara Foxley.) London: J.M. Dent & Sons Ltd. [1762]

1971 *Discours sur l'origine et les fondements de l'inégalité parmi les hommes*. Paris: Editions sociales.

1977 *Du contrat social ou principes du droit politique*. Paris: Editions du Seuil. Translated in 1767 by T. Beckett and P.A. De Hondt (London). New translation: Jean-Jacques Rousseau, *The Social Contract*. London: Penguin Books, 1968. [1762]

Rubinstein, E.
1982 "Technology in war and peace". *I.E.E.E. Spectrum*, Oct. 1982.

Rutkowski, A.M.
1982 "The global village: Getting there from here". *Chronicle of International Communication* 3:5. Washington, D.C.: International Communication Project.

Schanz, Hans Jørgen
1981 *Træk af behovsproblematikkens idéhistorie med særligt henblik på Marx og Engels*. Aarhus: Modtryk.

Schiff, Frank W.
1982 Unpublished speech, World Future Society's Conference, Washington, D.C.

Schiller, Herbert I.
1981 *Who knows: Information in the age of the Fortune 500*. Norwood, New Jersey: Ablex.

Science Council of Canada
1982 *Planning now for an information society: Tomorrow is too late*. Hull, Québec: Canadian Government Publishing Centre.

Serafini, S. and M. Andrieu
1980 *The information revolution and its implications for Canada*. Hull, Québec: Department of Communications.

Servan-Schreiber, Jean-Jacques and Nicholas Negroponte
1983 *Centre mondial informatique et ressources humaines: Mission and programs*. Paris.

Shaftesbury, Lord
1711 *Characteristicks of men, manners, opinions and times*. London.

Smith, Adam
1976 *An inquiry into the nature and causes of the wealth of nations*. Oxford: Clarendon Press. [1776]

Söderquist, Thomas
1982 *På väg mot ett informations(klass)samhälle?* Roskilde: R.U.C.

Thyssen, Ole
1976 *Utopisk dialektik*. Copenhagen: Gyldendal.

Tocqueville, A. de
1840 *De la démocratie en Amérique, vol.II*.

Toffler, Alvin
1970 *Future shock*. New York: Random House.

1980 *The third wave*. New York: William Morrow and Company.

Tourraine, Alain
1979 *Mort d'une gauche*. Paris: Galilée.

Tuschling, Burkhard
1978 *Die "offene" und die "abstrakte" Gesellschaft. Habermas und die Konzeption von Vergesellschaftung der klassisch-bürgerlichen Rechts- und Staatsphilosophie*. Berlin: Argument-Verlag.

Uhlig, Ronald P., David J. Farber and James H. Bair
1979 *The office of the future*. Amsterdam: North-Holland Publishing Company.

Wicklein, John
1981 *The electronic nightmare: The new communications and freedom*. New York: The Viking Press.

Yokoi, Mitsuru
1982 "Agencies and directions of Japanese policy". *Telecommunications Policy* 6:4.

In the PRAGMATICS & BEYOND series the following monographs have been published thus far:

I:1. *Anca: M. Nemoianu*: The Boat's Gonna Leave: A Study of Children Learning a Second Language from Conversations with Other Children.
Amsterdam, 1980, vi, 116 pp. Paperbound.

I:2. *Michael D. Fortescue*: A Discourse Production Model for 'Twenty Questions'.
Amsterdam, 1980, x, 137 pp. Paperbound.

I:3. *Melvin Joseph Adler*: A Pragmatic Logic for Commands.
Amsterdam, 1980, viii, 131 pp. Paperbound.

I:4. *Jef Verschueren*: On Speech Act Verbs.
Amsterdam, 1980, viii, 83 pp. Paperbound.

I:5. *Geoffrey N. Leech*: Explorations in Semantics and Pragmatics.
Amsterdam, 1980, viii, 133 pp. Paperbound. Temporarily out of print.

I:6. *Herman Parret*: Contexts of Understanding.
Amsterdam, 1980, viii, 109 pp. Paperbound.

I:7. *Benoît de Cornulier*: Meaning Detachment.
Amsterdam, 1980, vi, 124 pp. Paperbound.

I:8. *Peter Eglin*: Talk and Taxonomy: A methodological comparison of ethnosemantics and ethnomethodology with reference to terms for Canadian doctors.
Amsterdam, 1980, x, 125 pp. Paperbound.

II:1. *John Dinsmore*: The Inheritance of Presupposition.
Amsterdam, 1981, vi, 97 pp. Paperbound.

II:2. *Charles Travis*: The True and the False: The Domain of the Pragmatic.
Amsterdam, 1981, vi, 164 pp. Paperbound.

II:3. *Johan Van der Auwera*: What do we talk about when we talk? Speculative grammar and the semantics and pragmatics of focus.
Amsterdam, 1981, vi, 121 pp. Paperbound.

II:4. *Joseph F. Kess & Ronald A. Hoppe*: Ambiguity in Psycholinguistics.
Amsterdam, 1981, v, 123 pp. Paperbound.

II:5. *Karl Sornig*: Lexical Innovation: A Study of Slang, Colloquialisms and Casual Speech.
Amsterdam, 1981, viii, 117 pp. Paperbound.

II:6. *Knud Lambrecht*: Topic, Antitopic and Verb Agreement in Non-Standard French.
Amsterdam, 1981, vii, 113 pp. Paperbound.

II:7. *Jan-Ola Östman*: *You Know*: A Discourse-Functional Study.
Amsterdam, 1981, viii, 91 pp. Paperbound.

II:8. *Claude Zilberberg*: Essai sur les modalités tensives.
Amsterdam, 1981, xi, 154 pp. + 4 folding tables. Paperbound.

III:1. *Ivan Fonagy*: Situation et Signification.
Amsterdam, 1982, v, 160 pp. Paperbound.

III:2/3. *Jürgen Weissenborn and Wolfgang Klein (eds.)*: Here and There. Cross-linguistic Studies in Deixis and Demonstration.
Amsterdam, 1982. v, 296 pp. Paperbound.

III:4. *Waltraud Brennenstuhl*: Control and Ability. Towards a Biocybernetics of Language.
Amsterdam, 1982. v, 123 pp. Paperbound.

III:5. *Wolfgang Wildgen*: Catastrophe Theoretic Semantics: An Elaboration and Application of René Thom's Theory.
Amsterdam, 1982. iv, 124 pp. Paperbound.

III:6. *René Dirven, Louis Goossens, Yvan Putseys and Emma Vorlat*: The Scene of Linguistic Action and its Perspectivization by SPEAK, TALK, SAY and TELL.
Amsterdam, 1982. v, 186 pp. Paperbound.

III:7. *Thomas Ballmer*: Biological Foundations of Linguistic Communication. Towards a Biocybernetics of Language.
Amsterdam, 1982. x, 161 pp. Paperbound.

III:8. *Douglas N. Walton*: Topical Relevance in Argumentation.
Amsterdam, 1982. viii, 81 pp. Paperbound.

IV:1. *Marcelo Dascal*: Pragmatics and the Philosophy of Mind. Vol. I.
Amsterdam, 1983. xii, 207 pp. Paperbound.

IV:2. *Richard Zuber*: Non-declarative Sentences.
Amsterdam, 1983. ix, 123 pp. Paperbound.

IV:3. *Michel Meyer*: Meaning and Reading. A Philosophical Essay on Language and Literature.
Amsterdam, 1983. ix, 176 pp. Paperbound.

IV:4. *Walburga von Raffler-Engel*: The Perception of Nonverbal Behavior in the Career Interview.
Amsterdam, 1983. viii, 148 pp. Paperbound.

IV:5. *Jan Prucha*: Pragmalinguistics: East European Approaches.
Amsterdam, 1983. v, 103 pp. Paperbound.

IV:6. *Alex Huebler*: Understatements and Hedges in English.
Amsterdam, 1983. ix, 192 pp. Paperbound.

IV:7. *Herman Parret*: Semiotics and Pragmatics. An Evaluative Comparison of Conceptual Frameworks.
Amsterdam, 1983. xii, 136 pp. Paperbound.

IV:8. *Jürgen Streeck*: Social Order in Child Communication. A Study in Microethnography.
Amsterdam, 1983. vii, 130 pp. Paperbound.

V:1. *Marlene Dolitsky*: Under the Tumtum Tree: From Nonsense to Sense, a Study in Non-automatic Comprehension.
Amsterdam, 1984. vii, 119 pp. Paperbound.

V:2. *Roger G. van de Velde*: Prolegomena to Inferential Discourse Processing.
Amsterdam, 1984. viii, 100 pp. Paperbound.

V:3. *Teun Van Dijk*: Prejudice in Discourse. An Analysis of Ethnic Prejudice in Cognition and Conversation.
Amsterdam, 1984. x, 170 pp. Paperbound.

V:4. *Henk Haverkate*: Speech Acts, Speakers and Hearers. Reference and Referential Strategies in Spanish.
Amsterdam, 1984. xi, 142 pp. Paperbound.

V:5. *Lauri Carlson*: "Well" in Dialogue Games: A Discourse Analysis of the Interjection "Well" in Idealized Conversation.
Amsterdam, 1984 (publ. 1985). ix, 111 pp. Paperbd.

V:6. *Danilo Marcondes de Souza Filho*: Language and Action: A Reassessment of Speech Act Theory.
Amsterdam, 1984 (publ. 1985). ix, 167 pp. Paperbd.

V:7. *Lars Qvortrup*: The Social Significance of Telematics: An Essay on the Information Society.
Amsterdam, 1984 (publ. 1985). xi, 230 pp. Paperbd.

V:8. *J.C.P. Auer*: Bilingual Conversation.
Amsterdam, 1984 (publ. 1985). ix, 116 pp. Paperbd.